GOD
IS IN THE
CRAZY

**With Astounding Miracles and
Reflections on the Peaceful Life**

Dr. Chet Weld

ISBN 978-1-63885-627-6 (Paperback)
ISBN 978-1-63885-629-0 (Hardcover)
ISBN 978-1-63885-628-3 (Digital)

Covenant Books
11661 Hwy 707
Murrells Inlet, SC 29576
www.covenantbooks.com

The incidents described in this book are true. A few names and locations
have been changed to protect the privacy of the contributors.
When internet links are cited, there is no guarantee the links still
connect with the information the author collected from the website.
Library of Congress Cataloging-in-Publication Data
Weld, Devereaux Chester.

*God Is in the Crazy (With Astounding Miracles and
Reflections on the Peaceful Life)* / Chet Weld
Publisher is not responsible for websites (or their
content) that are not owned by the publisher.

God is in the Crazy provides a handbook of help for anyone struggling to know that nothing is too terrible or difficult for God to help you with. Dr. Weld is an excellent writer and conveyor of deep truths through stories that minister hope and faith. He masterfully reveals that although God sometimes miraculously intervenes, He often empowers us to overcome with His strength…an eternal gift.

I have not read a richer source of encouragement outside of God's Word. This is a book every person would benefit from reading. It's a "go to" wealth of inspiration that lifts the reader above struggle to a more accurate perspective of life—that the God of power and love is in the middle of the worst of circumstances. The stories within these pages are powerful reminders that every person matters to God, and no one is forgotten.

Capt. Dale Black
Retired Airline Captain, Bible Teacher, Author of *Flight To Heaven, Visiting Heaven* and co-author of *Life, Cancer and God*

This book introduces us to an unexpected world of surprise and rescue in the midst of suffering, confusion, and even death. I was hooked from the beginning and eager to turn each page.

The author reports otherworldly but very real experiences with humor and wisdom from a long career as a marriage counselor and individual psychotherapist, and from years of theological and psychological study. He's had a front row seat on the parade of broken minds and spirits that make up the human struggle. And from his own personal journey, he's learned how to impart hope to those he's encouraged in his office, church, and in the marketplace.

This book imparts hope! The stories will inspire you to listen for God's voice and look expectantly for that Unseen Hand that can alter circumstances in life-changing ways.

Happy reading and pass it on to a friend!

Bill Holloman, M.D.
Retired Internal Medicine Specialist, Geriatrician, and Hospitalist

This is an extraordinary book. Having pastored and counseled for many years, the author brings insights about the human condition and presents penetrating views about our possible relationship with God. By presenting so much evidence of the supernatural world, he challenges us to chase knowledge about God and the spiritual life. And his conclusions from examples of miracles that Jesus is performing in our time encourage me to keep looking for God everywhere!

I was surprised to also learn of the faith and miracles reported by heroes of the past such as George Washington and Winston Churchill, and by lesser-known heroes of both past and present. The book also directs our attention to the fact that we have met many people during our lives who are equally heroic, many of whom have experienced miracles. To learn of them, we simply need to ask if they've ever witnessed or experienced a miracle.

I learned from and enjoyed the author's anecdotes and personal experiences. I think there's something in this book for everyone, and I wholeheartedly commend it to you.

Ivan Rudolph
Author of *Your Origin and Destiny* and *Living Beyond: Making Sense of Near Death Experiences*
https://ivanrudolph.com/

Chet Weld has written a book that is sure to inspire! It has been said that no one can live without hope. This book is filled with hope and will touch your heart. "Is there supernatural in the ordinary?" That's the question that this book answers. Many years ago, Dr. Weld and I worked together. I've seen him find light in darkness, the work of angels that others may miss, and God's goodness where some may only see suffering. When we worked together, I felt Dr. Weld's warmth and saw how it touched others' lives. This book represents the deep faith and love of a man of God who cares for others.

We all need to be stimulated and encouraged to have faith and to love one another. I believe *God is in the Crazy* will inspire and help you see the good in the bad and positively reframe some of the difficult times in your life. Therapeutic insights and faith invite us to look through lenses that allow us to see things otherwise unseen. Dr. Weld tells great true stories and is honest about his own journey. How often can you see the world of miracles through the eyes of a therapist? This book will engage you and deepen your faith.

Randy Reynolds
Author, counselor, pastor, community developer and business man

In loving memory
of
Hiram and Mary Weld

CONTENTS

FOREWORD

Several years ago, Chet Weld counseled my family member who was in crisis. Dr. Weld's approach was empathetic and God-driven. In like manner, *God Is in the Crazy* gives us pause in anxiety-filled lives to see God's miracle workings on a regular basis. In a warm conversational tone, Dr. Weld leads us through a panoply of stories that place ordinary people in unique circumstances to receive abiding grace. The experiential variety of these stories is truly amazing. While we may not be part of a thunder and lightning miracle, God's continuous work in our lives is miracle enough. As Dr. Weld says, "And even if we don't understand all of God's ways, how much of God's light do we need to walk in, anyway? Here's the answer: just enough. He gives us all the light we need." *God Is in the Crazy* is a down-to-earth (and heaven above) manual where there is encouragement from the miraculous life stories of others and a promise of divine providence in our daily walk. Dr. Weld wisely states that "With the uplift and 'thermals' from God through His Holy Spirit, there is no need to struggle to gain altitude and soar. Like the albatross or the eagle, we can circle effortlessly in the sky for hours, with barely the twitch of a wing."

Robert Matte Jr.
Talkingthunder.com
Tucson, Arizona

SECTION 1

GOD IS BIGGER THAN CRAZY!

INTRODUCTION

BIGGER THAN THE WASTE HOWLING WILDERNESS

There are men and women so lonely they believe God, too, is lonely.
—Carl Sandburg[1]

As a faith-based counselor for many years, I hear of grueling struggles daily. Someone might experience a stolen inheritance, a home invasion, or betrayal by a coworker. A loved one might be murdered or drawn into the gravitational pull of a cult with a message from the Star Trek series, "Resistance is futile. You will be assimilated." I've heard more than once, "My brain broke," and even more often, *"He makes me crazy!"* When I was a new counselor, I would explain how we can only make *ourselves* crazy. Now I simply say, "That would make me crazy, too!" And when people ask how I can do my job without losing my mind, sometimes I jokingly respond that insanity is a hazard to my profession.

Nobody must tell me that we live in a world infected with evil. No one must tell you either. Pick up a newspaper, watch the news, or just live your life while heartaches ebb and flow around and inside you. None of us can escape what feels like conspiracies of unfairness. I've never met anyone who hasn't at some point been lightning-struck by cruel words, underhanded agendas, or unpredictable hardships. Certainly, there are few who haven't been adversely affected by the deadly pandemic and civil unrest that dominate the news cycles. Social mores around the world are dangerously unhinged.

Someone once said that life is a bad night in a cheap hotel.[2] This idea is like the theme of the book of Ecclesiastes—that everything under the sun is meaningless, or that life is a rat race, and the rats are winning! Of course, a full understanding of Ecclesiastes provides a more profound theme. "Under the sun" means "without God's influence." We all run a race in our lives, but we don't have to run a rat race. You can still come through it all with a victory shout!

Yes, life can be crazy! But if you're reading this book, the final curtain hasn't fallen. Chapter 1 will help you understand that there are many ways to look at the night in a cheap hotel. The rest of the book builds on the miracle experiences of people like you and me who have wondered, "Where is God?" Each chapter ends with a reflection that flows from the miracle accounts, leading us beside still waters of inner peace. I believe you'll finish this book with a sense—or a stronger sense—that God *is* in the crazy.

As the son of a minister, I wandered from faith in a personal God who loves me, to a drug-induced delusion that I was at one with the universe. I thought I was stardust and that my exciting destiny was to join with galaxies of infinite glitter. I didn't experience out-of-body travel through the universe, as one friend in a cult did, but I was confused!

I let myself be swallowed up by years of drug and alcohol abuse in my twenties. In addition to the damage I inflicted on my body, the axis of my value system leaned toward relativism. If the internet had existed back then, I would have been more interested in making it to Wikipedia than to Heaven. At age twenty-nine, I quit alcohol, weed, cigarettes, and hallucinogens on a single day. But I did not yet know God, and I was a nervous wreck. I could barely walk down a flight of stairs, and I should have sought medical help.

Three months later, a girlfriend suggested that I pray. I'm going to talk about my journey, what I prayed for, and how God answered in the chapter titled "Nil Sine Numine." That Latin phrase is the Weld family motto. It means "Nothing without Providence." In that chapter, I'll also talk about the problems, victories, and miracles of family members. My parents were more fortunate than they realized to leave Germany, then England right before German submarines started sinking ships that crossed the Atlantic. I'm inspired by their encounters with brainwashed Nazis, discouraged Jews, a pastor who saved Jewish lives, and Nazi resisters who survived concentration camps. You'll see why I named the section about my parents, "Heil Roosevelt!"

Beyond the usual thought of something that makes no sense, I'm defining *crazy* as dysfunction, danger, or distress. Any of the three conditions—which are sometimes embodied in a person or event—can be foreboding. Any of them can be unexpected. They might seem highly improbable and even unfair. They never make sense at the time and can often put our worldview on tilt! When I use the phrase "crazy-hard," I'm talking about tortuous evil that also makes no sense at the time and is life-threatening.

However, *when we look back through the eyes of faith*, we usually see ways in which God used the "crazy" for our benefit. In fact, the expanded view of crazy you'll get from reading this book will likely elicit praise and worship for our Creator who lives *in it* and reigns *over it!* And He can help us overcome all manner of crazy. He has performed miracles throughout history and is still moving supernaturally in our time. For example, He still answers prayer and still uses angels to intervene in our lives. He is the only one who can make sense out of "crazy."

In fact, miracles surround each one of us and are easily known. Now and then miracles get right up in our faces, and we can't ignore that one has happened. Other times, miracles are subtler. Friends and acquaintances often tell me they've experienced both kinds of miracles. Hundreds of books have been written on this topic. I wish you could see my library at home! And aside from what I've read, people have told me about supernatural events they've personally experienced. I've also prayed with many people, and I've seen God answer cries of desperation.

Each story is unique. Many people have heard an audible voice from out of nowhere that saved their lives. One family, on its way to my hometown on Christmas Eve, was rescued by an auto mechanic in a shop that turned out not to exist. A longtime friend was trapped in his crashed crop duster and was then instantly on the ground without moving. Right before a Tucson great-grandmother died of the coronavirus, the family received much comfort from her vision of a white chariot and of her desire to be on it. Two retired New York police officers tell mesmerizing stories. One saw the highlights of his life as if on a movie screen. The other believes it may have been two angels who lifted a wave of depression from him in a pizza parlor. A war hero, Lieutenant Commander (retired) Paul Galanti, survived almost seven years in the "Hanoi Hilton," a notorious prison camp in North Vietnam. He describes how Jesus Christ appeared and spoke to him between torture sessions. I'm not kidding when I say these stories are exciting, faith-building stuff!

Along with such accounts, you'll read about people who overcame great odds to even stay alive, including George Washington (bullets tore holes in his jacket but did not touch him), Winston Churchill (he walked the streets of London while German bombs fell), and Sergeant Carney of the all-black Civil War regiment who carried the flag through a barrage of bullets. Two "Heroes by Choice" chapters speak of these people and others who overcame great odds with God's help. One of these heroes is a distant relative who was, perhaps, the greatest anti-slavery advocate of the 1800s. He was called "the most-mobbed man in the United States."

Maybe you're someone who feels their prayers are never heard. Fortunately, God's promise is that He won't let you be completely cast down. Sometimes, He'll let you hit the ground hard—but He won't let you stay down permanently.[3] I saw a news report about a dog that was trapped on the median of a busy interstate. Traffic whizzed by from several lanes in both directions. The poor dog was trapped and could not stop howling. Traffic didn't slow down, and the danger didn't let up. I love animals, and I was touched by the dog's predicament. As I think about the desperate animal, I'm reminded of an Old Testament passage that speaks of God leading the Israelites out of the bondage of Egypt and through the desert: "He found him in a desert land, and in *the waste howling wilderness*; he led him about, he instructed him, he kept him as the apple of his eye."[4]

Most of us have at times felt trapped in the waste howling wilderness. At our wit's end, we may have attributed to God unlikeable qualities that are really true of the damaged parts of ourselves. For example, we may have said, "God must hate me!" when we have really learned to hate ourselves. I heard someone who *wanted* something to complain about say, "I don't even know what to complain about!" Even though most hardships don't have to be permanent, I've felt like that, not knowing what to complain about—but howling, nevertheless. As for the dog? A policeman spotted him, brought traffic to a stop, and rescued him.

St. Augustine said that *God loves each one of us as if there's only one of us to love.* The value of a single life is immeasurable. That means your life too! And as an ember has enough heat to stoke a fire, exercising small faith can lead you to a powerful destiny. You can stoke the fire! You can open up to God's revelation of Himself in the midst of the crazy! An unknown psalmist said, "He will respond to the prayer of the destitute; he will not despise their plea."[5] Nothing can stop God from accomplishing His good purposes for your life. He's right in the middle of crazy. Even better than this, He's also sovereign and in charge!

I heard a story about a Native American tribal chief who visited the Grand Coulee Dam. Looking at the immense engineering marvel, while others expected him to be impressed, all the chief had to say was, "But they couldn't stop the river!" The parallel to our lives is clear. Life's harsh realities can't stop God's unseen power. I haven't been able to see or feel God in *all* of life's craziness. God keeps Himself hidden at times. Scriptures say clouds and thick darkness often surround His bright presence.[6] But to those who have an open heart, God delights to make Himself known. Jesus said that God the Father *wants* to reveal Himself to us. He wants us to position our lives daily to receive more revelations from and about Him. Commentary throughout this book will encourage you to do the same.

When God led the tribes of Israel to Mount Sinai where Moses received the Ten Commandments, Moses and Aaron were instructed "to camp to the east of the tabernacle, toward the sunrise."[7] While I'm on this Earth, that's where I want to camp my soul. When I don't see Him, I'll keep looking and hoping for the sun to rise. I don't exclude myself from active participation in what's wrong with this world! Much of the time, my own heart is crazy. I'm only glad God lives in it.

Reflections on the Peaceful Life

You've probably howled in the waste howling wilderness. Fortunately, God sees the entire landscape of your past, present, and future. He sees the green grass, the streams of refreshing, and the mountain peaks of achievement just beyond your horizons. When you're despondent, or even desperate for hope, remember that the eternal God is your refuge, "and underneath are the everlasting arms."[8] No matter how deep your pain goes, God's love goes deeper still. No matter how far down you fall, His everlasting arms are there to comfort and lift you up. It's even okay to ask God for a tangible sign of His goodness. King David of the Old Testament did this when he called to Him with desperate sincerity, "Give me a sign of your goodness."[9] Ask Him today! He hears you!

Endnotes

1.   Carl Sandburg, *The Complete Poems of Carl Sandburg*, "They Ask: Is God, Too, Lonely?" (New York: Harcourt Brace Jovanovich, Inc., 1970), 393.

2.   Anonymous, In Chris Thurman, *If Christ Were Your Counselor* (Nashville: Thomas Nelson Publishers, 1993), 25.

3.   Psalm 37:24 KJV.

4.   Deuteronomy 32:10 KJV (italics added).

5.   Psalm 102:17.

6.   Psalm 97:2 and Psalm 18:12.

7.   Numbers 3:38.

8.   Deuteronomy 33:27.

9.   Psalm 86:17.

1

BE A FAITH-REALIST!

It is good to grasp the one and not let go of the other; the man who fears God will avoid all extremes [Hebrew: "will practice them both"].
—*Ecclesiastes 7:18*

Faith and reason are mutually reinforcing.
—*Clarence Thomas, Associate Justice of the Supreme Court of the United States*[10]

Most people believe in God, though many define Him differently. Most people also believe in miracles. I believe it's unrealistic to think we can live successfully without faith in a God who performs miracles. When King Solomon said God has *set the world* in our hearts,[11] he was talking about an intuitive sense of the eternal. This awareness can help us deal with our problems. When I have a problem, I sometimes think of King David. He had a really big one: Goliath! David was realistic about the strength of this fighting giant who wore a fortress of armor. He heard the talk of the soldiers. He saw the giant. And as Goliath daily taunted King Saul's army to send out someone who would fight him, David watched Saul's men cower in fear.

Yet David *ran toward* Goliath with only a sling and a stone. He had faith that God would deliver the arrogant challenger into his hands. David was a faith-realist—and you can be one too! You can grow to contain both the crazy things that happen to you and the peaceful presence of God at the same time. When He calls you to run toward battle, He will enable you to win!

Let's define "faith" and "realist," according to biblical theology. *Faith* is believing in an unseen God who is personal and loves us. Faith embraces the eternal realm as more real than the one we can see. One reason for that is because eternity existed before the world began, and unlike the temporal realm, the eternal one won't pass away. Faith includes believing God answers prayer and that He can make things happen that don't seem possible. Therefore, faith is being certain that, at any time, a burst of God's glory can set our dimly lit lives aflame!

What does it mean to be "realistic"? Most of us think it means being practical, pragmatic, and able to face painful life events head-on. These descriptors are partially true. But there's more than that to being realistic. Life contains multiple realities, and as we search for truths hidden inside them, we notice they don't contradict faith but *complement* it.

The Whole of Things

To be realistic means to see the *whole picture of things*. When an architect looks at Niagara Falls, he might see a beautiful structure. When an engineer looks at it, she might compute the power that's produced. When an artist sees this majestic waterfall, he might marvel at the rainbow sprays and *hear* the gentle sound of brush strokes creating a colorful painting. All three of them see a piece of the whole.

Part of my job as a counselor is to help people see the big picture. This perspective can help bring inner peace amid a swirl of problems. Problems usually have multiple dimensions that stay hidden unless we consider other points of view. Sometimes, a good friend or counselor can help us expand how we see people or situations. This can help us to be more compassionate, more forgiving, and more discerning.

Much of *reality itself* is often hidden or unnoticed. Obviously, we don't see everything God sees because He is infinite and everywhere. While we "see through a glass darkly"[12] here on Earth, God's understanding has no limit.[13] The more we see the whole of things, the more we look at life through God's serene and all-seeing eyes. The more we become faith-realists, the more we are able to lay hold of unfathomable peace.

Six Invisible Dimensions of Reality

At work, I have to keep in mind many clinical dimensions and how they influence each other. These include factors such as family rules, unmet needs, communication problems, and diagnoses. But this book isn't written from my office with deliberate clinical perspectives. We need to expand our understanding of reality beyond what we can learn from psychological testing and interview techniques.

Here are six non-clinical dimensions of human experience that a person who thinks realistically should consider. You'll notice that each dimension includes a view of life that considers more than what we can see with our physical eyes. The same would be true with any dimension you can name, and the list of these dimensions is extensive. When these *invisible realities* intersect with the world we live in, they become evident, and *miracles* can happen. These are the six dimensions we'll now consider: radiance, heartache, courage, kindness, redemption, and prayer power. Here's the first of the six invisible dimensions.

No Small Roles, Only Small Players[14]
The Reality of Radiance

One of my favorite books is *Anonymous: Jesus' Hidden Years and Yours* by Alicia Britt Chole. She ends the book with this story that challenges the typical definition of success:

> Whenever I am disappointed with my spot
> in life, I stop and think about the little boy who
> was trying out for a part in a school play. His
> mother told me that he'd set his heart on being in

it, though she feared he would not be chosen. On the day the parts were awarded, I went with her to collect him after school. The boy rushed up to her, eyes shining with pride and excitement. "Guess what, Mom," he shouted, and then said those words that will remain a lesson to me: "I've been chosen to clap and cheer."[15]

I'm still learning to appreciate that the opportunity to clap and cheer indicated a huge victory for this little boy. "God works within lifted spirits,"[16] and this little boy's spirit is an inspiration! The truth is that a role in a play is only as important as you *make* it. Can we say that a person so jaded that he can't rejoice with this little boy has an unrealistic outlook on life? That person's outlook is probably skewed toward a place where my brain wouldn't want to live. Russell Stafford says, "People who surrender joy are almost ready to surrender everything else. When humor and mirth and rollicking tunes die away, defeat is near."[17] I would add that in order to surrender to joy, we need to simply pay attention to what there is to be joyful about.

I almost didn't go to a Christmas church service because children were giving a concert. I was in the mood for worshipping and hearing a sermon, not watching a bunch of little kids. My wife said, "But we can clap and cheer!" Of course, I went and was glad I did. My wife Susan has taught many classes with me. She's heard me use this example, and she won't let me get away with much! King Solomon wrote in a proverb, the *realistic* voice of wisdom says, "I was filled with delight day after day, rejoicing always in his presence, rejoicing in his whole world and delighting in mankind."[18] A *wise* person *rejoices* in God's presence and *delights* in His whole world and also in mankind. A wise person pays attention to the many reasons we must rejoice.

Jesus must have been in a festive mood when He performed his first miracle at a wedding, providing the best wine toward the end of the celebration. This is the same Jesus who had "joy above his fellows."[19] Jesus was the most joyful man who ever lived, and He appreciated the good and beautiful in life. We're often surprised by what children do and say because they tend to pay more attention to the good and beautiful. They seem more likely to appreciate life's simple pleasures, such as Grandpa's lesson in how to tie a knot, their favorite teacher's kindness, the year's first appearance of snow, or the playfulness of a pet. Perhaps, with a poem by Elizabeth Barrett Browning in mind, one Bible commentator says the authors of the Psalms "may have reached the conclusion that earth was crammed with Heaven and every common bush aflame with God."[20] Do we see "common things" as the psalmists do? Do we clap and cheer at the smallest victories of others? Do we see the earth crammed with the glory of God? Most joy is sparked by noticing what there is to be joyful about. Joy reflects a realistic view of a notable part of the whole.

Fate of a Test Pilot
The Reality of Heartache

Uncle Bob was a humble man. My mother's only brother served as a test pilot during World War II. When he warned his superiors that the plane he often tested wasn't safe, no one believed him. The plane crashed and severely injured him. Uncle Bob remembered hearing a medic pronounce him dead. However, he lived to fly another day! Nevertheless, his life of bravery turned in a tragic direction. After the war, he opened a store that sold vacuum cleaners and sewing machines. Twenty-five years later, he loaned out a room on the second floor of his shop to a support group for alcoholics.

In May of 1975, after a group meeting, a man who had been prematurely released from a mental hospital walked down the stairs and shot my uncle dead. What could be more starkly realistic, as we typically define "realism"? What could challenge my mother's faith in God more than such a tragedy? I understand how she could later say, "The sunshine of one's life exacts its penalty of shadow."[21] I don't think she ever got over losing her brother, but you'd never know it by how she continued to give each day her best shot—as she always had.

While in college, my mother had been invited to try out for the Olympics in swimming, but she was too poor to afford to travel to the trials. She went on to triumph in other ways. As a pastor's wife, she was criticized for teaching high school rather than working more with her minister-husband without pay. But as a teacher, she did much good, helping poor students get into college and teaching the first Black literature course in Columbus, Ohio, at South High School. And she continued to lay hold of the best life had to offer, which included swimming. I'll never forget how gracefully she glided through the waters even in her late eighties. She still enjoyed her life, despite suffering from short-term memory loss.

Joy like my mother's can only be acquired on the hard path of realistic living. The meaningful life takes the hard path of joy (sometimes the very, VERY hard path)—not the enticing road to destruction I followed in my drug and alcohol days. Psychologists refer to my mother's path as "post-traumatic growth," a phrase coined in the 1990s by Richard Tedeschi and Lawrence Calhoun.[22] This increase in well-being is fostered by spiritual growth, personal strength, appreciation of life, relationships, and looking for new possibilities.[23] These attributes defined my mother to a great degree; and she proved what the apostle Paul said two thousand years ago, that suffering *produces* hope.[24] This is a God-designed process, and faith in Christ as our Healer adds hope in God to the healing.

Despite what I suspect was never complete healing (as with many who have suffered similarly), my mother knew the truth of Paul's statement, "In all our troubles, my joy knows no bounds."[25]

You've probably suffered a broken heart, an experience common to us all. Even a bird can have its heart broken...and mended. I saw an interesting newspaper photo of a twenty-three-year-old shorebird, a black-necked stilt named Skippy. Skippy is looking at a painting of his mate, which was part of a mural at a veterinary hospital at the National Aviary in Pittsburgh. The caption beneath the photo tells a story about how "the heart mends." A few years earlier, Skippy's mate had died. Seeming depressed, Skippy had stopped grooming and eventually refused to eat. However, when the long-legged, black-and-white bird saw the mural, he started to call to it. He even offered food to the bird in the painting. And then he started to eat again.[26] God fashioned a path to healing for Skippy's grieving heart.

When I think of heartache, I often think of Christ. He wasn't *just* the most joyful man that ever lived. He also knew greater sorrow than any other human being.[27] After an illegal trial, He died a torturous death, even though He had never sinned. According to His Heavenly Father's plan, the weight of the sin of the world oppressed Him. Because Jesus was the most emotionally and psychologically whole person who had ever lived (never having sinned), He possessed the ability to experience all emotions in deeper ways than are possible for the rest of us. As we become more like Christ—a spiritual process that changes our earthbound selves—we also experience a deeper and broader range of emotions. And when we look to God during times of heartache, we come into a closer relationship with Him. Therefore, if we run from suffering, we also run from joy.

Can we expect to know great depths of joy without knowing the depths of suffering that are woven into the fabric of our fallen world? George McDonald understood the importance of suffering. McDonald said, "The Son of God suffered unto death, not that men might not suffer but that their sufferings might be like his."[28] We'll consider how joy and suffering hold each other's hands in the chapter titled "God Draws Straight with Crooked Lines."

When His House Burned Down
The Reality of Courage

C.S. Lewis said, "Courage is not simply one of the virtues, but the form of every virtue at the testing point."[29] *Any* serious challenge could be described as the point at which all other virtues are tested and refined. A realistic view of life demands that we understand the importance of courage.

Dwight L. Moody demonstrated courage. Many of us know Moody as the man who founded the prominent Moody Bible Institute in Chicago. Dwight's father died when he was four years old. His mother, left to raise a large family, never encouraged his education. Dwight got no further than fifth grade. When he was converted by Christ at age eighteen, he knew so little about the Bible he wasn't even allowed to become a member of his church.[30] The beginning of his courage was his fight to overcome these handicaps so that he could be used by God in powerful ways. Moody later found himself seated on a platform with religious leaders. He heard a preacher say, "The world has yet to see what God can do with one man who is *utterly* committed to him." At that moment, Moody said in his heart, "I propose to *be* that person."

R.T. Kendall writes:

> We might think that anybody who would want to be used of God like that would get the applause of the angels—that everything would start going right. Within days, his church burned down. His own house burned down. It is through much tribulation that we enter the kingdom of God (Acts 14:22).[31]

Did Moody flounder in his faith? Was the fire a curse or a blessing? This book will consider many such stories that inspire us to persevere and to hold fast to our visions. We can expect any call to achievement to be accompanied by opposition. King Solomon said, "When times are good, be happy; when times are bad, consider: God has made the one as well as the other."[32] Was it worth it for Moody to hang in there through the trials? The answer is "yes!" Moody is known for his frequent sermons on the love of Jesus. Sometimes he held revivals that focused every night on John 3:16: "For God so loved the world that he gave his one and only Son, that whoever believes in him shall not perish but have eternal life." Pastors who were present marveled he could speak so long on one subject! And we know the world is a better place because of the thousands of students who have graduated from Moody's school since 1886.

Such stories make me think of the courageous Christ. He confronted the teachers of endless rules and regulations, knowing their show of godliness was a front for arrogance. He toppled the tables of greedy merchants in the Jerusalem temple, stripping their disguises. Sometimes, we must also *escalate* a conflict—increasing the risk to ourselves and others—to accomplish *anything* worthwhile in this life.

Christ was a master of knowing precisely *when* to escalate because He was always directed by His Heavenly Father. Then His painful execution was well-timed, a Rorschach image of His escalation of the conflict between good and evil. As the Lamb of God, His sacrifice occurred during the Passover, exactly when Jews sacrificed a lamb to celebrate God's judgment passing over them before their pilgrimage from Egypt. Christ's sacrifice was courageous, and His timing could only be perfect. He faced the realities of hypocrisy head-on. Now through faith in Christ, God's judgment passes over us, as it passed over the Jews. We are forgiven and can live with Him forever, free of fear.

Chomping on Cactus
The Reality of Kindness

Realistic people know what kindness is when they see it, and they know how to be kind. I witnessed a great example. I was crossing the street on my way to a drug and alcohol treatment center. As a wounded healer, I was one of the counselors, although I was also still in recovery. I saw a beautiful Irish setter on a back porch. She was lying uncomfortably on her side, whimpering and crying. As I approached the dog, I noticed a large piece of Tucson prickly pear cactus stuck to her hind end. Prickly pears have flat, round "ears" with fifty to one hundred needles per ear. In order to remove the needles, the setter kept chomping down on them—but she was unable to get hold of the cactus ear itself, and the needles got stuck in her gums. I wanted to pet the dog and speak soothing words as I removed the needles from her leg and mouth. But I was a stranger to the animal. I feared the dog might turn on me. Suddenly, the dog's owner emerged from the back door. Seeing what was going on, he spoke gently to his dog and petted her head as he removed the needles from her mouth. Of course, the owner had a unique bond with his pet, and he was kind to his best friend. After about ten minutes, the needles were gone and the chunk of cactus was dislodged from the setter's hind end. *Whew!*

I think we're much like that Irish setter. She had brushed up against a prickly pear, panicked, and then tried to save herself as best she could—but she made matters worse. She understood only one way to fix her problem. She was hurting so badly that she couldn't see beyond the one reality of pain and the one way she thought to fix it. The pain gave that dog a "worm's eye" view of the problem. She couldn't see the bigger picture of her master's love and the safety net that was always there for her. Her owner's kindness made all the difference to the dog. I'm not much different from the setter—are you? When caught off guard by a thorny problem, I can get reactive. After recuperating from valley fever pneumonia in my early thirties, I had a boss so mean it made him weak in the knees to be kind (not an uncommon experience for many of us!). I couldn't fix him or the problems he caused, and if I'd been reactive, I would have ended up with the emotional equivalent of "a mouth full of cactus needles." Fortunately, I didn't have to work that job for long and soon moved into full-time ministry.

What we need in difficult situations is kindness from another source…from a stranger or friend. One way or another, we need help from God Himself. We need the type of kindness Jesus extended to the crippled, the blind, and the lepers. We can also extend this kindness to those around us. And we can show people that there are realities beyond their pain.

Sun Boy's Fiddle
The Reality of Redemption

Definitions of *redemption* include being saved from suffering and having something made better. This was the case when a young boy heard the singing strings of an old violin. His identity was restored, and his heart became attuned to the missing chords his life was meant to play—all because of an unexpected visitor.

Bob Taylor was three times governor of Tennessee. His nickname was "Fiddling Bob" because, as a young man, he'd lived to play the violin. The beloved governor often called on many people around his state, whom he considered friends. One time, he visited a humble family in the mountains. Among the many children in the family, there was one they called "Sun Boy." This boy had hoped in a childlike way to become a great violinist. His family had obtained a violin for him, and he'd played it all day long. Every day brought joy because of the music he played. After a time, however, his violin became worn. Several strings broke, and the bow was badly in need of repair. Ashamed because he could no longer produce music from his instrument, Sun Boy hid the violin in the hollow of an old tree.

On the day he happened to visit the family, the governor noticed the old violin in the tree. Fond memories returned as he thought of his own first violin. He fixed the fiddle's strings as best he could, cleaned off dirt from the tree, repaired the decrepit instrument, tuned it, and began to play. He played song after song, the melodies echoing through the woods. Sun Boy heard the melodies and came running. His eyes were eager and bright with amazement and admiration as he gazed at the player who seemed to be so inspired. When Bob Taylor paused, the little fellow exclaimed, "Gee, I wish I had a violin like that." The governor stretched out his hands to the child. He said, "Take it, Sun Boy. It's your violin."

Do you have a gift that has gathered dust? Do you have a dream that's part of who you are but you've forgotten about it? God can redeem it! He can make it new!

One of my favorite examples of redemption happened at Christ's execution. Jesus was crucified with one criminal on each side of Him. One thief hurled insults at Jesus while the other defended Him and asked to be remembered by Jesus when He entered His kingdom in the afterlife. Jesus said that He, indeed, would remember the thief and that he would be with Him that day in paradise. That was a last-minute reprieve for the criminal who was honest about his sins and his need for a Savior. He was redeemed! That's also what happened to the disciples. Before Christ rose from the dead, they had a mission and an identity—but they somehow abandoned both at the crucifixion. When they later saw their risen Savior, they understood how God can make all who believe in Christ into new creations.

When things look the bleakest, I like to remember that Jesus said a grain of wheat must fall to the ground and die before the fruit could come forth. Time and environmental factors tend to smother the seed until germination bursts out. Jesus was referring to His impending death, which was necessary so that He could impart eternal life to humanity as the resurrected Messiah.

But Jesus had another message for us. In our everyday lives, we understand that we must be *realistic* when we experience the "death of a vision." That's probably happened to you—a dream you've treasured and nurtured simply died. When you must endure a sacrifice like this, that's exactly when you need to be *realistic* and keep the big picture in mind. If you're going through this now, you must allow the seed to fight on. Don't try to turn your dreams into reality through your own strength. Your waiting—and later your efforts, with His help—will produce results. Trust that the fruit God has in mind will come forth in His timing!

So, what do we need to be realistic about? We need to accept that only God can make our highest aspirations a reality. Without God, a vision will stay buried. The violin will stay stuck in the hollow of a tree. But with faith that God can do even the impossible, we can raise a triumphant shout over our doubts and fears. Like Sun Boy, we can reclaim our gifts and take our seat in God's orchestra, where all lives are made new. Our redemption and the reworking of our lives for God's purposes is the destiny of faith-realists.

Just Talking to God
The Reality of Prayer Power

My Experience in Counseling with Prayer

The last of the six invisible dimensions involves prayer. Several years ago, I asked myself, "What's the most effective thing I ever do in counseling?" I quickly realized the answer: *prayer*. I pray with almost all my clients. Research shows that the only kind of prayer that helps people feel closer to God is "colloquial" prayer—"just talking to God." At the end of this kind of prayer, clients often say they feel peaceful. They get other takeaways from the sessions, but praying always seems to lift their spirits. That's why I decided to write my dissertation on Christian clients' expectations of prayer when seeing a Christian counselor.[33] Among other conclusions, my study showed that 82 percent of Christian clients expect to share an audible prayer with their counselor.

Whenever I feel peace in counseling sessions that end in prayer, I am assured that my client feels peace too. I've found this to be always true! Clients often come to the next session reporting progress because of something that happened to them that had nothing to do with the counseling.

I see two dynamics going on here: 1) God hears the righteous cry of a sincere heart and answers prayer, and 2) God often honors the humility of people who are willing to see a counselor by causing life events to turn favorably for them. A client once told me counseling wasn't helping her get rid of her phobia, but she returned to her sixth session to tell me the phobia had disappeared. I don't know how else to explain this miracle except that God answered our prayers. Sometimes, I pray that God will heal someone's emotions, even in their sleep. And sometimes He does! When couples tell me that I "saved their marriage," I think the counseling helped to speed God's process. The couple followed through with their homework, and God performed the miracle.

Much Prayer, Much Power: Jessica Tanner's Miracle

Sometimes, we see that God has answered the prayers of many and truly made the invisible become visible. Jessica and Phillip Tanner, two hardworking graduates of Grand Canyon University, were still honeymooners—married a little more than two months— on September 26, 2017. Suddenly, Jessica felt ill and was rushed to an emergency room, where doctors discovered she had clots in both lungs. This medical crisis threw a meteoric curveball at the young couple. When I worked in an emergency room, I'd seen this situation many times. Blood clots in the lungs can be fatal. Jessica had thrown a massive clot that almost totally blocked the flow of blood from her right heart into her lungs. It was a worst-case scenario!

Jessica was clinically dead for *ninety minutes*, which is a long time for the brain to go without oxygen (five minutes usually means death or severe brain damage). A skilled ER team who refused to give up on her somehow brought her back to life. But the incident left Jessica comatose—no surprise there. Forty-eight hours after she was revived in the ER, the neurologist on call gave Jessica less than a 1 percent chance of survival. He said, if she did survive, she would be in a vegetative state. Pointing at the comatose young woman, the specialist told Phillip and the family, "That is not Jessica. That is just a shell of her."

There was no reason to hope she would ever again function normally in the land of the living. Jessica and Phillip later learned that a nurse of Jessica's went home that day and told his wife, "I don't think I can do this anymore." Jessica could not have been closer to parting the veil separating this life from the next. She needed a miracle. Phillip called his father and his mother, Deanna, to tell them of Jessica's crisis. They headed to Phoenix, put the word out on a prayer chain, and called Jessica's friends to get to the hospital immediately. When Phillip called, Jessica's parents and her two brothers, Kyle and Matthew, all caught the first flight from Idaho. They also sent texts, emails, and social media posts requesting prayer for Jessica. Prayers started going up immediately from people as far away as Germany, Australia, and Japan. The amount of support this young couple had was nothing short of spectacular. Jessica's eight-year-old brother, Matthew, said with childlike faith, "God would not put Jessie through this if He wasn't going to help her get better."

Friends and family started pouring in from Idaho, California, Nevada, and Texas. Throughout an interminable two-month ordeal, friends from Grand Canyon University were visiting and praying too. They were the first to arrive at the hospital, camping out in the waiting rooms, running errands, bringing food, and encouraging Phillip. While clot-busting drugs enabled Jessica's heart to begin pumping blood normally through her lungs again, it was a ventilator, multiple medical procedures, and as many as eleven IV infusions that kept her alive. Author and emergency room physician, Robert Lesslie, wrote in *Angels on the Night Shift* that if a patient has more than seven tubes connected to one's body, that's a "sure sign they wouldn't survive."[34]

Aware that the veil between Jessica's life on Earth and life in the hereafter was gossamer-thin, family and friends continued in prayer…and God heard them! On her third day in the hospital, Jessica was still in a coma, but doctors saw positive signs on her MRI. They said she still had a long way to go. Jessica's entire family kept a constant vigil by her side. Phillip spent almost every night at the hospital those two months. The family happened to be outside her room for one, especially momentous milestone.

On October 5, Jessica returned from another CT scan. The ICU nurse ran to the waiting room to tell the family that Jessica "smiled at us on command!" She was slowly coming out of her week-long coma. Over the next ten days, Jessica still dealt with various complications. She had an increased heart rate, a fever, and her bowels were shutting down, to name but a few of her medical problems. On October 17, the CT scan showed the clots were all gone. *All gone!* Those were soul-shaking words! Phillip and Jessica were told that the normal time for this to happen is nine months, not three weeks. Phillip was joyfully certain such a quick disappearance of the clots was not merely because of modern medicine or the expertise and hard work of the medical team. This was a miracle from God and a demonstration that God's infinite wisdom continually empowered everyone involved. The prayers did not stop.

I heard Jessica and Phillip Tanner speak at Alive Church here in Tucson on a Sunday morning, about six months after Jessica was discharged from the hospital. Associate Pastor Steve Tanner, Phillip's father, introduced them. Jessica spoke softly and humbly, saying her family adheres to a well-known adage:

> Little prayer, little power
> More prayer, more power
> Much prayer, much power

At the time of that church service, Jessica showed only mild, lingering effects of her medical crisis. I noticed nothing unusual about her. In addition to the physical therapy she received to help her relearn to walk and talk, she was still getting treatment to correct occasional tangled thoughts and residual visual difficulty. She'd been given less than a 1 percent chance of survival, yet she'd made a 99 percent recovery and was still improving! Jessica gives glory to God that He heard the prayers of so many and performed this miracle! Jessica learned not to take anything for granted. She said she now appreciates more than ever "a cup of coffee in the morning with her mom and time with her little brother."

It's no wonder that neurosurgeon David Levy says, "I have learned two important things: that there is a limit to what I can do as a highly trained and experienced surgeon and that there is *no limit* to what God can do to touch a person, emotionally and spiritually, not just physically."[35] Dr. Levy who prays with his patients cites a study that concluded 75 percent of a thousand physicians surveyed believe that "religion and spirituality are important in helping patients cope and in giving them a positive state of mind."[36] Another study of 124 ophthalmology patients at Johns Hopkins University found "prayer was important to their sense of well-being."[37] I cite two studies in my dissertation that indicate the positive effect of prayer on physical well-being.

Now that we've started down the road of faith-realism, where intellect and awe joyfully coexist, our miracle journey into *astounding* miracles begins to quicken! Our next chapter, "Life on the Wire," helps to show how natural and supernatural realities are often intertwined. If they weren't, no one could walk the high wire!

Reflections on the Peaceful Life

If you can look at life from multiple perspectives, you'll never be backed into believing a lie. When you value Christ's point of view on all of life's dimensions, you'll more easily tolerate uncertainties, see more to the heart of life's mysteries, and the truth will set you free… and give you peace.[38]

Endnotes

10 Clarence Thomas, *Imprimis*, November 2019, Vol. 48, no.11 (Hillsdale, MI: Hillsdale College), 1.
11 Ecclesiastes 3:11 KJV.
12 1 Corinthians 13:12 KJV.
13 Isaiah 40:28.
14 Constantin Stanislavski (1863–1938) of the Moscow Art Theatre, "Brainy Quotes," "Constantin Stanislavi Quotes," Stanislavski's quote is, "There are no small parts, only small actors." Accessed 11/25/2018, https://www.brainyquote.com/quotes/constantin_stanislavski_155177.
15 Alicia Britt Chole, *Anonymous: Jesus' Hidden Years and Yours* (Nashville, TN: Thomas Nelson, 2006), 181.
16 Jose Hobday, *Stories of Abundance* (New York, London: Continuum, 2004), 4.
17 R.H. Stafford, "The Singing Heart," from a sermon delivered in the Old South Church, Boston, 10/8/1939.
18 Proverbs 8:25–26.
19 Hebrews 1:9 KJV.
20 Clovis Chappell, *Sermons from the Psalms*, © by Lamar and Whitmore (USA: Wartime Books, 1931) 96.
21 Mary Weld, *A Beautiful Stride* (unpublished) 1994.
22 Richard Tedeschi and Lawrence Calhoun, Adena Bank Lees, "Posttraumatic Growth," *Psychology Today*, accessed 8/31/2020, https://www.psychologytoday.com/us/blog/surviving-thriving/201904/posttraumatic-growth.
23 Richard Tedeschi and Lawrence Calhoun.
24 Romans 5:3–4.
25 2 Corinthians 7:4; author hasn't researched the *extent* of healing by posttraumatic growth. Studies, however, show that such growth meets levels of statistical significance.
26 Keith Srakocic, "The Heart Mends," The Associated Press, *Arizona Daily Star*, 2/13/2011.
27 Isaiah 53 and Luke 22:44.
28 George McDonald, "Our Daily Bread," "The Ministry of Suffering," 12/5/2000, accessed 3/2/2018, https://odb.org/2000/12/05/the-ministry-of-suffering/. See also Romans 8:17.
29 C.S. Lewis, Twitter, @CSLewisDaily, accessed 2/22/2018, and C.S Lewis, "Brainy Quote," accessed 12/13/2020 https://www.brainyquote.com/quotes/c_s_lewis_100842.
30 Accessed 12/11/2017, http://www.inspirationalchristians.org/biography/dwight-l-moody-biography/.
31 R.T. Kendall, *God Meant It for Good* (Charlotte, North Carolina: Morning Star Publications, 1981), 62.
32 Ecclesiastes 7:14.

33   Chet Weld, "A Survey of Primarily Christian Clients' Preferences Concerning the Intervention of Prayer at Faith-Based Counseling Agencies," 8/2006. Dissertation available at ProQuest, accessed 12/13/2020, https://www.researchgate.net/publication/277559093_A_Survey_of_Primarily_Christian_Clients%27_Preferences_Concerning_the_Intervention_of_Prayer_at_Faith-Based_Counseling_Agencies_Dissertation_available_at_ProQuest.   Also, available at ResearchGate.com.

34   Robert D. Lesslie, *Angels on the Night Shift* (Eugene, Oregon: Harvest House Publishers, 2012), 52.

35   David I. Levy and Mark Anthony Lane II, *Gray Matter: A Neurosurgeon Discovers the Power of Prayer… One Patient at a Time* (Carol Stream: Tyndale House Publishers, Inc., 2011), 11.

36   Curlin FA et al., "Physicians' Observations and Interpretations of the Influence of Religion and Spirituality on Health," *Arch Intern Med* (2007), 167 (7) 649–54. Cited in Levy and Lane II, *Gray Matter*, 11.

37   Magyar-Russell G. et al., "Ophthalmology Patients' Religious and Spiritual Beliefs," *Arch Ophthalmology* (2008) 126(9): 1262–65. Cited in Levy and Lane II, *Gray Matter*, 11.

38   John 8:31-32, John 14:27, and 2 Corinthians 5:16.

SECTION 2

KINDS OF MIRACLES THAT DEFY CRAZY

2

LIFE IS ON THE WIRE

Life is on the wire. The rest is just waiting.
—Karl Wallenda

The onlookers below stared upward in shock as Karl Wallenda made his way slowly across a wire stretched high above the ground, with not even a net beneath him. At age nine, Karl had answered an ad for a "hand balancer with courage." Apparently, his skill took hold and grew. Years later he founded "The Great Wallendas." They performed high-wire acts throughout Europe and the United States—always without a net. The Wallenda's most famous high-wire routine was the seven-person chair pyramid. After a lifetime of amazing performances, Wallenda dropped to his death in 1978 while walking between the towers of the Condado Plaza Hotel in San Juan, Puerto Rico. Felled by a gust of wind, he died doing what he loved—the only pursuit that made him feel truly alive.

Wallenda understood a simple facet of life that many are unaware of: without taking risks, we're not stretched enough to know what we're capable of. His philosophy of living reminds me of the unofficial motto of the United States Life-Saving Service, the precursor of the Coast Guard: "You have to go out, but you don't have to come back."[39] These rescuers lived on the wire, using small boats to save sailors from larger ships that were capsizing or had run aground.

While my father was in graduate school, several members of the Coast Guard attended a small church he pastored in Hull, Massachusetts—only a block from the ocean. Dad was invited out to sea on several occasions, and he sometimes saw the rescuers in action. He was impressed by the skills and courage these men demonstrated. The motto of the Coast Guard became "Semper Paratus," which means "Always Ready."

What are the limits of your readiness? Do you live at the edge of your capabilities? Do you live there every day? God often assigns tasks to us that can't be fulfilled in our own strength. If we could do seemingly impossible things in our own strength, God's power would not be revealed through us. The truth is that our greatest triumphs come when we're at our weakest. Dr. Thomas Griffin, a Tucson physician specializing in psychiatry, once told me, "Sometimes we're reduced to the most powerful thing we can do." That truth is worth meditating on!

Think about Christ's life: Rising from the dead is surely the most powerful thing He ever did while on Earth. But He first came to Earth as a man, wrapped in vulnerable human flesh. He was then further "reduced" when He "made Himself of no reputation"[40] and died a humiliating death on a cross—the death of a criminal. The Savior of the world was reduced to *death*. And the most powerful thing He could do was to literally overcome death by arising from the grave. When we cooperate with what God allows in our lives—especially *during* the hard times—we may feel we have been reduced. But through hardships, we grow in character and might even end up doing the most powerful things we could've never dreamed of. That's because when we're weak, we're strong in God's strength.[41] Let's look at some exciting accounts illustrating the courage of those who live life on the wire.

A Jet Pilot's Last Roll at Heaven's Door

When I speak to groups about weak people who became strong and on miracles and answers to prayer, I always talk about Lieut. Commander Paul Galanti. I hold up a vintage copy of *Life* magazine from October 20, 1967, with his picture on the well-worn cover. It's a black-and-white photo of Paul dressed in gray—the attire of a prisoner of war—sitting expressionless in a dingy cell with a single light bulb hanging from the ceiling. Paul told me that the photo had been edited to eliminate a defiant gesture he made at the camera for his captors. I also hold up the February 26, 1973, *Newsweek* magazine with a picture of Paul and his radiant wife in an exuberant Valentine's Day embrace after his release. Then I tell the story of what transpired in the interval between the two magazine covers: his long and torturous imprisonment. In a constant struggle to maintain his balance "on the wire," Paul had been tormented and tortured almost beyond human endurance.

I first read about Paul in a 1997 issue of *Angels on Earth*. I never forgot the story of his nearly seven-year captivity in the North Vietnamese prison camp, the notorious "Hanoi Hilton." I sent Paul an email in 2008, telling him I was going to talk about him during a Christmas presentation. He responded that he didn't have anything to add but said I should feel free to call him at any time. Years later I dug into his story more deeply. Speaking with Paul, I discovered that it was the appearance of Christ Himself—and what Christ told him—that enabled Paul to endure his remaining years of imprisonment. As a faith-realist, Commander Galanti is supremely acquainted with evil in the world, while also being keenly aware of God's kingdom here on Earth.[42]

Paul Galanti had graduated from high school at Valley Forge Military Academy and then from the US Naval Academy. In fact, after returning to the US from his imprisonment, he was elected president of his class at Valley Forge, though a long time had passed. After growing up in a military family that traveled the world, serving his country in the Navy seemed to be a natural path for Paul. His father was a decorated colonel who had served in the Army Air Corps during World War II as an aviation engineer, helping build bases under enemy fire in towns of the Okinawa Prefecture. And Paul's brother was at West Point while Paul was at Annapolis. But when did Paul become interested in flying? In fourth grade! That's when he was lucky enough to see new, top secret jet planes at an air show at Fort

Leavenworth. Paul witnessed an F-80 Shooting Star being flown by Chuck Yeager, the first pilot to break the sound barrier. Yeager also happened to be a friend of Paul's father. Paul decided then and there that he would become a Navy pilot.

A few years later, while in Japan, Paul saw combat planes return from Korea riddled with bullets and shrapnel. He was quickly learning of both the thrills and dangers of flying into war zones. But he felt he had a destiny to fulfill. Even as a baby, his nickname had been "Scrappy." This attitude, plus a slowly growing dependence on God, would define much of his character. On June 17, 1966, Paul's A-4 Skyhawk was shot down on his ninety-seventh combat mission near the coastal town of Vinh, North Vietnam. His engine took a direct hit at 1,200 feet. After the Skyhawk had done an uncontrolled 720-degree spin, Paul regained control and hoped to land his plane on the ocean, where he could be picked up by Americans. But this was not to be. The plane was streaking at five hundred miles per hour—far too fast and low to jump safely—but Paul had no choice. He ejected. Although three panels of his chute were torn, air currents somehow wafted him toward land. But his peaceful descent into enemy territory was ruined when he took a bullet through the side of his neck. "Tracers were everywhere," Paul said. He swung two or three times in his chute before hitting the ground hard. Seeing his plane make it to the ocean was little comfort. Immediately, Paul used his survival radio to contact his squadron ops officer, Lieut. Commander Lew Chatham, a former Blue Angel pilot and the naval officer he most admired. Paul requested a strafing run—but it was too late for any kind of rescue. As he saw enemy troops approaching, Paul could only shout, "I'll see you in five or six months," before the connection went dead. He could not have known how *much* longer it would be.

On the twelve-day march to prison, he watched the kilometer signs counting down to the dreaded "Hanoi Hilton." They marched only at night. Two American Air Force prisoners eventually joined in the trek, and impoverished Vietnamese civilians hooted at them along the way. He had one thing on his mind now: escape. Whenever he saw water, he wanted to dive in and float to the ocean, but he never saw a good opportunity to make a break. Paul told me others who had tried were always caught. The worst of his trip to prison came after the bombing of Hanoi began on June 29—the very day he arrived in the Communist capital. One week later, Paul and as many as sixty other prisoners were paraded through downtown Hanoi in handcuffs, suffering the abuses of the mobs. After three days at the Hanoi Hilton without food, Paul yelled for attention. An angry guard jerked him from his cell and dragged him to interrogation.

Four days of mind-numbing inquisition followed. Paul was given some filthy, blood-stained "pajamas" and led out of the prison. He was promptly handcuffed to Lieut. Col. Robbie Risner, an Air Force pilot most known for his seven "kills" in Korea. Paul said that when Risner was captured, "They thought they'd captured [someone as famous as] Sgt. York," the American hero of WWI. Robbie and Paul were both mercilessly tortured. In fact, torture became an expected routine for all prisoners. To add to their indignities, they were forced to "confess" by signing statements detailing their "war crimes." Some prisoners broke down and did sign. When it came to torture, their captors were experts. "They didn't have to pull out our fingernails. They knew how to do it," Paul said. During intensely painful torture sessions, with his arms lashed to a stool, his fingers turned dark from bruising or lack of blood. "When the ropes were loosened, there was a flash of yet more intense pain. My arms felt like they were on fire. My fingers wouldn't work right. It took six months for me to feel better." Despite the excruciating interrogation, Paul tried as hard as he could to only state his name, rank, serial number, and date of birth. But on several occasions, "I gave them garbage to stop the torture."

Although Paul believed in God, he had not been a man of deep faith. He said he'd enjoyed military church services around the world, mostly "because of the good-looking girls." Nevertheless, Paul looked to God in prison. "*All* the prisoners did." Because they were always in solitary and had no chance to see each other, Paul and other prisoners communicated with neighbors by tapping on the walls. On Sundays, a senior officer gave three loud thumps, which meant it was time for church. What was church? Everyone stood in their private cells and recited the Lord's Prayer and the Pledge of Allegiance. But these holy moments didn't last long. Talking was not allowed, and at the slightest sound of voices, the guards quickly and gruffly commanded silence. Everyone denied that there had been any talking. The Sunday services continued, but the cruelty never stopped. Torture or isolation—it was always one or the other.

Two and a half years into captivity, Paul endured ten straight days of intense torture. Bound to a stool by ropes that were tightened beyond what he could bear, he still gave only his name, rank, serial number, date of birth, and—you guessed it—more truckloads of "garbage" information! Between torture sessions, he was usually given a serving of "food." It was little more than gruel "in a tin can covered with some kind of enamel," as Paul put it. "Something that we don't see anymore." On the enamel were painted words that appeared to say "Korean-Vietnam Friendship League."

An optimistic man by nature, Paul was nevertheless taken to his limit. At the exact moment he felt that all hope had faded, Paul had what he called "a very real experience" that he would never forget. He saw a glowing figure "materialize out of the wall." The apparition was gowned in luminous white, brighter than anything Paul had ever seen. The being also had a beard. Paul later came to believe this glorious figure was Jesus Himself...and Jesus had his attention! Jesus said to him, "Everything is all right." Paul was mesmerized. Within moments, the figure vanished.

Immediately, Paul felt "energized" and "filled with great peace." He knew Christ's appearance and words also meant that he would get out of prison. He was soon thrown back into his solitary cell, but now as a changed man, filled with hope and with an unshakeable commitment to Christ. He knew he could endure with confidence every torment his captors might come up with. When I asked Paul what he had learned from his prison experience, he said, "It takes a lot to get me down now. I so appreciate breakfast, dinner, driving a car." He takes nothing for granted. As a recruiting commander after the war, he would tell new recruits to "suck it up and press on." When I told Paul he was a humble man, he was quick to correct me, saying, "I'm not so much humble as I'm quiet." Paul's soft, raspy voice belies a heart of steel. If the definition of meekness is power under control, Paul has it. He also has a sense of humor.

At a later get-together of retired marines in Richmond, retired Marine Lieut. Col. Chip Houston put a tongue-in-cheek spin on Paul's experience. Chip drew uproarious laughter from the crowd when he introduced Paul as "the luckiest SOB in the history of the Navy because he lived in a gated community." Paul laughed as he related that to me.

Finally, after their release in 1973, Paul and his fellow prisoners were invited to the White House to visit with President Nixon. There, Paul met many of his surviving colleagues for the first time—the men he had been "tapping to" in the POW camp, whose faces he'd never seen. I asked Paul about his two Purple Hearts, Silver Star, Bronze star, combat air medals, and numerous other awards for valor and distinguished service. His self-deprecating response was that, nowadays, military personnel get medals like those as soon as they enter the service!

Long since getting on with his life, Paul managed Senator John McCain's Virginia run for the presidency in 2000 and worked with him again in his 2008 bid. He and John had been imprisoned in the same camp at about the same time and had endured similar torture. The permanent injuries and resultant disabilities McCain suffered were well known and were visible indicators of how bad it had also been for Paul.

In addition to his military honors, medals, speaking tours, and eldership at his church, Paul seemed most pleased with his connection to a war memorial. The Education Wing of the Virginia War Memorial was named in honor of Paul and his lovely wife, Phyllis (there are stories to tell about her too!). Phyllis passed away in 2014, and Paul now lives close to his two sons and their families with grandchildren in Richmond, Virginia. In the summer of 2019, he connected with many friends at a reunion of about 180 POWs in Portland, Maine. Paul remains a man whose deep faith resonates greatly with my own.

Close to the end of our first interview, I asked him how well he knew the famous poem, "High Flight." I've counseled many military pilots, and one of them told me that in his training, he was required to memorize it. (See the Appendix to read this inspiring sonnet.) Paul said he had memorized "High Flight" even before entering the Naval Academy. But Paul also likes another poem that he recited to me *verbatim*. It was written by Cpt. Jerry Coffee, a fellow POW. Jerry referred to the poem as "a toast" and tapped it through the wall to Paul an hour after Paul saw his vision of Christ. The poem, "One More Roll," is now well-known—and Paul had been the first to hear it! Jerry's wife tells me there are several versions of it on the internet; she gave me the correct version, which is also in Jerry's riveting book, *Beyond Survival*. In Paul's many talks over the years, he concludes each one by reciting Cpt. Coffee's poem. Having lost so many friends in the war, Paul choked up while reciting it to me:

> We toast our faithful comrades,
> Now fallen from the sky
> And gently caught by God's own hand
> To be with Him on high.
>
> To dwell among the soaring clouds
> They knew so well before
> From dawn patrol and victory roll
> At Heaven's very door.
>
> And as we fly among them there
> We're sure to hear their plea—
> "Take care, my friend; watch your six,
> And do one more roll...just for me."[43]

At the end of our time together, Paul started coughing. He told me he had a sore throat and had been ill. I was surprised he hadn't canceled our interview—but Paul must have decided to "suck it up and press on," giving it "one more roll" for his brave comrades and for you, the reader, to be encouraged by his account.

A Police Officer's Brush with Death and Glimpse of Heaven

Let's consider the heroics of others who also lived on the wire—and who also hit the wall of their limitations, only to discover that God's power has no limit. One such man was Paul Cerone, who inexplicably escaped death and got a peek into Heaven after a violent assault.

In his own words:

> At three AM on May 13, 1981, I was driving home from a night of drinking after the end of the night shift. I was stopped at a red light when a man approached my vehicle and proceeded to rob me. My driver's door window was open, and he stabbed me in the neck and asked me for my money. As I grabbed for my neck to stop the bleeding, the suspect noticed that I was trying to get my service revolver out of my holster. I wanted to shoot him, but I was getting weak from the stab wound and he wrestled the gun from my hand. He then told me to lie down on the front seat of my vehicle and placed the gun to my head.
>
> The next thing I remember is that I firmly believed I was going to die. My entire life just flew through my mind in a split second. I saw when I was baptized, when I took my first communion, and every significant event of my life. In an instant. How was this possible? All I know is that it happened!
>
> After this life review, I felt so happy and peaceful that I did not care what was happening to me. I remember that there was complete silence. Then I saw myself going down a path of brightly colored green hedges and beautiful

flowers. I was on a winding cement path. There were flowers of all different varieties and I could smell them. And I saw the most vivid colors of red, yellow, blue, orange, and purple. I knew that this perfectly manicured path was the path to Heaven. I was on my way!

Suddenly, and I have no idea why, the gunman ran away, keeping my gun. He was arrested within a few days, charged with multiple crimes, and spent several years in prison.

Now it's 2018 and I still think about the incident. I had many close calls as a police officer, but I never saw a passageway to the other side of this life. I can honestly say that at that time and place I was on my way to Heaven and wanted to go there. God had other plans for me, however.

Plain Pizza and a Slice of Heaven
One Brave Detective

New York City Police Department Detective A. also lived his life on the wire, with danger as his constant companion. Another unwelcome companion—depression—disappeared one day after he had an unlikely encounter with what just might have been a couple of angels. (Due to the nature of his work, I can't reveal Det. A's name.) He's made thousands of arrests, including over seven hundred as an undercover officer, during the crack epidemic of the 1980s. Det. A maintained a low profile as he mingled with dope dealers and buyers. No man-on-the-street would suspect that he was not someone to be messed with! It's no wonder he also worked for a global security company, protecting celebrities and a president. Det. A served fourteen years in the Army and then joined the NYPD, where he had several brushes with death. Once, a suspect shot at him, but he only heard the click of the pistol's hammer on the bullet in the chamber. Inexplicably, the bullet did not fire. Those who work in law enforcement, protecting people like you and me, often have such stories. Det. A has many more!

After his years of service on the front lines, including serving as the director of security at one of New York's Botanical Gardens, he met the chief of the animal police at Ground Zero on 9/11/2001. Animals had always been Det. A's particular love, and he decided to take a large cut in pay so he could become an animal cop. He did this for thirteen years and was often featured on a television program on the Animal Planet channel. His career as a canine-assisted officer came to a disappointing end. Many police officers have line-of-duty injuries, and Det. A had more than his share. He needed surgery for many life-altering injuries, with more to come.

The Plot Thickens

On a cold New York evening in mid-November of 2016, Det. A was driving down Main St. in Nyack on his way to Turiello's Pizza ("King of Pizza!"). His pet dog, Hannah, had just died at age five. Det. A had rescued Hannah, a Rottweiler-Doberman mix, and her pups. He kept Hannah, who became as close to him as any best friend. After Hannah was put to sleep in his arms, he remembers overpowering grief spilled out in sobs.

As he drove to enjoy some great pizza, he couldn't shake his deep sense of loss. He was also dealing with his young daughter's fight with cancer (she has since survived and now thrives cancer-free). Other troubles weighed heavily on his heart, and he found himself weeping again. He slammed his car door, and as he hesitantly walked into Turiello's, he had two desperate prayers on his lips:

1. "God, I feel like I'm losing my faith. I need a sign."
2. "If there's a Heaven, I pray my dog Hannah will be there and I'll see her again someday."

While waiting in line, he noticed a tall handsome Black man standing next to him at the counter. *Very* tall, Det. A told me. He was well-dressed and as athletic looking as any professional basketball player. The man asked, "What's good in here?" Years on the police force had conditioned Det. A to be guarded with strangers, and he was too troubled to strike up a conversation with anyone. Det. A managed to suggest the lasagna was good…and then he hoped to be left alone. But the tall gentleman said, "I'd like to buy you a meal." He seemed gracious enough, and Det. A was surprised! He said the fellow was adamant about paying for his dinner.

Less guarded but still a bit suspicious, Det. A hesitantly looked into the man's eyes where he saw nothing but kindness. He finally relaxed and told the man he'd like a slice of pizza. He also told him about his daughter and what she was going through, and about his beloved dog that had just passed away. He showed the man Hannah's picture. "She's beautiful," the man said. Guardedness became openness between strangers.

Then a petite, attractive white lady appeared "out of nowhere." To Det. A, she looked like a Hollywood actress. The kind, NBA star-like man introduced Det. A to his girlfriend, saying, "This is Det. A, and his dog just died." Again, Hannah's picture came out. Her immediate response was, "Awww, she's gorgeous. Don't worry, she's in Heaven." Det. A asked the stranger where he was from. "I'm not from around here," he said. The restaurant manager later told Det. A that he'd never seen the couple before. As they were leaving Turiello's, Det. A was still seated, lingering over his pizza. Det. A asked the stranger his name. "Faith," he replied, as he headed out the door. "How many men are named Faith?" the detective mused.

"Before I leave," Faith said, "let me ask you for a favor. One day, I'd like you to return the favor…pass it on." After the couple had gone, Det. A couldn't help but wonder who they were and where they were going. But he'd never know. The wheels in Det. A's brain were spinning. First, he had confided in a stranger. Next, it felt strangely as if both his prayers had been answered. He'd just been weeping about losing his *faith*, and the kind man's name was Faith. He'd also been worrying that Hannah might not be in Heaven. Without hesitation, the young lady had reassured him that Hannah was, indeed, in Heaven! Then the man said they weren't "from around here." At least, the man could have said where he lived!

When Det. A looked to the street, the couple had vanished. The encounter and the way they departed seemed stranger by the minute. But in the wake of the odd encounter, Det. A felt great peace. His deep sadness and despair had completely lifted. Immediately, he called his minister, Pastor Dan, and shared what he'd just experienced. It took only a few words and a few minutes for Pastor Dan to realize the full impact of what Det. A was saying. Det. A now believes that sometimes God uses people to encourage us and sometimes He uses angels. He isn't certain which category these two belonged to, and it's not all that important. He believes God showed up during that dark night of his soul, pure and simple. Det. A calls this "a mystery of faith."[44]

A Bullet versus the Supernatural

When I came to Casas Church as the director of counseling, one of the first sermons I heard was by an associate pastor on the preaching team headed by Dr. Roger Barrier. The pastor told a story I'll never forget. It was about his former Sunday school teacher and friend, Chuck Frank Hubbard. Not even his closest buddies knew Chuck's middle name. We'll shortly see why that's important.

Chuck served his military service in the jungles of Vietnam. During a brief visit to a nearby town, Chuck and some of his buddies were standing together on a busy street in the business district. Chuck got a huge surprise—one that saved his life. From a source Chuck could not identify, he heard a clear audible voice call him by his middle name: "Frank!" Chuck instantly turned his head toward what he thought was the source and felt a sniper's bullet whizz by his head. Chuck never did figure out where the voice came from, but had he not turned his head at that instant, he would likely have been killed. He found the bullet embedded in a nearby wall and dug it out to keep as a reminder of how God had miraculously spared his life.

When I recounted this story to a combined adult fellowship group at Casas, Chuck's sister-in-law just happened to be there. She was one of the group leaders and a charter member of the church. After my talk, she approached me and confirmed the story. She also reminded me of Chuck's middle name, which I'd forgotten while sharing the account. I've read many stories of people hearing an audible voice when no one could be seen at all. Several people have also shared experiences like this with me in which a life was saved or direction given at a critical moment. Three such stories appear in the next chapter.

Family Cafeteria or Funeral Parlor?

Jonathan Byrd dreamed of building and running the best cafeteria in the world. We're talking computerized kitchens, a drive-through for take-out, a bakery, innovative menus, banquets, weddings, concerts, and *long* lines to enjoy the best and greatest variety of food money could buy. It was such an ambitious project that Jonathan realized only God's favor could bring success, especially since almost everyone he knew told him his dream business was sure to fail. Why? Because Jonathan would not serve alcohol!

At age eighteen, he and his pastor had visited the relatives of a family member who had been killed in a head-on collision with a drunk driver. He was moved by the family's profound grief. Jonathan respected other restaurants' right to serve alcohol, but he didn't want to be remotely connected with anything that caused that terrible accident. He also didn't want to be associated with a man in a dark suit who would pronounce premature last rites over a failed enterprise. But more on that man in a moment.

Jonathan began working hard at an early age. His parents weren't well off, and he did everything from selling tomatoes to raising sheep to earn money to contribute to his family's survival. In speaking with Ginny, his wife of thirty-four years, and his son, David, I learned that Jonathan's dad, Carl, had started a frozen custard stand on one of Greenwood, Indiana's main drags, while Jonathan was still a baby. The custard stand morphed into the "The Custard Kitchen," and Jonathan was a teenager when the business became "The Kitchen Drive-In."

Jonathan was learning firsthand how God blesses hard work... with *more* hard work! When his dad became extremely ill, Jonathan took over the business with its sixty employees at the tender age of fifteen. Out of unexpected necessity, he had only begun to prove that the sooner one starts, the farther one can go. Jonathan found himself following in his father's footsteps in ways he'd never dreamed of. His dad had been the first member of the Byrd family to become a restaurateur, buying a Kentucky Fried Chicken franchise after meeting Col. Sanders himself. Jonathan bought his father's KFC, as well as another that was under construction. He eventually built and operated at least a half-dozen KFCs. Ginny told me that was when Jonathan got his idea to build an "exceptional cafeteria."

Jonathan had also bought a Christian television station in Minnesota and had become involved in Jack Van Impe's evangelistic crusades. Then he got into selling old books and rare Bibles. He even began stock car racing in 1985! In 1987, he sold five KFCs to help break ground for his dream cafeteria. He also sold his television station for added liquidity. Now he was putting his and his family's finances—and livelihood—on the line. Jonathan's was another life that involved balancing and moving on the wire! Most of us know how the realization of big dreams can be followed by bigger problems. That's how it went for Jonathan. Expenses increased far beyond what he had anticipated. Securing permits, grading the property, and installing high-quality oak trim interior added up fast. Then came actual storm clouds with a wind that blew the roof off the skeletal one-acre structure. Finally came a pronouncement—the kind that often follows the failure of even a worthy venture.

One day, Jonathan was sitting at a picnic table at the building site. His pastor showed up and warned him that a church member familiar with the restaurant business predicted that he'd go broke in six months. Then another man showed up—a man in a dark suit. Jonathan asked if he could help him, and the man responded, "Oh, just looking around. I own a chain of funeral homes, and I hear the fool who's building this place isn't going to serve alcohol. I figure he'll be bankrupt in six months and I can turn this space into the biggest funeral home in the Midwest." There was that six-month prediction again!

Jonathan was now understandably in despair. Then his friend Dr. Gene Hood showed up and said, "If you have enough faith to build this place, I have enough faith to help you keep those banquet halls filled with great gospel-singing groups." Wow! That was an incredibly different spin! Three months later, on November 7, 1988, "Jonathan Byrd's Cafeteria and Banquet Hall" opened for business. Before long, Bill and Gloria Gaither began giving concerts there each August, and that continued thirteen years. For twenty-eight years, long lines and great food were the rules there. Jonathan said, "If you count the cost, stick to your principles, and leave everything in God's hands, you'll have a menu that can't fail."

I'd like to add that when you have a big dream and think the worst roadblocks are behind you, be ready for "the man in the dark suit" to show up. When he does, remember that God is still in charge. Keep in mind the words of Winston Churchill who said, "Success is walking from failure to failure with no loss of enthusiasm."[45] Jonathan lost no enthusiasm and also built the first Cracker Barrel west of the Mississippi. Ginny told me this was in Surprise, Arizona—an appropriate place name!

Twenty-eight years is a long time for a cafeteria like this to serve up great meals, concerts, and smiles. But eventually, cafeterias diminished in popularity among the younger generation. Time brings change for all of us. Five million customers and thirteen million meals later, the huge cafeteria needed to shrink. The new business realities made Jonathan sad, but Ginny said that faith in God sustained him as he regrouped and moved in a new direction.

The Byrd family started another ambitious enterprise, the "502 East Event Center," which now provides attractive venues for weddings and social events. It also contracts food services and caters to the Army's Camp Atterbury in Edinburgh, Indiana. Then in 1996, Jonathan ventured into the hotel business to form "Byrd Hotel Group." A son, David, teamed up with him on two new hotels in Arizona. David built another hotel in Utah and started racing cars in Arizona.

Epilogue to the Dream: More Puzzle Pieces Fit Together

While he was building his fourth hotel in 2004, Jonathan suffered a stroke. He passed away in 2009. While Jonathan now enjoys his best dream of all in Heaven, David carries on the family vision of bringing enjoyment to many people through the hotel business and car racing. He's raced in the Phoenix International Raceway and manages an Arizona racetrack (where Ginny often helps on weekends). David even qualified and raced in the 2018 Indianapolis 500! Because he's headquartered west of Phoenix—about two hours from where I live—I'm looking forward to spending a night at one of those Byrd Arizona hotels!

Although Jonathan passed on, his dream continues to bear fruit. Ginny is the president of the Byrd Group. When I spoke with her recently, she'd just returned from a mission trip to Vienna. That morning, she had attended a Bible study and was beginning a five-hundred-piece puzzle while listening to gospel music. Ginny was kind, eloquent, and precise in sharing more details than I could easily record! She'd lovingly cared for Jonathan for five years after his stroke. Following his death, she'd returned to Greenville, Indiana, to manage the rest of the dream that God had enabled the family to realize. The original cafeteria has been beautifully renovated and repurposed as "The Nest," which accommodates "Brick House Coffee Roasters" (featuring fair-trade coffee produced by Christian nationals connected to missions' outreach), a day spa, a hair salon, and other businesses—even a chapel. David told me that "The Nest" became a "showplace" after being purchased by a man who had frequented the cafeteria most every day. David's brother is the president and manager of the Indianapolis Speedrome, where Ginny enjoys preparing food at the concession stand. The ripple effect of a young man's dream is still spreading. It went far beyond selling tomatoes and working at the drive-in to what, for a long time, was arguably the best cafeteria in America.

(From Doug Hill's How to Listen to God, "Failure Was Not on the Menu," 2004. Adapted by permission of Guideposts. All rights reserved. Additional information for an updated account was provided through interviews by author with Byrd's son, David Byrd, March 29, 2019, and with Ginny Byrd, Jonathan Byrd's wife, of thirty-four years, April 18, 2019, along with email exchanges with David and Ginny.)

The Balanced Life

How can we take risks and still "keep our head"? To answer this question, we must consider the importance of leading a balanced life. Karl Wallenda knew the importance of physical balance and coordination. He combined *balance* with great courage! Just as Wallenda had to maintain perfect balance on the high wire, when we take risks in life, we need to likewise be balanced.

I've known risk-takers who suffered from a lack of balance. They seldom succeeded unless they became balanced. A balanced life is a life of character lived out. It's a life that can resolve—or live with—seeming paradoxes. I'm talking about opposites of all kinds that can appear to be in conflict but are not. We balance sleep and work, spending and saving, emotional vulnerability and drawing boundaries, forgiveness and reconciliation, focusing and having fun, resting in faith and doing good deeds, not thinking evil of others while being cautious, and so on. The apostle Paul said he could rejoice in times of want and in times of abundance.[46] As a faith-realist, he valued multiple beautiful realities of this world. Despite the world's grotesque ways of molding people, God continually transformed Paul's character more perfectly into His image.

Lawrence Thompson, a biographer of the poet Robert Frost, described Frost as a man of balance: "He still had the power to consist of the inconsistent, the power to hold in unity the ultimate irreconcilables, the power to be in a bursting unity of opposites, and the power to make poetry out of these opposites."[47] In fact, the maturity of any person can be described as the ability to tolerate paradoxes and uncertainties. The ability to make poetry out of opposites is both an outcome of personal growth and a gift! I've observed that someone who is imbalanced in having faith without doing good deeds typifies a lazy faith, which is of no benefit to fellow humans. Furthermore, someone who emphasizes good deeds can become rigid and rule bound with diminished compassion and common sense. People of either extreme are destined to learn important life lessons the hard way. God does not lack in ways to teach us!

In one of my favorite Louis L'Amour books, *The High Lonesome*, an experienced cowboy says, "Never was a horse that couldn't be rode, an' there never was a rider who couldn't be thrown."[48] The apostle Paul phrased that sentiment more seriously: "Therefore let him who thinks he stands take heed lest he fall."[49]

Being in Balance Is Practical

Some years ago, I was surprised when a car mechanic told me that I needed new tires. My objection was that there was a forty-thousand-mile warranty on the tires and I'd only put on twenty-five thousand! Was someone scamming me into buying new tires sooner than necessary? I'd had a bad experience at a shop across the street. A mechanic there told me I'd need to fix a leak in my radiator soon. With a little additive, my car ran without any radiator problems until I traded it in fifteen years later. But the matter of my tires was different. The shop had kept a record of all my visits, and it turned out I needed an education in tire maintenance. I had neglected to have my tires balanced for a few years, so the tread had worn unevenly. While most of the tire surface looked fine, a closer inspection indicated zones of tire treads that were dangerously worn. I learned an important lesson: If we want to drive safely, and save money, it's important to keep our tires balanced! In the same way, we need to maintain balance in other parts of our lives as well.

What Does a Balanced Life Look Life?

If I want to live on the wire, on the edge of God's will, and often on the edge of the impossible, maintaining balance isn't optional. To endure bad times or enjoy the good, we must be able to embrace extremes of *both* joy and sadness—sometimes *at the same time*. I spoke earlier of "the hard path of joy" and how Paul experienced joy in the midst of trouble—even when he was beaten and left for dead. Of course, Paul could only experience this joy because he had lived a life of faith during troubles. Had he turned to another source of pleasure, he might have experienced some fleeting form of happiness. But Paul knew that mere happiness depends on circumstances, which are always fluid. True *joy* is profound and comes only from God, regardless of circumstances. Joy and not mere happiness should be our goal.

When we shrink from enduring tough times, we can never know what Paul knew: that in troubles, our joy can be boundless. Just as satisfying feelings only follow noble actions (never the other way around), joy only follows acts of faith. When I've hung in there through the dark periods, I've often laughed out loud, from the depths of my soul. Joy doesn't come from the outside in. I might briefly feel happy if I won the lottery. But when I haven't persevered through real suffering, I've gravitated toward pleasures that didn't last, and I was left emptier than before. It's better to admit painful emptiness, admit our need of God, and be filled with His joy rather than anesthetize our pain with temporary pleasures.

If you think of the great paintings of history, they speak through darkness and shadows as well as light and well-defined central figures. Without darkness, there would be limited depth to the painting. It's the same with our lives. If you want a boring and unfulfilling life, simply succumb to every temptation and seek only happiness. A painting depicting this shallow kind of life will end up at a garage sale, if not in some stranger's trash!

As I waded through the shallows of my drug and alcohol years, the meaning I pursued became more elusive. It was on a New Year's Eve when my roommate and I threw a party at our two-story, ramshackle townhome across the street from the campus of Ohio State University, where my roommate and I were enrolled. Our home was the last in a row that stretched from High St. to Wales Alley. We overlooked the alley with streetlights that I liked to throw beer bottles at.

As happens at parties, the big moment came when the door prize would be awarded. It was an actual door...which no one wanted, not even the winner! No amount of drugs and alcohol—that night or any like it—would have stoked excitement for that door! And just like our townhome was later demolished, I assume that door ended up in the rubble. Years later, I counseled someone who worshipped a doorknob he named "Chuck." I suspect that the doorknob may now be in a different pile of rubble. So much for the drunken parties and false gods. Now I know a good life is walking the wire, which requires balance and discipline!

In order to live on the wire, we must learn to tolerate tough times and even unjust suffering—the kind of suffering that Christ promised we were born into.[50] *We either do that or we fail to reach our true destiny.* And by living out our true destiny—no matter who we are, what our gifts and abilities may be, or whether our destiny is celebrated or unnoticed—we will be filled to the brim with meaning and satisfaction. Taking a stand, speaking out, taking risks, and doing things we could never do without God's help—noble acts like these are often necessary to counteract the darkness. They keep us balanced on the high wire. We frequently need help from our friends too. We gain true satisfaction in life from our relationships with God and with others. If we're not cultivating those, we're just spinning our unbalanced wheels and ultimately lose control!

I began the chapter about faith-realism with wisdom from King Solomon: "It is good to grasp the one and not let go of the other; the man who fears God will avoid all extremes."[51] The Hebrew for "avoid all extremes" is "practice them both." If we're going to walk the high wire, we need to be in balance, often practicing or believing two apparent opposites at the same time. Wallenda was in balance when he strode across the wire, carrying weight on each side that kept him upright! But his crowning achievement was to balance on a wire supporting *other people*—all on chairs in a pyramid formation. The weight of relationships adds stability and helps to keep one balanced! With more stories of miracles, great obstacles overcome, and even angelic appearances that you're going to read in this book, you'll understand how troubles handled well can be the beginning of new strength and creativity. Our struggles make us strong enough to climb the next mountain God puts in front of us.

Reflections on the Peaceful Life

Ernest F. Tittle said in *A Mighty Fortress*, "Plainly, life is not meant for cowards. It is so ordered as to call forth the latent heroism of the human spirit."[52] The good news is that no matter how rough the road you're on, God is with you and will show His tangible goodwill to you when you reach the limit of your endurance. It's God who allows you to reach precarious heights and depths so that He can call out your heroism. Many more people than you can benefit from the good you are enabled to do.

Endnotes

39 "United States Coast Guard. 2016-12-21," "Coast Guard History," Wikipedia, accessed 12/17/2017, https://en.wikipedia.org/wiki/United_States_Life-Saving_Service. Author heard this motto in his childhood. His parents saw it on a plaque in Massachusetts.

40 Philippians 2:7 KJV.

41 2 Corinthians 12:10.

42 Paul Gallanti, Interviews with author, March 10 and 24, 2018 and October 5, 2019. There is no duplicated material, or overlap, between the author's account and Paul Galanti's own account in *Angels on Earth*.

43 Gerald Coffee, *Beyond Survival: Building on the Hard Times—A POW's Inspiring Story*, rev. ed. (Aiea, Hawaii: Coffee Enterprises, Inc., 2013), 311. Permission granted by former Vietnam POW, Captain Gerald Coffee, US Navy (Ret.) who composed "One More Roll" sometime in 1968 while held in Hanoi's Hoa Lo prison.

44 Det. A, interviews by author, March 13, February 24, 2018, and February 12, 2019.

45 Winston Churchill, *The Epoch Times*, September 30–October 6, 2020.

46 Philippians 4:12.

47 Lawrence Thompson, *Robert Frost: The Early Years, 1874–1915* (New York, Chicago, San Francisco: Holt, Rinehart and Winston, 1966), 477.

48 Louis L'Amour, *High Lonesome* (New York: Bantam Books/Random House, Inc., 1962/2004), Kindle edition, 193.

49 1 Corinthians 10:12.

50 John 16:33.

51 Ecclesiastes 7:18.

52 Ernest Freemont Tittle, *A Mighty Fortress* (New York: Harper & Brothers Publishers, 1949, 1950), 23. Tittle was a friend of the author's family, and his ashes are buried in the chapel named after him at First Methodist Church in Evanston, Illinois (now a United Methodist church). The memorial services of the author's grandparents were held in that chapel.

3

DEUS EX MACHINA

"It may seem marvelous to the remnant of this people at that time, but will it seem marvelous to me?" declares the Lord Almighty.
—Zechariah 8:6

God from the Machine

To God the Supernatural Realm Is Natural

Deus ex machina is among the most-searched terms on the internet. Here's what it means: "A god introduced by means of a crane...in ancient Greek and Roman drama to decide the final outcome."[53] In a work of fiction or drama, it's "a contrived solution to an apparently insoluble difficulty."[54] The expression arose in the late seventeenth century, and the phrase is derived from the modern Latin translation of the Greek "god from the machine."[55] In Greek theater, actors representing gods were suspended above the stage by a crane made of wood and pulleys. The intervention of the god brought about certain occurrences to conclude the play well. Some works of fiction are ridiculed for use of a deus ex machina to cause an easy resolution to a plot that has reached a dead end. In fact, we all need supernatural intervention from time to time, if not every day. But not from a machine! From the *real and true* God!

Fortunately, the real God created time and space and lives inside and outside both. He can intervene at any time and in any way He wants. A Bible professor of mine, Ralph Hawk, used to say that the definition of God's sovereignty is that "God can do anything He wants, any time He wants, and He doesn't have to ask anybody." The real God is a compassionate miracle worker who can lift us above seemingly insoluble difficulties. And He doesn't need wooden cranes or pulleys!

Nothing New under the Sun

Although the "gods" suspended by planks and pulleys can't save any of us from real-life danger, the true God can intervene in our lives at any time. What must have been "high-tech gods" back then reflected the ingrained belief that there must somehow be a God who can control the ebb and flow of our lives. Most agnostics I've met freely admit they do hope God exists.

Miraculous interventions have been inspiring awe and increased hunger for God for thousands of years. I'm talking about awe as an emotion that never leaves us the same. When the Assyrian army surrounded Jerusalem around 700 BC and sealed the fate of the outnumbered Israelites, much desperate prayer ascended to God for deliverance from the invaders. Then, in a single night, an angel of the Lord slew 185,000 Assyrians.[56] To witness such a thing would leave most of us changed!

Another time, two foreign armies surrounded Jerusalem. King Jehoshaphat prayed publicly on behalf of the city. God assured Jehoshaphat, "You will not have to fight this battle. Take up your positions; stand firm and see the deliverance the Lord will give you."[57] The next morning it turned out the two invading armies had destroyed each other overnight. God had used flash-flood waters that appeared like pools of blood in the clay dirt to confuse the armies.

Living in Arizona, I know how flash floods can suddenly fill dry arroyos and wash away anything in their path. Here in Tucson, cars can be swept away, and sometimes lives are lost. Surging water can be so powerful that it can take only a few inches of depth to pull someone off their feet. I knew a man who kayaked down a flooding arroyo with the police chasing him, speeding down an adjoining roadway. My friend somehow escaped—alive.

Two more biblical examples: When the parents of Samson saw an angel, they did not know it was an angel speaking to them until after it had disappeared. Similarly, when an angel told Gideon to rally the Israelites to throw off their oppressors, he didn't know it was an angel until it vanished before his eyes. Samson's parents and Gideon learned the truth of a New Testament Scripture before it had been written: "Be not forgetful to entertain strangers for thereby some have entertained angels unawares."[58] You'll read more about such heavenly strangers who still visit us, even in our times. Let's first consider their *voices*, then explore credible accounts of angelic interventions, as related by friends and acquaintances.

Audible Voices (as Opposed to Imagined) from Heaven

Hearing supernatural voices is a relatively common experience. I've read more than a hundred such stories, and many people have told me of hearing a voice that can only be explained as coming from God or an angel. These occurrences are analogous to what we read in biblical accounts. The great prophet Samuel was a powerful man who appointed kings and pronounced blessings or judgment on the nation of Israel. He regularly heard the voice of God. But early in his life, he did not recognize God's voice.

Samuel's mother, Hannah—who was barren and bitter—had cried out to God for a son. She promised to dedicate her son to the Lord to serve in the temple where Eli was high priest. When Samuel was born, she said, "I prayed for this child, and the Lord has granted me what I asked of him."[59] God had heard her prayer and answered. Then Hannah kept her promise, and beginning in his childhood, Samuel served in the temple. "Samuel!" God called to him in the temple one night. Three more times: "Samuel!" Samuel responded by going to Eli, who told him to go back to bed—the first two times. On Samuel's third trip to the priest, Eli realized that it was the voice of God that was calling the lad.[60]

Samuel grew up to become the great prophet that God used to anoint the first Israelite king, Saul, and then King David. God directed him as to the specific men to proclaim king. On such occasions, Samuel no longer needed to hear an audible voice. His remarkable life began with a voice that bewildered him. But as he grew, he became so close to God that he could recognize His voice *however* He spoke.

The following are examples of similar occurrences in modern times.

Peter Marshall Feels the Call to Ministry

Peter Marshall's wife wrote the book *A Man Called Peter* following her husband's untimely death at age forty-six. It later became the basis for a movie. Peter was a humble Scotsman with God's call on his life. As a young man, he worked in the English village of Bamburgh near its castle and sixteen miles southeast of the Scottish border. This area of England was known for its limestone quarries. One dark and starless night, Peter took a shortcut home over the barren moors. He knew there was a quarry close to the Glororum Road but thought he could skirt it. He heard only the sound of the wind, his footsteps, the occasionally flushed wildfowl, and the distant bleating of sheep. Catherine explains what happened next:

> Suddenly he heard someone call, "Peter!" There was great urgency in the voice. He stopped. "Yes, who is it? What do you want?" For a second he listened, but there was no response, only the sound of the wind. The moor seemed completely deserted. Thinking he must have been mistaken, he walked on a few paces. Then he heard it again, even more urgently: "Peter!" He stopped dead still, trying to peer into that impenetrable darkness, but suddenly stumbled and fell to his knees. Putting out his hand to catch himself, he found nothing there. As he cautiously investigated,

feeling around in a semicircle, he found himself to be on the very brink of an abandoned stone quarry. Just one step more would have sent him plummeting into space to certain death.[61]

That experience gave the future Dr. Marshall a sense of destiny and purpose. He soon determined "to give my life to God for Him to use me wherever He wants me."[62] He became the pastor of New York Avenue Presbyterian Church in Washington, DC, and was twice appointed chaplain of the United States Senate, making him one of the most remembered ministers of his time. Known for both his brilliant, down-to-earth messages and his Scottish brogue, he led many people to faith in Christ. His sermons and quotations are now available online.

Drs. Roger and Julie Barrier Know Who Called Their Names

When I was a young pastor and counselor in Tucson, my favorite voice on the radio was that of Roger Barrier, minister of the largest church in Tucson. He and his wife, Julie, pastored Casas Church as it grew from a quite healthy two hundred fifty people to an exciting Sunday morning attendance of more than three thousand. As the minister of music and orchestra director (with a PhD in orchestra), Julie's musical productions became as well-known as Roger's sermons. When I later performed a song for her that I'd written, I was awed watching her hands glide over the keys, bringing the song to life more than I ever could on my guitar alone.

Roger and Julie's outreach has expanded beyond Tucson to more than thirty-two countries. Their website, PreachItTeachIt.org, has had more than seven million visits in 231 countries and territories in recent years. Roger is the featured pastor of "Ask Roger: Ask a Pastor" on Crosswalk.com, the largest Christian website in the country. I never dreamed I would one day join his staff. Here's a miracle story from PreachItTeachIt.org in Roger's words:

> I've heard scores of personal stories from people who have interacted with angels who protected them from physical danger. For example, in our first house, Julie and I had a large, floor-level, sunken tiled bathtub when the children were little.
>
> I was working in the front of the house when Julie screamed for me to run to the bathtub. As I raced down the hallway, I ran into Julie, also racing for the tub. As we reached the bathroom, our two-year-old was tottering on the raised-tile edge, about to fall headfirst into the three-foot-deep pool. We grabbed her away from danger.
>
> I said to Julie, "Why did you scream for me when you were already on the way?" She said, "I didn't scream for you. You screamed for me." I said, "I never screamed for you." At that moment, we both thought we saw a wisp of white robe departing the room. We were stunned. As we later debriefed the incident, the only conclusion we could draw was that Brianna's guardian angel was "wide awake" and on duty and screaming for both of us to run to the bathroom as quickly as possible.[63]

The Voice That Saved the Life of Her Grandfather

In *God Answers Prayer*, by Allison Bottke with Cheryll Hutchings, Renie Burghardt tells of a harrowing experience she had in post-WWII Hungary.[64] Soviet troops had filled the vacuum left by the defeat and expulsion of the Germans. Those who spoke against the new government were quickly "disappearing." Renie—who is from Doniphan, Missouri—tells how Russian soldiers came to take away her grandfather, a retired judge. He asked if he could wash up first. He was allowed to do so and quickly escaped through the bathroom window. Renie constantly prayed that he would return, but the danger awaiting him made it unwise for him to do so.

When Renie was ten years old, in 1947, it was announced on the radio that the Communist Party had been defeated in an election. Renie didn't know that the Communists were not about to release their grip on power, so she raced off to her grandfather's hiding place. She was startled when she heard a man's voice. Stopping dead in her tracks, Renie said, "Who are you? Where are you? I can't see you." The voice responded, "It isn't important who I am. I am here to warn you that you are about to put your grandfather in grave danger, for you are being followed. Turn around and go back to your grandmother immediately, and know that you will all be together soon."

Understandably frightened, Renie turned and ran past a man on a bicycle, whom she recognized as a member of the secret police who had once been at her house. She *was* being followed! Two weeks later, Renie and her mother were led one night to the Austrian border where her grandfather waited, along with other Germans who were about to be deported to Austria. They all were taken to a refugee camp in Austria, from whence Renie's family was given the chance to move to America in 1951. She's since given much thought to the voice of warning:

> Over the years, I often wondered about the voice I heard on that fall day in 1947. Could the voice have belonged to some kind neighbor who had guessed my destination and decided to warn me anonymously? Or perhaps it really was the voice of God that prompted me to turn around. But whether the voice was human or Heavenly, of this I am certain: God answered the prayer of my heart, and it was His hand that guided us safely back together so we could be a family again.[65]

I've personally been told by at least ten people that they heard an inexplicable voice that saved or helped them. I remember being in the airport several years ago and seeing someone talking to himself. I assumed he was schizophrenic and hearing voices. As he turned his head, I saw something blue in his ear. I realized he must be on the phone, using "Bluetooth connectivity" that I'd been hearing so much about. So I was actually correct. He *was* hearing a voice—just not a supernatural one!

What I find amazing is that books, magazines, and personal testimonies that tell of what had to be *authentic* heavenly voices are available everywhere. I've read and heard of hundreds, and I'm just one person. There must be tens of thousands of similar stories out there. If God created the Heavens and the earth, and if Christ talked about how "my sheep hear my voice,"[66] and if the New Testament speaks of God the Father speaking audibly to Jesus, how could we not believe that God speaks—both silently and audibly—to people in our time? Jesus said that He is the same yesterday, today, and forever.[67] If God spoke in the past, it's no surprise He speaks today. For Roger, Julie, Peter Marshall, Renie, and many others, God is the real deus ex machina—and that's a good thing! He doesn't *need* a machine!

Provision from the Sky
The Tanguays' Miracle

Early in my Christian life, I used to house-sit for Dr. Richard and Laurie Tanguay. Richard was a former Jesuit priest—a loving man of faith. He preceded me as the director of counseling at a church on the east side of Tucson. I was hired to that same position about ten years after house-sitting for the Tanguays.

In a sermon, Richard told a story of how he and Laurie needed new insulation for their water heater. Without proper insulation, there was a danger of fire. Lacking money at the time, the two of them prayed fervently for God to provide the needed funds. One afternoon, Richard was looking out the back window of his home. He saw a large object fall from the sky into his backyard. It was a package about the size of a bale of hay. Unwrapping the package, Richard and Laurie were stunned to see the exact type of insulation they needed! There was no road behind the house, so the package could not have been dropped off by a truck. There was simply no other explanation except that what Richard saw was what happened. Insulation *dropped from the sky!*

Years later, I became Facebook friends with Richard. I sent him a message and repeated what I remembered about the story of the insulation. I asked him if I had it right. Was the story he had told in his sermon really true? (I'm less skeptical now of such miracles!) Richard confirmed every word.

Richard has since gone on to glory, where this miracle is nothing compared to the wonders he now beholds. In 2018, I spoke with Laurie at a memorial service for a fellow minister and friend. I recounted the details of the story with her (did I say I was now less skeptical?). Laurie lit up with a huge smile and confirmed all the details. Yes, it really happened! I think I'm done asking!

Charlotte's Protectors

I asked an acquaintance, Charlotte Poe, if I could tell you her story of the appearance of three angels at a time she was injured and desperate. She wrote it out and gave it to me, writing with such persuasive clarity that I share it here verbatim:

> As I sat in the van in the driveway, Lydia was waiting inside for help to move Mom. Lydia was a caretaker for my mother. I didn't want to leave the motor running for long, so after making sure everything was in place for transport, I turned to get out the driver's side. As with most vans that can accommodate a wheelchair driver, there was a small ledge between the driver's seat and the exit. I quickly lifted my left foot high over the ledge. I was in a hurry and I prepared to run to the house, giving a little hop to begin

my dash. As my right foot followed my left, I felt a tug around my ankle, as if a cord to the leg of my jeans had caught on something and was pulling me back. My entire body went flying out the car door. With no time for support from hands and arms, I landed face down on the concrete driveway.

Stunned and fearful of broken bones or internal injuries, I dared not move for the next few moments. When I was finally able to lift my flattened head, I felt a wet pool surrounding my face. I briefly opened my eyes and saw broken bits of teeth in a sea of blood on the pavement. When I caught my breath and was able to speak, I started screaming, "Lydia, Lydia, help me, help me!" Lydia could not hear me. The distance to the front door and the sound of the motor made that impossible. "I gotta get up or just lie here until she finds me" kept running through my head. "What'll I do? What'll I do?"

There was no mental attention to seek God's help. Having neglected God for a long time, trust in God was lacking and I didn't even pray. It was obvious there were facial injuries and I knew I needed medical attention. But still fearful, I remained immobile, waiting for…for what, I still don't know. However, verses from Psalm 91 have great meaning to me now: "Those who live in the shelter of the Most High will find rest in the shadow of the Almighty… For he orders his angels to protect you wherever you go. They will hold you in their hands to keep you from striking your foot on a stone" (Psalm 91:1, 11, 12).

Billy Graham once said, "God has no favorites and declares that angels will minister to all the heirs of faith. If we, the sons of God, would only realize how close His ministering angels are, what calm assurance we could have in facing the cataclysms of life."

Looking back now, I remember relaxing, but at the time I knew and heard only the quiet, faint sound of voices approaching my outstretched body on the walkway. I slowly lifted my head and looked up through blood-filled eyes. Coming toward me were three young men—preteens—possibly from the middle school nearby. Strangely though, at two in the afternoon, students were in classes. These teens did not appear to be truants. Also unusual was the fact that my home is in a closed neighborhood where residents are quite familiar with each other.

These boys were strangers...unusual strangers! All wore similar white or light-colored clothing. Each boy wore a buttoned shirt with a mandarin collar—my first notice. None had typical jeans of today but dressed in light-colored slacks, not of the younger generation. Each had blond hair and a manner of maturity beyond his apparent age level. Speaking quietly and without alarm, they approached me and encircled my body.

"Ma'am, may we help you?" In this prone position, I felt protecting and helpful eyes staring downward, ready to assist. A wave of unexplainable peace flooded my body. I was clearly conscious of this wave! Only a supernatural intervention could have created this, especially when undesirable renters had invaded our neighborhood a few houses away. Their gang activity had robbed many residents of peace. We lived in fear. But now—with the car door open, my purse lying on the seat, key in the ignition and motor running—no thoughts of vulnerability came to mind.

"Yes, yes," I hastily explained. "Can you go inside and get the lady for me? Her name is Lydia. And can someone please get me to a hospital?"

After carefully turning to my side, the three faces were now visible. They each looked at each other and back to me. "Well, Ma'am, I think that could be arranged," one replied.

Without further communication, one boy headed for the front door, passing Lydia, who had finally heard the commotion and was on her way out. She gently lifted me to a sitting position, and we watched the unfolding scenes in complete awe. One young man went to the car, reached under the dash, pushed the hidden button, and lifted the electric ramp. He turned off the motor, picked up my purse from the front seat, locked the car door, and carried keys and purse into the house. The first boy was coming from the house with a wet washcloth for my face. The remaining lad found a rolled water hose behind a front yard bush and proceeded to clean the bloody driveway while Lydia helped me into the living room.

Mom was sitting in her wheelchair and had a shocked, surprised look on her face. "What is happening?" is all she could say. She later told us what occurred inside. The boy who had entered the house for the washcloth had walked directly to the front bathroom, retrieved a washcloth from under the sink, wet it, and took it outside. The other brought keys and a purse into the house. The purse was placed on a chair and keys were delivered to a key hook in the kitchen. All was done quickly and in a silent, almost robotic manner. As if unaware of her existence, no one said anything to Mom, nor asked for directions around the house.

Outside, all three were completing the clean-up and replacing the hose. They entered the house briefly, made brief comments like, "Hope you get better, Ma'am...goodbye" and were out the door. Still in a daze, I managed to get my senses together enough to realize there must be compensation for the deeds done. I had not come to grips with the impossibility of human beings at this age and at this time of day having the knowledge to carry out the tasks they performed.

At the very moment they closed the front door, I yelled to Lydia, "Get them. Go stop them." Lydia ran for the door at almost the instant they closed it. There's an atrium right outside with a gate that opens to the outside yard. It's not possible for one to cross the atrium and get to the gate in the amount of time it took Lydia to reach the door. She jerked open the door to see a closed gate and no one present anywhere. She turned, wide-eyed with mouth gaping open, while all three of us looked at each other and shouted in unison, "THOSE WERE ANGELS," meaning supernatural angels... God's angels.

It seemed an easy chore now to get Mom into the car, and with Lydia driving, we quickly reached the emergency room where attention was given to the broken teeth, lacerations, scrapes, and bruises on my face and body. Fortunately, there were no broken bones, and x-rays revealed no serious damage. After many exams, medication, and observation, I was ready to go home within a few hours. Lydia, Mom, and I could not stop telling our story to many unbelieving hospital personnel.

I'm acquainted with the people in my neighborhood and had not encountered these three prior to this day. And I've never seen these young men again. I don't look for them, as I know in the depths of my being, they do not exist here.

I've told my angel story to others. Some are blessed in hearing. Some are skeptical. However, I know God had a purpose in revealing Himself in a visible way to ME. That day, my physical experience was neither of life or death but was simply of body, soul, and spirit being in trouble. The danger of depression and mistrust had distanced me from my Lord, and I needed a trail back. Even if the trail put me face down on the ground. I believe this was God's way of bringing me to an awareness of Him. Hebrews 1:14 says, "Angels are only servants. They are spirits sent from God to care for those who will receive salvation." I needed a servant sent from the Lord God Himself. I did not need rest from the constant care of Mom—as many friends and family members had suggested. I did not need to be relieved of this daily service. I needed God to fill my soul with His Being and to show me He was ever-present and that He would not allow me to bear more than I was able. Peace had filled my soul! Awareness of His omnipresence ascended from deep inside of me—from deeper than I knew was part of who I am! He was there, He is here, and He reveals Himself in everything in every way!

I know God's angels are often near, available to us, and I know He will make them known in whatever way, for whatever reason, and whenever

He may choose. I am at peace, at rest, and I have no fear about what tomorrow may bring.

Angels on Black Ice

When Ruth Grossman told me this story around 2005, I also asked her to write it down in her own words. She was pleased that I would include her story in this book. Sometimes, things take time! So after some fifteen years, here is Ruth's account:

It was mid-winter in Buffalo, NY. For anyone who has ever been in Buffalo at this time of year, you can still see a vivid picture in cold grays and icy whites. Living at Houghton College's extension campus, I knew some basic Buffalo winter facts. One of these was that you can't leave a car to sit out in the cold wind for a whole week and then expect to start it up.

My friend, Gary, was traveling with a college music group. In exchange for keeping his little blue Toyota in running order, I could avoid a chilling wait at the bus stop. For a week, I enjoyed scraping ice off the windshield, instead of fishing ice out of my boots and shaking it off my wet socks. When Gary returned, I wanted to be able to start that car up!

Another Buffalo winter fact is black ice. While traveling Route 90E to the airport to pick up Gary, I found myself in three lanes of bumper-to-bumper traffic. Buffalo folks know the danger of black ice, and all cars were traveling a slow 55 mph. I was in the far-left lane when the black ice found my tires. Instantly, the rear of the car moved ahead of the front tires and within seconds I'd spun three times counterclockwise. Then the Toyota stopped dead. The driver's side door was facing into the median's dirty, crusty snowbank. I was now an easy target for even the slowest of cars, and I knew my chances for survival were slim. I braced for impact and breathed a prayer.

Then a most unusual question formed in my fearful mind: Where was the traffic? There were no oncoming cars. Only two four-door sedans. With their flashers on, one of the sedans parked in front of me and one behind me. As if rehearsed, two men stepped out of the cars. They were dressed in similar, dark green parkas with gray fur-trimmed hoods pulled over bearded faces. I rolled down my window and followed directions to turn my wheels. In seconds, they had me pushed out and pointed east. "Go! Don't stop!" they said. I turned to wave and shout, "Thank you!" but found myself speechless. Which I remain today!

The Angel that Helped Me Slow Down

After hearing my friend, Merr Threesens, tell this story, I asked him if he too would write it down and let me publish it. (Thank you, Merr!) Here it is:

This happened sometime in 2010. My wife, kids, and I were shopping at the VF Outlet near Calvary Chapel on Julian Drive. We checked out and proceeded to walk toward the front door. I opened the door for my family. I then looked back to see if I would need to hold the door for anyone who was behind me. When I looked back, I noticed an elderly woman about forty feet away. She was walking toward me. When I made eye contact, she said, "You do not have to," meaning, "You do not have to hold the door

for me." I answered, "I want to." Again she said,
"You don't have to," and I replied the same thing.
We repeated all this one more time. With the
distance between her and the door, we probably
could have said it a few more times!

When she got to the door, she had a smile
and said, "Thank you." She said something about
how she moved a little slower now in life. I said,
"Well, I hope I make it that far," meaning that
far in life. I will never forget the beautiful smile
and look on her face when she replied. Looking
into the sky, she said, "I do, too." She also said,
"I have someone that takes really good care of
me." I knew exactly what she meant. Her heart
belonged to Christ.

Now my wife and kids were almost across
the street, which is right by the sidewalk in front
of the entrance. I hurried to catch up to them.
When I did, my wife asked me what I was doing.
As we both looked back toward the front door,
I said, "I was holding the door for that elderly
woman." My wife said, "What woman?" I stared
behind me, trying to make sense of where the
woman would have gone. I didn't see her anywhere. And she had moved so slowly, she could
not have gone far. Also, no cars had driven behind
me to either obscure my vision or pick her up.
And it had only been a few seconds to walk from
the VF Outlet to catch up with my wife and kids.

The front of the store has a long sidewalk
on both sides of the entrance. Being a perfection-
ist and one who pays close attention to detail,
I scanned the sidewalk and the entire area. I'm
very logical, too, and there was no logic to her
absence.

Across the street, I stopped and reflected on what had just happened. Replaying the woman's long trek to the entrance, her beautiful smile, and what she said to me while she looked to the sky, I listened to my heart. I then realized she was an angel. I believe this is the only explanation. And if you knew me better, you'd know God's purpose in providing this experience for me. I tend to struggle with my work/life balance. That means I sometimes get out of balance in the direction of working too long and hard. I think God was sending me the message: Slow down and listen to Him more carefully.

I will carry this wonderful memory forever. During times of struggle, I reflect on this event. I think of the woman's disappearance, how she looked, and what she said. I *do* slow down and listen to his voice. This helps keep my busy life in perspective. I'm so grateful for the reminder! Thank you, dear Lord God, Heavenly Father, for loving us all so much.

The Miracle of the Pipes

Katrina Ward has seen Heaven burst into her ordinary life on several occasions. Katrina is a licensed clinical social worker whom I've known for more than thirty years. She has many stories to tell of God's faithfulness. Here she tells one of them—about frozen pipes... and the breath of God:

I recall one miracle that happened to me in 1983 when I was living in a small farming town in Oklahoma. My family lived in a mobile unit that didn't have insulated pipes and we didn't have the money to insulate them.

The winter brought many snowstorms and then freezing ice blizzards. That's when our water pipes froze. We didn't have water to bathe, cook, or clean with. For two weeks, my mother, two older sisters, and I drove several times a day to a nearby gas station and filled up a five-gallon cooler with water.

One day, my mother rushed out of her room to tell us God told her He was going to breathe life into our water pipes. We were commissioned to turn on every faucet in the house. So that's what we did. Still no water, of course. That evening, we attended our mid-week church service and the pastor preached on "the breath of God." That's exactly what we would need for the pipes to provide water, and I remembered what my mother had said. Our family gleamed with joy and amazement. We suddenly had the faith to believe that God was about to do a miracle. Although the temperature hadn't changed, when we arrived home, we heard water flowing. I know now more than ever that His grace is sufficient!

My wife and I recently had lunch with Katrina and her mother, Martha. They shared more of the story. When they returned from church, the house was completely flooded, and it took them a long time to scoop the water out—but they sang praises all the while. They never did insulate their mobile home's plumbing, but for the next six winters, before they moved somewhere warmer, the pipes never froze.

Imelda's "Harley" Angel

In her first year at the University of Arizona, Imelda Buchanan worked part-time at a distribution company. Driving to work, she was singing along to her favorite music when something distracted her out of the left corner of her eye. She didn't see that traffic was backed up in front of her until she *did* see! Imelda slammed on the brakes but couldn't prevent hitting the car in front of her. She heard a loud "pop." Smoke filled the air, and the smell of gas overwhelmed her senses. She became disoriented and filled with dread that she might have hurt someone. Then things got worse. She felt her face swell, and she was having trouble seeing because a chemical that leaked from her airbag had gotten into her eyes. Her sunglasses had also become wedged in her eyebrows. She unstuck and straightened them and feebly attempted to get out of the car.

At that moment, she heard a motorcycle pull up. Harley-Davidson was the only motorcycle she knew the name of, so she's always referred to this one ever since as a Harley. Though she couldn't see it, she knew it had pulled right next to her car. The rider opened Imelda's driver's side door and said confidently, "You're going to be all right, and no one was hurt." What comforting words! He then said he would stay with her until the paramedics arrived. He covered her face with a towel, helped her out of the car, and gently walked her to the curb. Sitting with her by the side of the road, he held his hand to her back while they waited.

When Imelda heard the sirens, she finally heard her good Samaritan say, "The paramedics are here. They'll take care of you now. You're going to be okay." He then removed his hand from her back, and she took the towel from her face. Because of her blurred vision, she saw only his shadow as he walked away. She says she can still hear the revving of his motorcycle as he roared away.

One of the paramedics was a cousin of Imelda's. While being transferred into the ambulance, she recognized his voice. But because of her injuries, he didn't recognize her at first and was astonished to learn she was Imelda! He asked why she had gotten out of the car before the ambulance arrived. She told him about the man who helped her out of the car and sat with her—the man who said he'd stay with her till the paramedics arrived. She didn't think to wonder how the motorcycle man happened to have a towel.

Imelda could barely hear her cousin's voice, but she heard him say that as he and the other paramedics approached, no one had been sitting with her. The kind man *did* leave right before they arrived, but she believes they had to have seen him roar away just as their ambulance arrived.

Imelda's eyes sparkled when she told me what went through her mind in the next moment—thoughts that continue to increase her inner peace and trust in God. Her words:

> That's when I knew. God had sent an angel to comfort me and be with me, someone to assure me that I was going to be okay and care for me until help arrived. To this day, I refer to him as my Harley angel and pray that one day I will get to thank him for helping a scared girl feel the comfort and love of God.

Time to Pause

Now is a good time to pause and reflect on what you've read so far. Simply relax and meditate on whatever times God has revealed Himself to you in a big or small way. Sometimes, to negate regrets or fears, it helps to dwell on positive memories and situations when you felt happy or peaceful. The best relaxation method for me is to meditate on God's word. One way that I especially love is to float in a swimming pool and recite favorite scriptures I've memorized.

You may simply want to read Psalms such as 1, 23, 34, or 138. They will help calm your heart and mind. When I was the pastor-on-call at the first church I served, I counseled a man who said that the "secret place" spoken of in Psalm 91:1 is the Word of God. I haven't plumbed the full depths of that passage, but I've nonetheless found it to be true for me. When you meditate on the Word, you open more space within you where God can live. That's a secret place where only God and you commune.

Reflections on the Peaceful Life

When something happens to you for which there is no explanation except that you've just experienced a miracle, that's a perfect time to meditate on God's boundless power and love for you! The same is true if you hear of a miracle that happened to anyone you know well or trust (or read in this book!). James 1:17 states, "Every good and perfect gift is from above, coming down from the Father of the Heavenly lights, who does not change like shifting shadows." The Creator of the universe lifts the veil between eternity and where we live to give us good and perfect gifts. Many of these are obvious miracles, and thanking God for them helps us set aside our worries and trust more in Him. God will help you to trust Him and help you to *enjoy* trusting Him!

Endnotes

53 "Deus ex machina," Wikipedia, accessed, 12/15/2017, https:/en.wikipedia. org/wiki/Deus_ex_machina.

54 *Merriam-Webster*, s.v. "deus ex machina," accessed 12/15/2017, https://www. merriam-webster.com/dictionary/deus%20ex%20machina.

55 Ibid., https:/en.wikipedia.org/wiki/Deus_ex_machina.

56 2 Kings 19:35.

57 2 Chronicles 20:17.

58 Hebrews 13:2.

59 1 Samuel 1:27; Hannah literally "asked" or "petitioned" God.

60 1 Samuel 3:4-8.

61 Catherine Marshall, *A Man Called Peter* (New York: Avon Books, 1951), 23–24.

62 Catherine Marshall, 24–25.

63 Roger Barrier, "Do We Have Guardian Angels," Preach It Teach It, accessed 12/13/2020, http://www.preachitteachit.org/ask-roger/detail/ do-we-have-guardian-angels/.

64 Renie Burghardt in Allison Bottke with Cheryll Hutchings, adapted from *God Answers Prayers* (Eugene, Oregon: Harvest House Publishers, 2005), 172–175.

65 Renie Burghardt.

66 John 10:4 and 27.

67 Hebrews 12:8.

4

Extraordinary Miracles

*Miracles do not happen in contradiction to nature, but only
in contradiction to what is known to us of nature.*

—St. Augustine

Inside and Outside Time and Space

We know that because God created the universe, He lives outside
time and space, as we understand these concepts.[68] As God told the
prophet Isaiah, He "inhabits eternity."[69] We also know that, because
He speaks to people and has performed wonders throughout history,
He lives *inside* time and space as well. That's where miracles happen
that we can witness. The mere contemplation of such "impossible"
events invites us into a deeper understanding of God's fascinating
and unpredictable ways. They help us to know Him better and see
the world through His eyes.

In a sermon about Christ's belief that anything is possible for
those who believe, Pastor Bobby Schuller told of miracles he witnessed while on missionary trips. He said he prayed for a man in
Thailand who hadn't been able to walk for ten years. After prayer, the
man stood up and ran. Schuller prayed for a woman with a tumor
on her neck, and the tumor vanished. He was in a town where there
had been no rain for three months, and as he and others prayed, it
began to rain.[70]

Dr. Bob Sawvelle describes similarly astounding miracles. I'm struck by a statement in his book *Receive Your Miracle Now: A Case for Healing Today* that "There are healings and miracles, and then there are extraordinary miracles. In Acts 19, we read, 'God did extraordinary miracles through Paul'" (Acts 19:11).[71] I'll speak more about Dr. Sawvelle later in this chapter, including a miracle his wife experienced.

You've already read of several extraordinary miracles. This chapter contains *nothing but* that variety! Missionary friends have told me of witnessing many more such miracles. They believe these events are more often seen in poorer countries than in the United States because the needs are so much greater. Few clinics or nearby hospitals are available, and there are no social service agencies or 911 assistance. In short, resources we take for granted are severely lacking. The desperation for medical attention and other life-saving care is greater—and hence, the prayers are more passionate and faith-filled. Nevertheless, the mightiest influencers of history are sometimes awakened to their mortality and certain need of God. Hezekiah was such a man.

Seal of the Two-Winged Sun

God told King Hezekiah that he had only a few years to live. Hezekiah pleaded with God to heal him. God heard the king's prayer and gave him a sign that He would heal him. God said that He would make the shadow of the sun on the temple stairs go back ten steps. That's exactly what happened, and Hezekiah lived fifteen years longer.

A recent archaeological dig in Jerusalem uncovered a three-thousand-year-old object with an ancient Hebrew inscription: "Belonging to Hezekiah [son of] Ahaz king of Judah." At the center of the seal is a two-winged sun that is flanked by two symbols that mean "life." Archaeologists believe King Hezekiah began using this seal as a symbol of God's protection after He answered the king's desperate prayer for healing from his life-threatening illness.[72] Hezekiah's seal is a reminder that God can intervene in time and space. A modern-day example of that happened near where I grew up.

The Mayor of Bexley

There wasn't a back road or diner for miles around
that my grandfather didn't know about.
—Melanie Clark, Tucson, Arizona

Mom and Dad had recently moved all the way from Ohio to be closer to me. I loved spending more time with them and sharing even the littlest details of our lives. Like the morning Dad and I were talking about a television show I had watched the night before. A show about angels. My all-time favorite subject.

"It was amazing," I said. "People getting rescued, for example, just in the nick of time."

"That same thing happened to us," Dad said. "Driving home to Ohio, Christmas Eve."

"I don't remember that."

"It was way back in '45. You didn't come on the scene until 1953! We were flat broke and didn't have any money to get the kids presents for Christmas. I called my dad. He told us to get in the car and get home, and they would take care of Christmas for the kids."

I'd heard stories about my folks and older brother and sister making the 500-mile drive from up north to spend the holiday with Dad's family in tiny Bexley, Ohio. But nothing involving a rescue. This was long before the interstate system. Definitely no cell phones or Google Maps. My dad was an expert with maps. Give him a good map and he could find anything and remember it. But the drive was at least twelve hours, easy, with my siblings in single digits. *Ugh.* I couldn't imagine how stressful it must have been.

95

"We'd almost made it to Bexley," Dad said. "We were thirty miles away. It was dark and cold. We'd hoped to make it by dinnertime." Dad had moved the family to New York City from Toledo, Ohio, to pursue his dream of singing opera. His parents missed him terribly. Back then, even making a long-distance phone call was a big deal.

Grandpa, Dad's father, had been the mayor of Bexley for ten years. He knew every back road, every store, every nook and cranny like the back of his hand. He couldn't imagine why anyone would ever want to leave his town, let alone venture outside of Ohio, including his own son.

"What happened?" I said.

"Well, we had engine trouble," Dad said. "We were on some deserted back road, and the car just died."

I imagined Mom and Dad with their two young children. How cold and tired they must have been.

"There wasn't another soul around," Dad said. "No house. No other cars. I mean, it was Christmas Eve. Everyone was in for the night. I admit I was kind of worried what might happen to us."

Dad had always seemed bigger than life to me. It was hard to imagine him being afraid or even feeling lost. Remembering landmarks, having this sixth sense for direction, seemed like a trait that had been passed down from father to son. He looked a little like Jackie Gleason, with an outsized personality to match. When he entered a room, all eyes turned to him. But he was good under pressure, focused, determined. I could see him doing his best to keep everyone calm.

"I got out and opened the hood," Dad continued. "Shone a flashlight in there. But it was nothing I could fix on my own. I needed a mechanic. Of course, that wasn't going to happen. Then I looked up, and in the distance, I saw lights. Started walking toward them. There was a diner and a garage. In the middle of nowhere!"

"Wow! Lucky for you," I said. It was a good story and all, but not really as exciting as the TV show I'd told him about. Still, I didn't want to hurt his feelings. I could tell he was enjoying reliving the memory.

"I managed to push the car over to the garage," he said, "with your mom steering. And there was a mechanic still on duty. Mom and the kids went in the diner. We were the only customers there, of course. I couldn't believe they were even open. I called my dad from the shop phone. Told him where we were and what had happened. He kept saying, 'Where? I think you must be confused.' You know how he could get. There wasn't a road or a diner he didn't know, and that was that. I told him I was tired and wasn't going to argue with him."

I laughed, thinking of the two of them, both men headstrong, certain of their opinions.

"So we got the car fixed," Dad said. "Got everyone loaded up and drove to my parents' house. Had a nice Christmas. But my dad, he just wouldn't let up about where this diner/garage was. Kept insisting I was wrong. Telling me how he knew every diner in the area. 'I know what I saw,' I finally told him. He was really starting to get on my nerves."

Was this all there was to Dad's tale? Two men arguing about a restaurant's location? The

TV show that had started this whole conversation was all about angels. Stories that gave me goose bumps. Not...

"So when we left," he said, "just to prove him wrong, I drove back the exact way we'd come. We got to the place where the diner was." Dad stopped. There was a little catch to his voice. "There was nothing there. Only an empty field. I drove all around the area, but it was just desolate. Not another building for miles."

I could feel my jaw falling open. "That's... that's...incredible," I said.

"God had to have put that operation there just for us," Dad said. "It's the only thing I've ever been able to come up with. The diner, the garage. The mechanic, and the waiters in the diner. They must have been angels."

But I'd never actually known anyone who'd come face-to-face with one. Or at least, I didn't know I did!

"Dad," I said. "How could you have not ever told me this?"

Dad shrugged. "I don't know. I guess I didn't think it was all that unusual. I mean, there was the other time. I was in an airport..."

("The Mayor of Bexley," Jan./Feb. 2018, "Angels on Earth." Published by permission of Guideposts. All rights reserved.)

I've read many accounts that exemplify the meaning of *baffling*—stories of time stopping for all but one person who continued to move through time and stories of lives saved because strangers appeared at the right time in a house that turned out to be nonexistent or abandoned. Clearly, it is small potatoes that the Creator of all things can manipulate the universe however He wants to! In the story that Melanie told about her father and the mayor, the mayor was right. But Melanie's dad, mom, and brother were the ones who experienced the miracle. Although there was nothing in the field, *there had been, just when needed!*

I'm still learning that things like this happen more frequently than I'd ever dreamed. Melanie's account expands my view of the spiritual perspective of reality, as do all credible miracle stories. We need only talk to the right people and read easily available sources. My bookshelves are filled with these accounts.

Another story of God intervening in time and space involved David Ammon. Susan and I have been friends with David and his wife, Christina, for more than thirty years. I was honored to perform their wedding ceremony. I'd forgotten most of the details, so—as with other stories in this chapter—I asked David to recount this story from his perspective as an experienced pilot.

Angel Rescue from My Crashed Aerial Applicator

It was the spring of 1974. I attended Cal-Ag-Aero, an Aerial Applicator School in Hanford, CA. I received training and testing, earning licenses in both Arizona and California as an aerial applicator operator and pilot. Some of you may have heard the term "crop dusting," but the phrase is not an accurate descriptor, so it's no longer used. Aerial application of chemicals, seeding, and fertilizing is conducive to less soil compaction and healthier plant growth.

Flight training was in a stock Stearman, a WWII trainer. I soloed in a 450-horsepower Stearman sprayer and did practice runs on crops with only water on board. Just some background info on the angel rescue:

I returned to Yuma, Arizona in early June and was employed by Marsh Aviation. I spent the next month working with the aircraft mechanic to complete the engine installation and annual inspection of the Cessna 188 Ag Wagon, tail number N9825V. It's important to know everything there is to learn about your plane so that you could fly it in your sleep!

On July 11, I familiarized myself with the aircraft on a thirty-minute maintenance check flight. Then on July 13, I continued with slow flight, turns and stalls. On July 15, with seventy-five gallons of water on board, I tested the spray system with simulated field runs. On July 19, with one hundred gallons of water on board, I did shallow and steep turns. These were simulated field runs. On July 22, with another 100 gallons of water, I sprayed a field, performed letdowns, spray runs, pull-ups, and turnarounds. By now, I had fifteen landings in the C-188A. I was comfortable with the craft. I was also having fun!

My first paying job was on July 25: seventy-four acres of cotton on the Jim Barkley Farms in Yuma. Over the next two months, I flew 175 hours with about 517 takeoffs and landings and sprayed the following crops: alfalfa, cotton, lettuce, soybeans, and sugar beets. I was also seeding alfalfa from the air and spreading sulfur powder on cotton. I didn't know that I was soon to experience a miracle.

On September 26, 1974, after flying a field or two, I was on my way to a cotton field about one mile south of Gadsden on the east side of Highway 95 (southwest of Yuma). I circled east of the field over a crop of tall date palms, waiting for my flag crew to arrive. I was a little angry that they were running behind schedule. As I circled, my chief pilot, Delbert R. Mahon, was working a field about one mile south of the cotton field, and we were watching out for each other as we turned.

As I continued turning, I got a little slower and lower over the palm trees than I should have. The flag crew finally found the cotton field and was heading for the north end of the field. The wind was out of the south, so they would be walking into the wind and away from any spray drift. I would be spraying east to west, then turning around to fly a west-to-east pattern. The cotton rows ran east to west, so the flaggers would count the rows for each swath/pass.

Since the flag crew was approaching the northwest end of the field, I decided to make my first pass, and they would then count off for the next swath. As I came over the west side of the tall date palms, I pushed down for my first pass, started the spray, and leveled off. The aircraft lost lift and then touched the top of the six-foot-tall long-staple cotton. This felt like the brakes were applied. I would later find out how another factor was involved in the loss of lift.

The main wheels touched the ground as the tail of the C-188A rotated up and over the top, flipping the craft, slamming me upside down while skidding on the ground. Coming to a stop, I felt a blow to my head and the control stick glanced off my helmet face shield. The filtered air system was still blowing air into the helmet. I turned off the master switch, cutting off all DC power at the battery. Then I unbuckled my five-point shoulder and seat belt harness and felt myself drop slightly.

The hopper was full of toxic chemicals and I knew I had to get out. Then I saw a spot of light about the size of a softball. I thought to myself, "That must be the way out," and the next thing I knew, I was lying on the ground by the wing of the upside-down Ag Wagon.

A helper was there immediately and assisted in the removal of my helmet. He asked how I was and said an ambulance was on the way. The next thing I remember was being put on a backboard and loaded into the ambulance. On the way to the hospital, I remember asking the crew, "If you talk to my wife, Sandy, let her know I am okay." I arrived at the hospital where I was examined, but I don't remember much about that.

An x-ray showed my sternum was cracked and the T-12 vertebra was crushed about 3/8 inch on the inner side. Years later, I found out my L-1 vertebra was also crushed. The cracked sternum hurt worse than the back, but I had to rest and sleep with my head raised. This was painful.

The next afternoon, the chief pilot came into my hospital room. Delbert said, "I made my next turn and was looking for you. Not seeing you, I figured the only place you could be was in the field." He may have made a radio call to the office asking for an ambulance, but I never knew this for sure. Delbert and the Marsh Aviation crew recovered the aircraft from the cotton field that morning.

Then Delbert asked, "How did you get out of the aircraft? We saw no evidence of how you got out. In fact, the canopy was sheared off and the seat back was on the ground. We thought there was no way you got out alive." I told him I did not know. All I remembered was seeing the spot of light and suddenly being by the wing of my upside-down Ag Wagon. There was no passage of time between the light and lying on the ground.

Later, as I was giving thanks to the Lord for my recovery, I looked at my jumpsuit and shoes that were in a hospital plastic bag. They weren't dirty or green from plant chlorophyll. If I had crawled out of the wreckage—and there was no evidence of that—I would have been muddy and green, especially because, as I found out, the field had been irrigated the night before. This still made no sense to my natural mind.

It took me a while to realize that no one had helped me out. Also, since no one saw me crawl out and since I was suddenly by the wing without mud on my boots or chlorophyll on my jumpsuit, there was only one explanation: I was extracted in less than an instant from the aircraft by an angel, the Heavenly Helper. Yes, a miracle, just as the resurrected Christ could disappear and appear. Just as Phillip was transported in an instant from the south of Israel to the north. Acts 8:39–40 records what happened to Phillip, after he baptized an Ethiopian eunuch:

"When they came up out of the water, the Spirit of the Lord suddenly took Philip away, and the eunuch did not see him again, but went on his way rejoicing. Philip, however, appeared at Azotus and traveled about, preaching the gospel in all the towns until he reached Caesarea."

I realized later that circumstances had mitigated against a safe pass over the cotton field all along. I was circling east of the field and my airspeed was slower than it should have been. The irrigation of the field caused the density altitude to be very high, producing less lift.

High-density altitude means there are fewer air molecules in a given volume of air, resulting in reduced lift from the wings and reduced propeller efficiency. Like climbing a mountain, the higher you go, the more the lighter air makes you breathe harder and probably have less energy.

My judgment was also not at peak performance. Big mistake. At least three things contributed to my accident: (1) I had a bad attitude about the flag crew being late; 2) I flew too low and slow before entering the field, and (3) high-density air over the cotton crop.

By December, workman's comp released me to go back to work. The wrecked Ag Wagon was not going to be replaced. I was unemployed. But the next miracle was in the making: I mapped out an interview trip from Yuma to most all the aerial applicators throughout California to the Oregon border. I became determined to find another pilot job.

I started out from Yuma in March 1975 with the first stop being Ripley, CA and Wotton Aviation. Bob Wotton interviewed me and asked about my experience and what I'd learned from the accident. I was hired and started working in the shop, helping with the repair of cloth-covered Stearman wings. I was sent to Brawley, CA for a recheck-out in the Stearman N4412N. My first paying flight was thirty-one acres of alfalfa in a Stearman N4685N on April 15, 1975.

I was so thankful. I believed that had I not planned the entire job-seeking trip through CA, I would not have been offered the job with Wotton Aviation. Wotton was the first stop on my itinerary after the accident and only seventy-nine miles from home. I was an aerial applicator for the next

six years in California and Arizona. I remain a
believer in God's miracles and a follower of Jesus.

Dr. Julie Barrier's Account on PreachItTeachIt.org

In the last chapter, I introduced you to Roger and Julie Barrier,
who thought they heard the other's voice and rushed to their daughter at the bathtub. I spoke of their website and the growth of Casas
Church under their leadership. When attendance was at its peak, it
was Julie who directed the music and drama ministries. Large crowds
flocked in from all over southeast Arizona each year for the church's
Christmas musical extravaganza.

Julie has published several of my articles on PreachItTeachIt.
org, along with many more of her own. A recent one by her advances
the narrative of this book. Julie retells a miracle account that was
shared one Sunday at Casas by two visiting missionaries. After I
posted the story on my Facebook page, Roger and Julie's daughter,
Brianna Barrier Wetherbee, commented, "I remember getting to talk
with them [the missionaries] and asking every question that came to
my little mind at the time—and I've never forgotten it." (Brianna
was the little girl who nearly drowned in the bathtub!)

Here's that extraordinary miracle story from Julie's article:

The Axe Murderer and the Missionary's Miracle[73]

The sharpened steel axe blade cracked her
skull like an eggshell. Awakened out of a deep
sleep, Beth fell to the floor in a heap, limp and
blood-soaked. Despite her gaping wound, she
spied the hulking forms of two men pummeling
her husband with rough-hewn axe handles. But
Dan fought like a wild man, fiercely hovering
over his injured wife, determined to serve as a
human shield to spare her life.

Suddenly, the two masked intruders heard
their superior officer barking orders in Russian

outside the bedroom window. A passerby had heard the screams and the assailants did not want to be discovered. One of the brutes carefully placed the bloody axe in Dan's hand to frame him for his wife's murder. The missionary family had caused quite a stir among their neighbors with the teachings of this heretic, Jesus, and the secret police were determined to shut them up for good.

Dan grabbed a large bath towel and fashioned it into a makeshift tourniquet [to wrap around] Beth's head. Beth, blinded by the blood and brain matter, managed to cry out, "Dan, the girls! Find the girls!" Faint from the agony of his broken ribs and clavicle, Dan stumbled to his daughters' bedroom. They were nowhere to be found. Had they been abducted? Were they already dead? Susie, seven, and Ellie, five, had disappeared without a trace.

Immediately, Dan called his mission organization's emergency number to get a Medevac for Beth. She would be airlifted to Vienna, the closest and safest hospital. As reinforcements arrived, Dan's beloved Beth was motionless, brutally bludgeoned but breathing.

Mom and Dad refused to leave until their daughters had been found. Just as the helicopter revved its engine to airlift the patients, Ellie and Susan emerged from the backyard shed, shivering and unscathed. Mom and Dad wept that their babies had escaped the soldiers' brutal attack.

The medics bundled the trembling girls in wooly blankets and placed them in the front seat of the copter next to the pilot. Dan demanded that his precious cargo remain beside him on the gurney. He held their tiny hands tightly. The medics whisked the frightened family through the frozen darkness to safety.

Vienna was three hours away. The medical team on board stitched Beth's gash and hoped for the best. As Dan's arm and shoulder were stabilized, he was conscious enough to ply his little daughters with questions.

"What happened? Where were you? Did the men chase you outside? Did they hurt you? How did you ever escape?" asked Dan.

Susie spoke first, quietly and simply.

"Jesus woke us up, Daddy. He told us to follow Him and He carried us to the shed and pushed us under the bench behind the garden tools."

Ellie chimed in, "He looked just like I thought He would, Daddy. I wasn't scared or nuthin.' He was there and then He wasn't."

Susie added, "The big man with the hood opened the door and stared at us. He was holding a big stick in his hand. He lifted it up and then dropped it on the ground. Ellie and me didn't say anything. He just ran away. We stayed 'til we heard the helicopter noise and came out to find you."

Dan collapsed on the stretcher, groggy and relieved. The girls' strange story would have to be processed tomorrow. The morphine drip was taking effect.

Beth lay comatose in the Wiener Krankenanstaltenverbund (hospital) for two months. After multiple brain surgeries, she regained consciousness. Her physician reported that she had suffered minimal permanent brain damage—only slight memory loss. When she awoke, Beth spoke clearly and articulately, as if the attack had never happened and her brain had suffered no injury.

Beth related her miraculous experience in the Heavenlies.

"I found myself in a great hall. They cheered as they looked down at me…my role models, just like the Bible said in Hebrews 12:1.

"'As for us, we have this large crowd of witnesses around us. So then, let us rid ourselves of everything that gets in the way, and of the sin which holds on to us so tightly, and let us run with determination the race that lies before us. Let us keep our eyes fixed on Jesus, on whom our faith depends from beginning to end' (GNT).

"Moses, Paul, Abraham, Daniel, and Jesus… I recognized them all. They stood, applauding and shouting. I felt so warm and happy and proud. I didn't know if I would return to earth, but I will never forget Jesus' smile as He gazed into my eyes.

"I couldn't believe it. I was there among all the heroes of the faith I'd read about and admired. Somehow, I knew I had won a great victory. I had held onto my faith and completed the task that God gave me."

Beth continued, weeping softly.

"I awoke with a blinding headache. I could only see shapes, but I knew that it was you, Dan, stroking my hair and holding my hand. Then I knew. Jesus had more for us to do. We will finish His work together, fearlessly and joyfully."

She sighed, exhausted from her brief conversation with her beloved.

Years later, as she told me her story, I marveled at her courage and perseverance. Dan and Beth didn't see themselves as missionary material.

Dan was an esteemed professor at an Ivy League university and they lived a charmed life. But God called them to take another road to a hostile country full of enemies, hardships, and poverty. Even after such persecution, Beth confided that she longed to return to her loved ones and ministry partners in that dark place.

God had yet another calling on the lives of this amazing family. They now lead a massive missionary organization with dedicated servants throughout northern Europe and Asia. Ellie and Susan are young ladies now and serve the Lord alongside their parents.

Few of us have faced torture and persecution as Beth and Dan have, but they will both testify that, in the gray mist between life and death, Jesus was there.

And so He shall be for you, too.

(Julie's conclusion: This story is not urban legend. These precious missionaries are our personal friends. We have seen the scars and can validate the facts. However, all names have been changed to ensure their safety and security.)

Barring a Miracle
Who Can Stop God?

I led worship for four years at New Life Wesleyan Church in Tucson. I worked full-time as a Christian-based counselor; my worship position was part-time. I loved the people at New Life, and that's where I met Tom and Trudy Prescott. Their miracle happened after I left New Life to become the director of counseling at Casas Church.

On March 3, 2010, Tom had surgery to remove his cancerous prostate. A week later, Tom began to bleed and was rushed back to the hospital. Fearing another operation would do more harm than good, the surgeon decided to simply monitor the bleeding. Five days later, his bleeding had not fully stopped. Tom's catheter was clogging with clots, and his urine as well was mostly blood. It was clearly time to re-operate, after all.

Tom says, "Two nurses were in the room, and the surgeon asked them to get a urine sample. The doctor then said, 'Barring a miracle, we will be in surgery at 10:00 a.m. tomorrow morning,' and he left the room. At that exact moment, the nurses took the urine sample from the catheter. It was clear. No blood! One nurse said, 'What just happened? This can't be.'" Since Tom's readmission to the hospital six days earlier, the catheter bag held nothing but very bloody urine. Why would it suddenly be clear, right after the surgeon said, "Barring a miracle?" Tom's wife, Trudy, who was in the room, said, "You just witnessed a miracle."

The surgeon didn't believe this report and blindly refused to cancel the surgery. Tom says that the surgery was still a "go" for 10:00 a.m. But the surgeon reluctantly agreed to hold off another two hours. Two hours passed and still no bleeding. "The surgeon finally canceled the surgery," Tom says. "I remained in the hospital for another three days, and the nurses started calling me 'the miracle man.'" Tom concludes, "It has been eight years since the surgery, and the cancer is undetectable. Praise God! I still smile every time I think of the doctor saying, 'Barring a miracle.'"

A Case for Healing Today

Dr. Bob Sawvelle is a pastor and Bible scholar who has witnessed all manner of healings, many occurring after he prayed. He and his wife, Carolyn, have traveled with Dr. Randy Clark and other Christian leaders to pray for thousands of people around the world. Both Bob and Carolyn heard God's call to promote the gospel. The former engineers went into spiritual deserts around the world to demonstrate God's power and preach the good news of Jesus Christ. Part of their life journey to this point involved seminary for Bob, then founding a church in Tucson in 2002. That's where I met them.

I had been invited by several friends to visit Passion Church, but because I was a pastor at a church on the other side of town, I couldn't leave my Sunday responsibilities. Quite a few years later, my wife Susan and I were finally able to attend. We loved the worship as well as the inspiring and compelling messages.

Bob's book *Receive Your Miracle Now: A Case for Healing Today* draws on the collective wisdom of many theologians, historians, and other biblical scholars to again show that God is good and every bit as active in healing people today as He was in biblical times. The dead are still being raised. The blind are still receiving sight. The crippled still rise up and walk, and the deaf still have their hearing restored. Bob's book is a theological work that is punctuated with miracle stories like those I hear from many missionaries as well as from other friends and acquaintances. Bob believes that God works miracles in each of our lives—as what you've read so far should have made evident! His theological view supporting that God performs miracles even in our time has been established by the writers of the Bible, by the church fathers, and by Bible preachers and scholars since the time of Christ.

Here is another miracle that I hope will boggle your mind and make you want to shout! Since I can't tell this story better than it's already been written, I'll let Bob tell it.[74]

Healing through a Stranger

Several years ago, my wife, Carolyn, suffered for months from an unknown intestinal condition that caused her extreme pain, discomfort, fatigue, and weight loss. She was unable to keep food in her system for very long, robbing her of important nutrients. At the time, we were small business owners with poor health insurance. We avoided seeing a doctor because our finances were limited and we thought her condition, although severe at times, would eventually heal.

One morning, her symptoms became severe and we discussed seeing a doctor. We began to pray, asking God for her healing and for clear direction as to what to do next. Carolyn left for work, and within two hours God answered our prayers.

After visiting a client's business that morning, Carolyn entered her truck and was ready to drive out of the parking lot when she noticed two men who looked to be homeless sitting on a bench outside the business. Suddenly, one of them came and knocked on her truck window, motioning for her to roll down the window to speak with her. Cautiously, she rolled the window down a few inches and asked what he wanted.

He stated that he and his friend were visiting from the west side of the state. The man then asked her what church she attended. Carolyn was puzzled. How did this man know she was a Christian and was involved in a local church? Neither she nor her truck gave any indication of her faith, so she asked him, "How do you know I am a Christian?" The man responded by explaining that the Lord had revealed this information to him and had instructed him to come over and pray for her healing. He went on to ask if she would like to receive prayer.

Carolyn thought to herself, "Yes, I want prayer for healing!" Not knowing the stranger and being unfamiliar with prayers for healing, she was very cautious at first, but [after a few minutes] she agreed to allow the man to pray for her. He said a simple prayer: "Lord, heal this woman in Jesus' name!" Then he asked her if she was healed.

Carolyn tried to explain that she would know as soon as she ate something, but the man would not let her finish a sentence. She tried again to explain it, but the man interrupted her again and insisted she give him a simple "yes" or "no" answer.

Finally, frustrated with the man, Carolyn responded, "Yes!" Later, she explained to me that it did not make sense for her to say "no" to the man. The moment Carolyn said "yes," she felt a burning sensation in her lower abdomen near her colon. She was stunned, but she knew that God had just healed her. Her pain and discomfort were gone. It was her first healing experience with God.

Carolyn described this encounter to me later at lunch. She had no ill effects from eating lunch and worked the rest of the day with no discomfort. That evening, we went out to eat Mexican food—the spicier the better, we thought. Carolyn enjoyed her dinner pain-free with no additional side effects! Carolyn received her healing and has not suffered from this condition since. We believe the heat she experienced in her abdomen after the man had prayed for her was God healing her digestive tract.

A random encounter with a stranger awakened both of us to the reality of Jesus as healer. God not only healed Carolyn, He revealed something important to us about His nature and His ways.

God Speaks to Her Heart, and a Baby Is Healed

You heard from my friend, Katrina Ward, in the last chapter. In the next one, you'll read about a minister who became a rocket scientist. Katrina is her daughter, and faith in God is the vital core of the family. Here she tells another amazing miracle story:

A few years ago, I was working the night shift at a rehabilitation center for women with children. When I took the job, I thought I would be able to get a lot of homework done. After all, I'd be on the night shift.

One night, a mother burst into my office with her ten-month-old child lifeless in her arms. We called paramedics and they rushed the baby to the emergency room. The next morning, I learned the baby had been diagnosed with meningitis.

After a couple of days, the baby remained comatose. On the third day, I heard the Lord speak to my spirit: "Go see that baby." Non-family members weren't allowed in the room and I had no idea what the baby's name was or what room the baby was in.

Well, I wanted to do the "Christian thing" and I tracked this baby down, hoping to find the mother in the room. I wanted to show the mother that people cared. No one was in the room and the baby lay lifeless in a steel, cage-like crib. Tubes penetrated his little arms and legs. My heart was so touched.

I sat down and whispered to the Lord, "What do you want me to do, Lord?" He answered, "Just sing." So I began singing little songs, songs I'd sung to my children when I would tuck them in at night. "Jesus, sweet Jesus, what a wonder you are. Brighter than the morning star…"

Soon, nurses crowded around taking vital signs. They seemed not to see me—which was strange—as they poked and prodded to find a vein and hurriedly drew blood samples. The baby whimpered. I could tell the child was in pain, drained and fragile, hanging on to life.

When they left, I again inquired what the Lord wanted me to do. He said, "Touch him."

So I reached my hand through those steel bars and softly touched his hand and whispered the only name I know to call when I'm in trouble: Jesus! Suddenly, the baby opened his eyes, sat up, and smiled at me. What a shock! The baby with meningitis was comatose a moment ago. Now he seemed attentive and happy!

His machines were beeping and the nurses rushed into the room and asked, "What is going on?" They took the baby's vitals again and were in awe that they were completely improved. That was fast! The nurses looked at me and I said, "I think he's hungry." They were thrilled. Soon, I was spoon-feeding him Jell-O and helping him to drink.

His mother finally arrived and was stunned by the whole situation. Who was I? How was her baby feeding and sitting up, wanting her to hold him? Her confusion quickly turned to joy! Two days later, the baby returned home.

I don't like going around praying for people, as though I have any power. I knew I had no power in me to heal the baby. Without the Healer, there is no healing. I stretched out my hand and He stretched out His love and made the baby whole. Praise you, Jesus!

When an Angel Speaks, Her Child Is Healed

Rev. Cynthia Palmer hosted two Christian radio programs in Zeeland, Michigan, for two years. She focused on the news and interviewed extraordinary women. Cynthia is now an associate pastor at Grand Rapids First, a megachurch in Wyoming, Michigan.

Twenty-nine years ago, she was told that her daughter would be born with either spina bifida and/or anencephaly. The latter is an absence of major portions of the brain and skull. On a scale of one to ten, the baby was predicted to have a 9.3 probability of such mal-formations. Cynthia's doctor advised a "therapeutic" abortion near term. But Cynthia would not even consider abortion and decided "I will take what God gave me."

Cynthia's blood sugar levels notched the baby's risk factor up to 9.5. The verdict for the child being severely deformed was all but certain. With such odds, what could reverse the inevitable? *Only prayer.* Cynthia was a new believer in Christ, but she had enough faith to ask everyone she knew to *pray.*

The doctor scheduled Cynthia for an ultrasound to measure the baby's organs and their vital function. Cynthia was warned that the results would horrify her. Surely she would be convinced to have an abortion! She was scheduled for the ultrasound in three weeks. Then, something amazing happened. The night before the ultrasound, an angel appeared to Cynthia in her bedroom. The angel was rocking a baby. The angel told her, "Do not fear. You are going to have a very healthy, normal child. Not only that, your child will be a world-changer. Your main mission in life is to get this baby to Earth."

Immediately, Cynthia was filled with great peace, and she slept for the first time in three weeks. The next day, she went to Northwestern Hospital in Chicago for the all-day procedure. At the end of the ordeal, the technician did something he wasn't supposed to. Knowing that Cynthia must be worried sick from all she'd been told about her baby's prognosis, he read the results to her before the doctor saw them. The technician showed her the images of the very healthy baby girl!

Cynthia says, "When my baby was born without the 'inevitable' deformities, she did have a huge scar across her back that she still has to this day where the Lord Jehovah Raphe ['the God who heals'] laid His hand across her and healed her." As is so often the case with scars many of us bear, they remind us of a victory or a miracle. Cynthia says this scar carries a special message: that her baby would become the world-changer the angel had spoken of! In fact, her daughter—who just gave birth herself—now works in a pediatric neonatal unit at Chicago's Lurie Children's Hospital. She helps save the lives of countless newborns. Cynthia says that "by the world's standards [these babies] would mostly have no hope but God!"

Unseen Hand Saves Pastor Andy

On a cool December Sunday in Tucson, I drove to Lifepoint Church with expectations of good fellowship and a solid message by Pastor Andy Tracy. It was the second Sunday of Advent, 2019, and his sermon topic was "Angels." I didn't expect Andy to share a personal angel experience!

A graduate of Covenant Theological Seminary in St. Louis, Missouri, Andy is a diligent student of God's word and a man of humble and good character. After the second Advent candle was lit, Andy began his sermon with an account of a personal experience with the supernatural—the kind of story that kindles the wonder angels can inspire all year long. I was finishing my first draft of *God Is in the Crazy* at the time, so as he shared this miracle, I really perked up!

When Andy was six or seven years old, his father took him hiking in a mountain range near Tucson. The towering and rocky terrain that surrounds most of Tucson is known for its sheer cliffs and occasional serious accidents for even professional climbers who try to scale them. Casual hikers need to be cautious on simple trails.

As Andy and his dad approached a crevice, it was clear they would have to leap a yard or so to reach the other side. To their right was a cliff, and near the crevice was a prickly cactus. His dad, Howard, made an easy hop to the other side, but Andy tripped on the cactus and slid to the edge of the cliff where there was a nearly thirty-foot drop to a dry, boulder-strewn riverbed. There was no time for him to cry out. Howard recalled, "By the time I knew what had happened, it was over." This is what happened:

Suddenly, Andy felt a strong arm grab him, saving him from a death that'd surely be on Tucson's nightly news. When his dad called from the other side of the crevice and asked what happened, all young Andy could blurt out was, "Someone grabbed me, Dad!" He believes he was saved by an angel. Howard says the incident "has been a reminder down through the years that there *is* a God who intervenes in the affairs of men to accomplish his purposes."

An experience of my own impacted me the same way. When I was climbing Mt. Katahdin in Maine, I'm sure God was looking out for me. I was about fourteen years old, and my small group was hiking the northern end of the Appalachian Trail. This 1.1-mile stretch that leads to the summit is called the Knife Edge. Do a Google Image search on the Knife Edge and you'll wonder what in the world I was doing up there! Some stretches of the trail are only four feet wide with two-thousand-foot drops on either side.

I remember having to descend a cliff by hanging from ledges and lowering myself to the next one. When my feet wouldn't quite touch the next ledge, I had to simply *drop and trust!* I didn't feel a force holding me, but I believe that God was mindful of danger with the series of steep drop-offs. And it wasn't my day to take a fatal fall off the cliff! I have no memory of the rest of the hike except to know I landed safely on that next ledge!

Concluding Thoughts on God's Sovereignty

Whether God holds the sun still for an hour, transforms the rod of Moses into a snake, makes the enemies of the Israelites turn on each other, or allows angels to appear to humble people—such as Abraham, Gideon, Samson's parents, and Jesus Christ in the Garden of Gethsemane—tens of thousands of people around the world and through history can testify to witnessing equally incredible miracles. But we often struggle to comprehend them with our finite minds.

We understand just as little about the natural realm, which is every bit as amazing! For example, how much do we know of the human brain? When we see a car moving down the street, different brain structures track different aspects of the scene, such as the color and speed of the car. Yet we see the moving car as a unified picture. And no one really knows how. And does a caterpillar say to itself, "I'm tired of this slow body of mine. All I can do is crawl up and down trees. I think I'll spin myself into a cocoon and emerge as a brilliantly colored butterfly?" Hard to grasp!

How much do we know of anything? We mostly know there's much we don't know about most everything! The most common non-medical doctoral degree is the PhD, which stands for "doctor of philosophy." When we study any discipline enough, we eventually end up having to philosophize about all we've learned. We don't know the entire truth or all the facts, but we can construct philosophies to point toward them.

At Ohio Wesleyan, I had an English professor named Dr. Marshall. He asked the class to imagine that there was a cricket in the corner of the classroom. Then he said, "As much as that cricket knows about what we're talking about today, that's how much we know about the truths of the universe!" One edition of the student newspaper featured a photo of Dr. Marshall and me laughing uproariously. Now that I live in Tucson, Arizona, it's hard to relate to the long winter coat I was wearing—but it was a moment of sheer delight. And I have no idea what we were laughing about. Hardly more than the cricket knew!

Although the sorts of stories I've been relating saturate the lives of many friends and neighbors—and the lives of people in every culture—we don't speak of miracles like these very often. Or not often enough. Many people wait a lifetime to share their story— if they ever do. When I've asked people to write down a personal miracle story for me to publish, I get a lot of excuses: "My miracles are too mystical and personal to share—no one will believe them." Or "I meant to write it down but didn't get around to it" (for some unknown reason). How wonderful that miracles, like the expanse of Heaven itself, are "the mere edges of His ways!"[75]

The apostle Paul wrote that God's creative power has been *clearly* evident since the creation of the world so that people have no excuse to not believe in Him. As if the creation of the universe isn't enough, God still piles on more miracles that emanate from His sovereign greatness and His holy goodness!

Why doesn't He do *even more*? I don't know. If I knew, I'd be God. According to Paul, it's not as if we need miracles to believe. Jesus even said that you are especially blessed if you have not seen Him and *yet* believe. But my experience, observations, and many supporting Scripture passages make it clear that God is more likely to reveal Himself to those who believe in—and pray to—Him. Such folks might be seen by unbelieving eyes as weak and foolish. Count me among the weak and foolish! In a speech at the Premier Business Leadership Series in Amsterdam, Malcolm Gladwell made the pivotal point that humility enables wiser decisions than expertise. Too much knowledge can lead to overconfidence that leads to "miscalibration" and colossal failures.[76] My friend Pastor Jack Lankhorst gave a candid and humble response to someone who told him that God was "just a crutch for you." Jack joyfully replied, "He's not just a crutch. He's my wheelchair!"

Reflections on the Peaceful Life

Time as we know it did not exist before God created the universe. Most scientists also believe that space did not exist either.[77] God now exists inside and outside of both space and time. Relax in the knowledge that you'll never understand—and therefore don't need to understand—how God can manipulate both time and space for our benefit. There's a reason Jesus said we must become as little children to enter the kingdom of God.[78] Most children can easily accept what Jesus, the disciples, and many other authors of the Bible have said that when people believe, nothing is too hard for God!

Endnotes

68 For an in-depth perspective on a biblical view of time and space, especially exegeting the Septuagint, see Ivan Rudolph's *Your Origin and Destiny*, (Mount Pleasant, South Carolina: Bublish, 2020).

69 Isaiah 57:15 KJV.

70 Bobby Schuller, "Falling in Love with Possibility," Hour of Power—Official Site, accessed 9/16/2018, http://hourofpower.org/episode/falling-in-love-with-possibility/.

71 Bob Sawvelle, *Receive Your Miracle Now: A Case for Healing Today* (New Kensington, PA: Whitaker House, 2014). 72.

72 Isaiah 38:1–8; see numerous internet sites for other interesting facts about this seal.

73 Julie Barrier, "The Axe Murderer and the Missionary's Miracle," Preach It Teach It, accessed 12/13/2020, http://www.preachitteachit.org/articles/detail/the-axe-murderer-and-the-missionarys-miracle/.

74 Bob Sawvelle, *Receive Your Miracle Now: A Case for Healing Today* (New Kensington, PA: Whitaker House, 2014/2017), 21–23.

75 Job 26:14 NKJV.

76 Malcolm Gladwell, "Malcolm Gladwell: Incompetence Annoys, Overconfidence Terrifies," Premier Business Leadership Series in Amsterdam, "SAS Blogs," Hetty Boerakker on "SAS Voices," July 4, 2013, accessed 10/14/2020, https://blogs.sas.com/content/sascom/2013/07/04/malcolm-gladwell-incompetence-annoys-overconfidence-terrifies/.

77 Greg, "Did space exist prior to the big bang? Does not matter create its space? Can space exist without any matter of any kind?", UCO/Lick Ask an Astronomer Question Archive, accessed 4/10/2019, http://www.ucolick.org/~mountain/AAA/aaawiki/doku.php?id=did_space_exist_before_the_big_bang.

78 Matthew 18:3.

5

GOD DRAWS STRAIGHT WITH CROOKED LINES

*And we know that in all things God works for the good of those
who love him, who have been called according to his purpose.*
—Romans 8:28

Miracles of Unlikely Overcomers

I once heard someone say on the news, "When you look around the poker table and don't see a chump, you know you're it." I don't play poker, but I've looked around a table or two and not seen a single chump!

When will I adjust to the fact that life doesn't usually seem fair? But it doesn't *have* to be! I think of the biblical view that God makes all things work together for our good and for His glory. I also think of the Portuguese proverb that says, "God draws straight with crooked lines." He can turn a tangled web of setbacks and heartache into straight lines of joy and meaning.

God drew straight with the crooked behavior of Jacob, the father of the twelve tribes of Israel. Jacob's name means "deceiver." At his mother's urging, he deceived his father and stole the blessing that rightfully belonged to brother Esau. When Esau discovered Jacob's deception, he looked for Jacob to kill him. Jacob ran for his life!

More than twenty years later, after being cheated numerous times by his Uncle Laban, Jacob returned to face his brother. The night before the meeting, Jacob wrestled with an angel until dawn. During this confrontation, the angel wrenched Jacob's hip out of its socket. Because Jacob's struggle with the angel was noble—to obtain God's blessing—the angel changed Jacob's name to "Israel," which means "struggles with God." God came to regard as noble Jacob's exhausting attempt to receive all that He had for him.

Jacob limped to meet his brother, knowing that he might be killed. But Jacob was no longer a deceiver; the direction of his life had changed, and he was completely committed to God. Hence, God's crippling became his crowning.[79]

We all are "out of joint" in various ways. Our limp calls out to God for help beyond what man can provide. I've heard such frailties called "grace-getters." One of my personal grace-getters has been an essential tremor. When we are honest about our weaknesses and sins and turn to God as our only source of strength and whatever else we need, our crippling can morph into a crown.

Honesty about our imperfections doesn't usually come naturally, does it? But God reminds us of them from time to time, and He helps us look at them in a broader context. That happened to me at Christine's Antiques in Tucson. I saw a small bookshelf I liked, but I noticed it had a scratch on top. Hoping to bring the price down, I said to the elderly salesperson (who would surely understand my concern), "I'd like to buy this shelf, but there's a scratch on it." The woman didn't respond in a way I expected. She moved close to me and carefully examined my face, almost touching it with her forefinger. She said with a scratchy voice, "You've got a few on you too." This woman turned out to be Christine, the owner, and she'd been around the block. I bought the shelf immediately!

I had an opportunity to offer an alternate view to an impatient woman in a grocery line. She was complaining that the person in front of her had too many groceries and was holding us all up. I could have said to her what I read on a plaque in a coffee house: "Well, aren't you a little ray of pitch black." But after her third complaint, I took a different tack. I startled her with, "Excuse me. Has it ever occurred to you that because we're taking so long, you might not get in an accident on the way home?" She turned her head and stared at me like I'd just stepped off a spaceship. Then I asked, "Do you believe in God?" She seriously pondered this for a moment, smiled broadly, and said, "Yes! I do! And I'll buy your items!" Unfortunately, I'd only purchased gum and M&M's. A friend told me I should have thanked her and ran to get some steaks!

God Bless Our Ship (Piloted by George Lymburn)

The book *Target Berlin: Mission 250: 6 March 1944* tells of the first daylight bombing raid over Berlin, the capital of the Third Reich. The raid was carried out by the US Eighth Air Force. The *Los Angeles Times* details the backstory of one of the bomber crews.[80] Twenty-year-old Lieut. George Lymburn piloted a bomber named "God Bless Our Ship." The *Times* article celebrates a reunion with some of Lymburn's Army Air Corps friends and his commemorative parachute jump near where the plane went down. His first jump was during this celebration—not during the mission. On the original mission, Lymburn chose to make a rough landing instead.

> If something had wings, and even if it didn't, Lymburn *knew* he could fly it. This was the kid who used to spend hours in his basement sand-papering balsa wood airplanes, the kid whose heroes were the daring World War I pilots.[81]

As a stock clerk at Woolworth's in Plymouth, Massachusetts, in 1942, he had no idea how his passion for air combat would soon become reality. Lymburn's first combat mission was during that historic daytime attack over Germany. Sixty-nine four-engine US bombers and eleven escort fighters did not return. But many of our bombs hit their targets. The Germans sent up four hundred fighter planes and lost at least sixty-five.

After Lymburn's crew dropped their bombs, his plane was hit at twenty-two thousand feet. Its gas tanks caught fire, and flames quickly began erupting from the wings. Lymburn said the only reason the entire plane didn't explode was that the bomb bays were open. The in-rushing air burned up the gas before it could accumulate. Then he ordered his crew to bail out. A Nazi fighter was flying so close that he and Lymburn almost waved. The pilot decided not to kill the men in their chutes. One of Lymburn's buddies later told him that it was safer in the air than on the ground, where a woman from a German village once hit him on the head with a hammer handle.

The story becomes yet more suspenseful—because Lymburn was too scared to bail. Despite the thrill of flying a mission like his WWI heroes, he was now paralyzed with fright. He could maneuver his badly damaged plane to avoid hitting his seven crew members who had parachuted out—but he never worked up the nerve to grab his own chute and jump!

At sixteen thousand feet, George was able to maintain a glide over Berlin and guide "God Bless Our Ship" just above treetops and into a crash landing. I saw the photo of the flipped fuselage being inspected by German officers. It was featured in articles in both the *Times* and *Target Berlin*. Lymburn managed to climb out of the wrecked plane through a window.

He at first thought himself a coward. But when he landed on the ground, he was flabbergasted to see his tail gunner, Frank Cittadino, running around the wing. Lymburn greeted him with "Hi, Frank! Just landed in your parachute here?" No, Frank hadn't just landed in his parachute. He had also been too afraid to jump and *also* stayed with the plane! Because George Lymburn steered the bomber to a rough landing instead of bailing out and letting it crash, both his and Frank Cittadino's lives were saved!

Lieut. George said his fear could have been self-destructive, but he chose to think of it as God's wisdom, with God saying, "You've got a guy in the back seat, a chum who's gotta go home and have seven children"—which Cittadino did.[82]

Tragedies that Couldn't Stop a Victorious Life
Ben Hogan

My dad and brother shot below par through their peak golfing years, which added to their enjoyment of the game. As enthusiastic golfers, they seemed to remember every stroke on every hole! And I heard the name of Ben Hogan most of my life. I still have a letter Dad received from Ben after he won his last tournament in 1959.

As I read about Ben's life, I was inspired by his story of success emerging from tragedy. When he was only nine, his father committed suicide right in front of him. I've counseled people who've witnessed similar horror. Such tragedies have derailed many people from pursuing productive lives. But this was not the case with Ben—and more tragedy was yet to come.

Ben entered the pro golfing tour—unsuccessfully, at first—but met Valerie, who became the love of his life and a devoted fan. They married in 1935. Ben's first two entries on the tour were met with disappointment. On his third try in 1938, he finally won a tournament. But WWII stalled his golfing career from 1943 to 1945 while he helped save the world from Hitler's dark intentions.

After the war, Ben's plan was to continue to climb the tour ladder. But as Mike Tyson once said, "Everybody has a plan until they get hit in the mouth." That's what happened to Ben, in the form of a tragic auto accident in 1948. While driving with his wife, Ben's car collided head-on with a Greyhound bus. He managed to throw himself across Valerie's body right before impact. Ben didn't know that he was not only saving his wife's life—he was saving his own. The collision shoved the car's engine into the driver's seat, which would have killed him. Ben barely survived with multiple fractures. It was doubtful he would ever walk again. But against all odds, he returned to the PGA tour in 1950, hobbling the courses as best he could.

Besides his physical limitations, the tour posed other challenges: relatively low pay and reporters who sensationalized and didn't always tell the truth.[83] And according to Hogan, "I found myself in a situation of proving I was as good a golfer as those who had won the

British Open before me."[84] Having to prove himself over and over "eats at you," he said.[85]

Between 1938 and 1959, he won sixty-three professional golf tournaments, despite the injuries. Ben was one of only five golfers to have won the top four major championships. The other four players are Jack Nicklaus, Tiger Woods, Gary Player, and Gene Sarazen. You can imagine that Ben's inspiring legacy was sealed by what he accomplished after the accident.[86] My dad wrote a chapter in my mother's book, *A Beautiful Stride*, in which he told Ben's story. Here's what Ben commented, after many unlikely wins in a single year:

> I don't think anybody does anything unless the Lord's with them. I think it's fate, and supposed to be, that I won those tournaments… All those victories required more guidance than one human being can give another, and I've been fortunate to receive that guidance. I think the Lord has let me win those tournaments for a purpose. I hope that purpose is to give courage to those people who are sick or injured and broken in body as I once was.[87]

I doubt if Ben ever understood in this life why God allowed the suicide of his father, his auto accident, and the long return to winning again at golf. But I know one thing for sure: Ben Hogan knew that God was in the crazy—and in the crazy *hard*—with him!

Seabiscuit
Life's "Losers" Are Often the Real Winners

Many of you are familiar with Seabiscuit, the horse that thrilled racing fans during the desperate times of the Great Depression. People especially then needed to be reminded that losers could become winners.

Seabiscuit was considered a loser in the beginning. One of his first trainers thought he was lazy. He ate more and slept longer than other racehorses. And Seabiscuit's left foreleg made a sideways movement when he ran called "dishing out," which can hinder speed. He seemed destined to be a pacing horse that would help other horses gain confidence and speed. This unlikely racehorse was the butt of stable jokes. After completing his training to lose, he was sold for a cheap price. I once heard about a horse who was trained not to eat. When the horse was fully trained, it died. Seabiscuit received similar training but ultimately would have no part of it!

Seabiscuit's new owner, Charles Howard, had just gone through a divorce. His marriage had collapsed from the shocking death of their son in a car accident. Dejected and feeling as much a loser as Seabiscuit, Charles sought a new challenge to lift his spirits. That's when he hired a tall and lanky jockey named Red Pollard to ride his underachieving horse. Charles also hired Tom Smith as Seabiscuit's trainer. Soft-spoken "Silent Tom" was in his fifties, which was considered "over the hill" in this business.

But the dejected owner, oversized rider, and aging trainer were about to electrify the world! What could they possibly do with a lazy horse and trained loser? Let's start with some big surprises! Silent Tom sensed the horse's promising temperament and potential, and with Tom's coaching, Seabiscuit began to win races! In 1938, "Seabiscuit & (unlikely) Company" made history. Anticipating what was dubbed the "race of the century," stores around the nation closed, and forty million people were glued to their radios while Seabiscuit raced War Admiral, the defending Triple Crown winner. This was a head-to-head race at Pimlico. And Seabiscuit won by three lengths!

Unsurprisingly, "The Biscuit" was voted 1938 Horse of the Year and ultimately was enshrined in the Racing Hall of Fame in 1958. And in 2001, Tom Smith was inducted into the National Museum of Racing and Hall of Fame. And do you remember the foreleg that was malformed? Seabiscuit later injured a ligament in that leg, but after months of recuperation, he raced again—and won yet again—on the leg that was finally straight!

Wow, what a lesson! I'll take being the unlikely and against-all-odds winner over a dashing and born-to-be-a "winner" any day! God seemed to have the same attitude toward many of our Bible heroes, including the ordinary men whom Christ chose to be His disciples. I think most of us can relate to the sort of people described in the following Scripture passage. The apostle Paul here speaks of those whom God chose to be His followers and representatives:

> Brothers, think of what you were when you were called. Not many of you were wise by human standards; not many were influential; not many were of noble birth. But God chose the foolish things of the world to shame the wise; God chose the weak things of the world to shame the strong. He chose the lowly things of this world and the despised things—and the things that are not—to nullify the things that are, so that no one may boast before him… Therefore, as it is written: "Let him who boasts boast in the Lord."[88]

Paul also said more than once that when he was weak, God made him strong. God seems to take great pleasure in calling forth and enabling apparent losers to become winners. Christ even said, "It is not the healthy who need a doctor, but the sick; I have not come to call the righteous [those who think they are righteous], but sinners."[89] Just like a defective and rejected horse became more than he appeared to be, anyone who believes God is bigger than their defects can overcome all odds and achieve spectacular success!

From Minister to Rocket Scientist

When my friend, Pastor Martha Wallace, was laid off by a large church, this was a major crooked line and a detour for her. Martha had been loved by the church and staff. In the course of her pastoral duties, she'd put much effort into designing each Sunday bulletin. This was back when many of us pastors used a Macintosh Plus. Martha used the PageMaker program on her Mac Plus for the bulletins. Prior to PageMaker, she wrote her own code.

Martha was about fifty and had already overcome childhood trauma, betrayal by close friends, and a marriage that left her shattered. I wanted to tell some of her backstories, but Martha preferred to keep them private, so I'll leave them alone. Besides, she's forgiven those who meant her harm—and her light shines even brighter, in contrast with the darkness that couldn't smother it. And you'll like the happy ending of this story of hers:

Among many gifts, two would soon serve her in good stead. Equal to her Southern charm and great sense of humor are her IQ and determination. After her layoff, an old friend contacted Martha and asked if she was looking for a job. The friend was a secretary at a major defense contractor. She was about to enjoy an extended vacation and needed someone to take her place. All Martha needed was a visitor's badge—which the friend obtained for her.

After Martha had worked two weeks at the top-security contractor, she received a call from its human resources department. HR wondered how Martha had even gotten into the place! She was told to go to HR and then to a temp agency to apply for an independent contractor position. Martha obtained another visitor's badge at the temp agency (probably just like the one she already had!) and returned to the secretary position—this time as a hired independent contractor.

The only computer program Martha knew was PageMaker on her Mac Plus. But she was a fast learner and rapidly picked up programs in common use at the company. Thanks to her friend's call and the visitor's pass she probably shouldn't have been given, Martha's foot had gotten the rest of her in the door. She soon became a full-time employee without benefits, and before long *with* benefits. A few years later, she was put on the team for a top-security defense project, right alongside some of their best and most brilliant engineers. She could only describe in general terms what she did—and I could hardly understand, anyway. But for a laid-off pastor, what an amazing move "up" for Martha! She hadn't even finished college, so clearly her intelligence, hard work, and eagerness to learn trumped any lack of education!

Several years later, Susan and I were celebrating my birthday with Martha at an Italian restaurant. I asked if she still had that job I didn't understand. She said, "No, I don't do that anymore." She then talked about her newest job with vagueness and sophistication I might hope to understand in Heaven! It may have been at that moment I realized I wasn't called to be a rocket scientist!

Martha said she liked her newest job so much that she rarely left her desk until her entire body had become stiff and numb up to her eyeballs! Not one to work only ten hours a day, she returned to college in her "spare" time and soon earned her BS in software engineering. Had she not been laid off by the church in the first place, she never would have found her life's greater calling. She now has five beautiful daughters and thirty-two grandchildren. I tell this story of Martha a few times a year in the course of my counseling. She's a joyful soul and a comfort and inspiration to many. And she still counsels others who look to her for wisdom.

I recently met Martha early one afternoon at a Mexican restaurant to fine-tune these snapshots from her life. Even though she's now retired from missile design, she'd been up since 5:00 a.m. working on her computer. I don't think she can help herself! She stays busy on the internet, including website engineering and consulting work. I didn't ask if she still got "numb up to her eyeballs" at times. That would have been a rhetorical question! Back at church, she'd probably been among the first of what we now call "computer geeks." But whoever would have guessed she'd become an actual rocket scientist too? *You go, Martha!* (She did!)

Quit Your Life
Victory over Brokenness[90]

I first met Michael Romero after I'd led worship at Casas Church one Sunday. Michael had just finished teaching a Bible study and had drifted over to the traditional service in Barrier Chapel. I've led contemporary worship most of my adult life, but for a couple of years, I led this service with the older hymns while weaving in as many contemporary songs as I could get away with.

Michael and I made a good connection right away. It wasn't until later that I learned more fully about his victorious life. Michael had been afflicted by grand mal seizures from birth. These are the scary kind. When Michael was old enough to be embarrassed by his uncontrollable and unpredictable seizures, he often hid in closets. Living in such confined spaces wasn't much of a life. At age six, he was mistakenly given an adult dose of Dilantin and lapsed into a coma. He was totally unresponsive; the doctors said that he would either die or be in a vegetative state for life. Michael calls his early childhood "a rough start." *You might say that!*

Michael's dad asked his pastor to come to the hospital to see him and pray. One look at Michael and the pastor choked up. But then he prayed. The result? Michael came out of the coma! It was a clear miracle that confounded the doctors. But the young boy remained on medication that harmed his teeth and damaged his liver, leaving him with a condition similar to alcoholic cirrhosis. Michael remembers being "zombified, spacey, and disinterested in everything" due to seizure medication. Both his parents were convinced Michael's current condition could not be God's plan for him. His parents decided to stop *all* Michael's medication for this serious medical condition—rarely recommended. Miraculously, however, Michael never had another seizure. In this case, medical advice was bested by God's wisdom and care.

But Michael remained awkward and clumsy, tripping while walking and knocking things over and breaking them. His body didn't always do what his mind wanted it to do—but at least he seemed to have a new lease on life. But once again, things got *much* worse. A casual observer of Michael's once suggested to him that he should quit living in such a haphazard way: "You train yourself to be better." Michael took this seriously. He decided, "Today, that stops being my life!" But then came another huge setback: his parents divorced before he was eight.

After being healed of grand mal seizures and surviving the coma, he ended up in Washington state with his mother and an abusive stepfather who did unthinkable things to his sister. Michael, by then a teen, told his mother what he'd seen, and she screamed, "Lies!" She told him to hit the road. Though his mother still believed in God, Michael told me that her faith was dwarfed by her codependency on men. But Michael did as he was told. He hit the road—which quickly proved to be a major mistake.

Landing in the middle of gangs, drugs, prostitution, and violence in downtown Tacoma, he was lured into sex trafficking. After his first night exposed to bitter cold, a man offered to let him stay at a hotel. That was the beginning of his being raped innumerable times by mostly men for the next two and a half years. But one of his most vivid and degrading memories was being abused by three women. Michael says they chained him to a radiator and for several days, beat him, threw him scraps of food, and violated him with every "toy" imaginable.

"Dangerous Dan"—the man who enslaved Michael—convinced him he was gay and made money off Michael's misery. Penthouse criminals had their way with him. But when he finally became useless as a boy prostitute, there were still lower depths of degradation to plumb. Michael became a drug abuser and dealer. He became known as a Latino gang member with the nickname "Grasshopper." He "slang dope for the family," robbed houses, and fought to defend the gang's turf. By that time, he'd been in and out of foster homes, attempted suicide three times, and dropped out of two drug rehab programs. Hopelessly trapped in a different kind of "closet," Michael no longer cared if he lived or died.

But he was still alive, depending on one's definition of "alive," and he still recalled the past miracles of his young life. Michael says,

> One particular day, after attempting to kick my addictions again, I told God if this was life, I didn't want to continue living it. If He was real and there was a better life for me then He would have to give it to me, because I couldn't find it. His answer? God said, "Give me your life."

In his short book, *Quit Your Life*, Michael quotes Jesus's words, "Whoever tries to keep their life will lose it, and whoever loses their life will preserve it."[91] Michael lost all desire to "keep his life." Through faith, he quit his life of prostitution and drug trafficking. He changed his thinking about violence and hopelessness too. "I quit being an angry gang-banger and began serving and loving people… I quit my trauma." At the age of twenty-three, Michael was married, and now has two courageous boys and one strong and beautiful daughter. *Against impossible odds come impossible miracles!*

What might surprise you is that Michael has developed a zeal to not only snatch other *victims* from lives of defeat but to invite *evildoers* to seek God's forgiveness, forgive themselves, and quit their self-destructive living. If anyone knows how hard this was, Michael does.

Michael is realistic about our broken world, saying that "millions of people don't want you to succeed in overcoming your trauma, addiction, hurt, pain, tragedy, or situation… Quitting the life you have for a better one is an internal decision." We must let our dreams "come down," he says. This is what Christ's disciples did when they dropped their fishing nets—their very livelihoods—and followed Christ. God used these unlikely candidates to change the world, and He still uses people like Michael, you, and me for holy purposes.

Planting churches and speaking around the world has been Michael's mission over the past twenty-six years. He believes that Christ was treated much worse than he was, yet Christ forgave everyone and said we must all do the same! Jesus isn't walking around in Heaven bitter, as Michael says, but confident in the power of His forgiveness. When He died on the cross for the sins of the world, He thought that each of us was worth the sacrifice. He now lives to impart new life to all who believe in Him—to everyone who will quit destructive lives they mistake as their destiny.

Near the conclusion of his powerful book, Michael says:

> I knew [that in order] to be free I had to continually follow Jesus who set me free. However, I also knew I could not follow Jesus if I was unwilling to QUIT MY LIFE and leave my past *continually* in order to find the future our Father had for me.

If you are struggling with thoughts and trauma in your life, I want you to know you can leave that behind, and you must, to have your hand fully grasp the future our Father has for you. QUIT YOUR LIFE...AND FOLLOW JESUS.[92]

Reflections on Frailties and Miracles
Stress Wood and Character

Less than an hour from our house is the Biosphere 2, a totally enclosed ecosystem occupying several acres. My wife and I drive past there whenever we want a great slice of apple pie at the Oracle Inn in Oracle Junction—a restaurant with terrific homestyle meals and an old west ambience.

The Biosphere gives scientists the opportunity to do research under closely controlled conditions on how living systems interact and how humans deal with isolation. But despite its worthy goals and being a popular tourist site, the facility has had its problems. The biggest one happened when trees inside grew faster than in a real-world environment—and then simply collapsed before maturing. No one knew why. It turns out that trees need wind in order to achieve maximum strength. Wind makes trees bend and sway, which creates *stress wood*, which is *strong*er wood. Stress wood is just what it sounds like: wood created by stress, which strengthens the trees to withstand the elements and live longer.

Let's reflect again on King David and his connection to this same principle. He possessed character like stressed wood. When King Saul's army of Israelites faced a Philistine army that was led by Goliath, the Israelites were close to teetering and collapsing like trees without roots. Goliath taunted Saul's army, shouting that if any man could defeat him, his entire army would surrender. Goliath seemed to be the opposing army's only root. That's when the wind blew toward the root-poor Philistines—and David arrived. An unlikely contender against a seasoned warrior, David proved to be God's *strong* wind of victory!

David's older brothers made fun of him for coming near the battle lines, but David was unafraid of Goliath. He told Saul that, as a boy, he had killed a lion and a bear to protect his sheep. He had already been strengthened by winds of opposition. Taking on Goliath was simply the next step in David's growing strength through stress. We see how the apostle Peter also grew stronger through stress. After Jesus was taken prisoner, Peter denied Him three times to avoid prosecution. He was wracked with guilt for his cowardliness. But Jesus, following His resurrection, appeared to him and the disciples. Jesus invited Peter to the same kind of fire he warmed himself by when he denied his Lord, a charcoal fire. This fire brought back the troubling memory of Jesus asking him not once but three times if he loved Him. Peter was not even chastised by Christ, and his relationship with Him was fully restored. Sometimes we too must return to a place of pain to obtain needed healing.[93] And look what happened in Peter's life next!

Within days after the disciples returned to Jerusalem for a religious holiday, God unleashed the Holy Spirit as a mighty, rushing wind among them. On the day that commemorates when God gave the oral Torah to the Hebrews on Mount Sinai,[94] the Spirt suddenly appeared in the form of flames above the disciples' heads. To the skeptical and bewildered onlookers who heard the sounds and may have seen the flames, Peter and the other apostles boldly proclaimed the need for repentance, the marvelous gift of forgiveness, and the promise of eternal life through faith in the resurrected Christ. And they spoke in languages unknown to them which enabled the Hebrews from many different countries to hear these proclamations in their own language! Thereafter, Peter and the apostles stood firm for the rest of their lives against torrents of hatred and persecution while proclaiming the message of Christ and His resurrection.

The apostle Paul, who originally persecuted Christians as Saul, was empowered to spread Christ's message all over the known world. He endured prison, floggings, and being stoned and left for dead, as well as other hardships before fulfilling his destiny to be martyred in Rome. The winds of adversity develop stress wood character in all who seek and yield to the Character Builder. The strength of stress wood is like God's character living in us.

It's easy to run from an unfair boss, an embarrassing defeat, or a struggling marriage. Sometimes, of course, one needs to "get out of Dodge." But before you decide to bail from adversity, consider again those trees at the Biosphere 2. Without being rooted in faith, one will tend to rot from the inside and fall over in the face of adversity. But if you turn your eyes to Heaven and fall into God's arms, He will help you endure hard times, misunderstandings, and all manner of evil that runs rampant everywhere. Hold your ground and you'll only get stronger. Recall this Bible verse: "A bruised reed he will not break, and a smoldering wick he will not snuff out."[95] Stand strong for Him, and He'll stand strong in you. He will not allow you to suffer more than you can endure![96]

Why I Needed to Be in Pain

The southwestern states are known for a type of pneumonia called valley fever. If the infection spreads to the brain, the outcome can be fatal. This illness is caught by inhaling fungus spores that had lived deep in the ground. The spores become airborne when construction causes their release—which happened on the church property where I once worked.

When I went to the emergency room with chest pain in my early thirties, I was told I had a simple "walking pneumonia," and that when I felt better, I could go back to work. I did, but it was a big mistake. It turned out I had the pneumonia of valley fever, although I obviously wasn't tested for this in the ER. This disease can require a long recovery period. Those who return to work too soon will get worse—and that's what happened to me.

As soon as I returned to work, I became so weak I could barely stay awake. I went home and stayed there, barely able to venture outside for months. Just taking a shower wiped me out for the day. If someone said something negative to me, I would feel a painful "pinch" in one of my lungs. This was certainly proof of the mind/

body (psychosomatic) dichotomy well known in both science and the Bible.

I flew to California to recuperate at my brother's condo. My parents flew out to help take care of me. I saw a physician in Rancho Mirage named Dr. Cohen, the foremost expert in the US on valley fever. He told me I had the worst lung function he'd ever seen.

My father suggested that I visit a chiropractor to see how she could help. She told me that x-rays showed my lower back was out of alignment. But because I had no pain, I didn't see the problem. Then she said, "I'm going to put it back in line. Then your nerves—which have been shut down—will come to life, and you will be in pain."

True to her word, the chiropractor straightened my back…and the pain started, as predicted. But the treatment worked! It was the beginning of my healing process. To this day, when I'm under great stress or when I overwork (which is my tendency), my lungs hurt. One doctor told me that the pain indicated inflamed scar tissue. This pain is a beneficial physiologic cue that says, "Slow down. Take five."

Another personal illustration is that, after a fall over four years ago, I still experience pain in my left shoulder. I can't swim except with short strokes, and some simple movements are limited. But this pain is a reminder to thank God that I have an arm with fingers I can move and use. The ability to move is something I've always been grateful for. Veterans with wounded or missing limbs no longer have the luxury of full use of an intact body. When my arm and shoulder hurt, I marvel at God's gift of finger dexterity and that I can move my arm at all!

I've learned another lesson from Mike Tyson: His trainer carefully studied him as a teenager. He called him a "sucker—but you're a great fighter."[97] Tyson said the trainer, Gus D'Amato, was telling the truth when he said, "You've got to be in trouble before you learn… that always happens to suckers… They've got to feel the fire to know that it's hot."[98] That reminds me of the poker player I mentioned earlier who looks around the table and doesn't see any chumps! If someone besides him doesn't leave the table straightway, he's going to feel some pain—in his wallet! D'Amato wanted Tyson to be aware of his blind spots…and to learn from his pain.

Understanding Life Backward

I read a popular book some years ago about why bad things happen to good people. I expected to learn something—and even to be encouraged. Instead, I found little wisdom and hardly any hope. What the book left out is the most profound truth that relates to suffering: God works *all* things together for our good when we love Him and when He has called us to serve Him.

I was serving Him when I was let go from a job I loved. At a staff meeting, we were told that two employees needed to resign to free up funds for the salary of a new employee who was gaining national recognition. That person would need to be paid twice what one of us earned. No one resigned, so two of us were let go. A friend encouraged me with Ephesians 1:11: "[God] works out everything in conformity with the purpose of his will." God was true to His word, after my dismissal. I quickly found a position at a Christian counseling center where I worked fewer hours, made more money, and had time off to earn my doctorate. That counseling agency became a launching pad for greater challenges that I'll mention later. God heard my desperate cry to provide for my wife and myself while serving Him in Christian ministry.

Robert Frost once told a friend, "I alone of English writers have consciously set myself to make music out of what I may call the sound of sense."[99] A realistic and faith-filled perspective on things we don't understand can tune our spirits into the musical sound of sense. This is usually the gift of poets like Frost. They refresh our souls with beauty and meaning. But it's also a gift any of us can possess when we have positive expectations for coming attractions, despite life's inscrutables or unknowables. When good things start to happen, it's like the audible music that was previously heard only in our spirits.

What we all need—and always need more of—is a renewed perspective on life. A good example of how this can help us is God's answer to David's desperate prayer. David said, "In all my distress I called to the Lord; I cried to my God for help."[100] The root Hebrew word for *distress* is "small place." Later in the psalm, David said, "He brought me out into a spacious place."[101] What joy to arrive where there are broad horizons with new opportunities! Psalm 4:1 goes even farther by affirming, "Thou hast enlarged me when I was in distress" (KJV). When God allows us to be in a small place, his desire is to increase our contentment *in* that place—even before He brings us out! This was true for Paul who learned "both to abound and to suffer need," and to be content in *any* situation.[102] Wherever we find ourselves, and in whatever the season, God can fill us with contentment and vision. He can impart confidence that He will provide *whatever* we need *when* we need it—which He *always* does!

I think of how my father-in-law experienced the Himalayas during WWII. The snow-crowned peaks appeared large from the ground but small from his plane. I've faced challenges that loomed as mountains and later looked like speed bumps. I remember when I was first asked to preach in the Sunday services of a large church. During the week, I was petrified. But as I sat in the first service, I thought to myself, "No one in here has a message to deliver to the congregation but me. Surely, God won't let all these people down by letting me fall on my face" (though I committed to accepting any outcome because I knew I was in God's will). After committing the sermon to God, I was eager to speak, and the anxious feelings disappeared as I spoke. I've celebrated other victories after asking myself, "What would I do if I weren't afraid?" and then doing that very task that had caused me to fear.

When I took a philosophy class my junior year of college, I read that Sören Kierkegaard said we *live* life forward but *understand* it backward. Jesus said something similar. When Peter questioned why Jesus should wash his feet, Jesus replied, "You do not realize now what I am doing, but later you will understand."[103] When I lost the job I spoke of, my view was limited, and my spirit was constricted. But looking back, I understand the benefit of that temporary loss. What looked like chaos was in sync with God's harmony. I've since been more aware of the beautiful and intricate workings of God's plans, in spite of my fears and misgivings.

Downward Mobility
God Uses Men from the Gutters

During my life, "downward mobility" has happened to me from time to time. As I look back, it clearly sharpened my understanding of how God's incarnate Son Jesus was downwardly mobile. But that was His *intention* and *not* something that happened to Him. He actually *practiced* lowliness so that He could more easily reach others who had been brought low in life one way or another—and for one reason or another. I alluded to this in chapter 2 when I spoke of people being reduced to the most powerful thing they can do. It's at the end of our own ability—at the end of one's rope, so to speak—where the quietest prayer or smallest act of faith can yield surprising results. John the Baptist was reduced by living his first thirty years in the wilderness where he worked hard, matured, and laid low. He then entered the moment that defined his mission, dramatically announcing the coming of the long-awaited Savior of the world. Similarly, Moses spent forty years in the wilderness until God declared it was time for him to lead the Israelites from centuries of wretched slavery to freedom in the promised land.

These two principles hold true: There's a connection between downward mobility and wilderness experiences; and if we commit to remain humble and never give up, these difficult seasons translate into power. Best illustrated by Christ, His reward for leaving His home in Heaven, and finally submitting to death on a cross, was the resurrection and the purchase of all who look to Him in faith. Even during His three final and most intense years on the earth, He embraced "intentional demotion" as He completed the full course of His Father's assigned world-changing ministry. And let's not forget that Christ's three years of ministry began after forty days and forty nights in the *wilderness* where He was tempted by Satan. That is the way of life for anyone who moves forward in God's will: to pass through seasons that we don't understand (though Jesus clearly understood the necessity of His!), including times of debasement—and even persecution—before finally experiencing transformation and breakthrough into God's larger plan for our lives.

141

Saul of Tarsus called himself the worst of sinners, primarily because he had violently persecuted the early church. Despite continued struggles with human frailties, he became the noble-hearted Paul, an apostle of Christ. St. Augustine was a sensuous reprobate as a young man, but he became a revered father of the church in the fourth century. When General William Booth began the Salvation Army in London, he was asked where he would get his helpers. His instant answer: "I'll use the men from the gutters whom I transform into Christian characters!"[104] When the future King Saul was still a humble and unknown man, God told him, "You will be changed into a different person."[105]

Do you want to be a man or woman who is used powerfully by God? Simply cooperate with God's process of downward mobility—with all its hardships. Spiritually speaking, if not literally, God found all of us in the gutter of sin and self-seeking. In fact, He especially *chooses* "the lowly things of this world and the despised things...so that no one may boast before him."[106] And the even *better* news is that He *delights* to change us into people after His own heart!

Changing Our Expectations

Robert Henderson's family had a little dog named Otis who was fourteen pounds of shaggy fur. Robert said, "We loved the little guy."[107] One morning, Robert's wife overheard their six-year-old grandson, Jackson, talking to Otis. Jackson was holding Otis and looking into his eyes. This is what Jackson said to his friend:

> Otis, if you want to be a superhero, you're going to have to change the way you think. The first thing you have to do is get a cape. The second thing you need is a superhero name like Super Dog. And the third thing you need to do is learn how to fly.[108]

Robert's book, *Accessing the Courts of Heaven: How to Position Yourself for Breakthrough in Prayer*, builds the scriptural case for needing to change our way of thinking about prayer in order to live victoriously with the power and authority God has given to his children. My application of the story is simple: As many Scriptures advise, we need to change how we think about many things. This includes our expectations—just like Otis had to somehow realize he could learn to fly!

People may hope for material reward from an act of kindness. Others have learned to expect ridicule even for a job well done. Our only expectation should be that God will be pleased. What better reward could we receive? Also consider that when we're kind, we gain *greater capacity* to be kind. When we're good, we can do even greater good—and do it *well!* And because many jobs well done *are* recognized, our reward is often another job that may be harder to do well. God asked Jeremiah, "If you have raced with men on foot and they have worn you out, how can you compete with horses?"[109] What was Jeremiah's reward for racing with men on foot? He could become fast enough to compete with horses![110]

Such rewards are less obvious than receiving a raise, a watch, or a prize...or the clapping and cheering of a crowd. But they are more valuable because of the value God places on them. Do you have God's expectations of life? Then you will look first for immaterial rewards from all you do and all your pure heart strives to do—even if it's no more than falling on your face and being able to get back up.

When God straightens our crooked lines, He usually uses our faith to turn possibilities into realities. Sometimes we spin like billiard balls on a pool table, being hit from every direction. People of faith can let go of needing to understand which ball started the collisions. Rather than try to understand many of life's mysteries and learn nothing, we're better served to stand in awe. With the eyes of the spirit, we can see that in every moment, God makes a grand debut—through an astounding miracle, a blessing, a lesson, or simply an appreciation of our five senses. We can choose to trust the Creator of all things to make straight our crooked lines, or we can choose despair. When the choice is between despair and "Wow!"—I choose "Wow!"

God knows all our thoughts and motives. He sees all we've been through and what we're going through now. Each moment has the possibility of being redeemed and working for good. Can we understand this? Not really—or *not fully*. It's tempting to ask, "Why?" Because there's no end of life's "whys?" it's even addicting! But I've rarely found this to be a productive question. A better question is, "*What's next?*"

Reflections on the Peaceful Life

Don't let your failures define you; rather, focus on how God has used them or will *yet* use them. You'll likely understand why God allowed certain heartaches when you look backward someday. We've all suffered and failed. We're all crippled in some way—we are the walking wounded. Let God's Spirit in you turn your crippling into a crown that you wear with gratitude. Beth Moore said it in a way that is potently inspiring: "I am better off healed than I ever was unbroken."[111]

Endnotes

79 Roy Hicks Jr., *A Small Book about God* (Sisters, Oregon: Multnomah Publishers, 1997), 63.

80 Beverly Beyette, "Ex-Bomber Takes the Plunge: Army Air Corps Veteran Waits 40 Years for His First Jump," *Los Angeles Times*, March 11, 1984/Part VII. The entire story of Lymburn's experience is taken from this article. Also, the story is noted briefly in Jeffrey Ethell and Alfred Price, *Target Berlin: Mission 250: 6 March 1944* (London: Arms and Armour Press, 1989), 100. Both the article and the book contain the same photograph of the downed plane.

81 Beverly Beyette, 100.

82 Beverly Beyette.

83 Gene Gregston, *Hogan: The Man Who Played for Glory* (Grass Valley, California: The Booklegger, 1978), 128. This publisher and author cannot be located. If anyone has this information, please contact the author and he will request publishing permission for the next edition of this book.

84 Gene Gregston, 1938.

85 Ibid.

86 Ibid.

87 Gene Gregston, 153. Also quoted in author's mother's book. See Acknowledgments for more information.

88 1 Corinthians 1:26–31.

89 Mark 2:17.

90 Michael Romero, *Quit Your Life* (Chesterfield, Virginia: Turning My Own Pages Legacy Publishing, 2018). This account is a summary of Michael's book.

91 Luke 17:33.

92 Ibid., 42.

93 Tauren Wells, "God's Not Done with You—A 10-Day Devotional, Day 9," YouVersion app, accessed 10/16/2019.

94 The Torah contains the first five books of the Tanakh, the Hebrew Bible, called the Pentateuch in the Christian Bible: Genesis, Exodus, Leviticus, Numbers, and Deuteronomy. The Torah also refers to the broader body of Jewish teachings, customs, and ceremonies.

95 Isaiah 42:3.

96 1 Corinthians 10:13.

97 Brendon Cronin, *The Wall Street Journal: Life & Arts*, May 25, 2017.

98 Brendon Cronin.

99 Lawrence Thompson, *Robert Frost: The Early Years, 1874–1915* (New York, Chicago, San Francisco: Holt, Rinehart and Winston, 1966), 434.

100 Psalm 18:6.

101 Psalm 18:19.

102 Philippians 4:11–12.

103 John 13:7; see also Jeremiah 30:24.

104 William Booth, "The Signs of the Times," a sermon delivered by Hiram C. Weld at the Hull Village Church, 11/7/1937.

105 1 Samuel 10:6.

106 1 Corinthians 1:28–29.

107 Robert Henderson, *Accessing the Courts of Heaven: How to Position Yourself for Breakthrough in Prayer* (Shippensburg, PA: Destiny Image Books, 2017), 9.

108 Robert Henderson, 9–10.

109 Jeremiah 12:5.

110 Tittle, 19.

111 Beth Moore, "Life through My Rose Colored Glasses," accessed 12/13/2020, https://forgetmenotak49.blogspot.com/2017/07/i-am-better-off-healedthan-i-ever-was.html.

SECTION 3

FAMILY MATTERS AND MIRACLES

6

NIL SINE NUMINE
FAMILY MATTERS AND MIRACLES

*I am the vine; you are the branches. If a man remains in me and I in
him, he will bear much fruit; apart from me you can do nothing.*
—John 15:5

Nil sine numine means "nothing without providence." This chapter highlights the theme of that motto. It's been the motto of the
Weld family from hundreds of years ago and is on its crest. It's also
Colorado's state motto. All the Welds I know have needed God's help
to overcome evil or difficult circumstances, and He's always proven
faithful. *Nil sine numine* could also be the motto of many other families. Whether we acknowledge it or not, we need God all the time.
But there are times we *know* it more! That's when *extraordinary* miracles are more likely to occur. This book has reported many miracles
of that kind.

But God performs other types of miracles too. We often stand
in awe of a sunset that can affect us as gloriously as the appearance
of an angel. A sunset is a *recurring* and predictable miracle. The more
we open our eyes to miracles—extraordinary, recurring, or seeming
"God-appointments"/"coincidences"—the more we understand that
miracles happen often and that we all need them.

What I'll tell you about my family constitutes what Malcolm
Gladwell calls "thin-slicing." That is our ability to perceive patterns

in situations and behavior based on very narrow slices of experience.[112] Researchers have proven how quickly our brains can process information and discard what isn't necessary in order to understand people or circumstances. In thin-slicing examples that follow, you'll understand how my family survived the crazy and proved the family motto over and over.

I begin with an account of my parents' experience in pre-war Nazi Germany, along with accounts of uncles and extended family during the war. My parents met many brave German religious leaders who would not be silenced. I'll speak of three of them that God kept safe in dangerous situations—*the crazy-hard.*[113]

Part 1
"Heil Roosevelt!"

When my dad was pastoring a small church in Hull, Massachusetts, and pursuing his doctorate at Boston University, he was awarded a fellowship to study abroad from 1938 to 1939, before the US joined World War II in late 1941. He chose Heidelberg University in Germany and Oxford in England. Although he was advised not to go to Germany because of dangerous Nazi domination, Dad had an interest that outweighed these concerns. Heidelberg was a great center of theological thought, and he wanted to meet the brave theologians and pastors who had not yet been imprisoned. He had many reasons to attend Oxford, including the chance to study at the Bodleian Library that dated back to the fourteenth century and is one of the oldest libraries in Europe.

Mom and Dad were thrilled to board the *SS Columbus,* a luxury cruise ship and the third largest of German ships. Less than two years later, when US naval vessels provocatively pushed it toward British ships, it was scuttled by the Germans only four hundred miles off the east coast of the US.

As soon as my parents landed in Germany, they began to vividly experience the horrors of the Nazi regime. On July 8, 1938, they boarded a train from Bremerhaven to Frankfurt and thence to Heidelberg, where the oppression of Nazism was palpable. The chiseled message over the stone entrance gate to the university had previously read *In the Human Spirit*. Now it read *In the German Spirit*. Many pastors and scholars who had refused to embrace Hitler's perverse doctrines had been sacked. Some had been imprisoned. My parents were in the heart of crazy-hard—in the belly of the beast.

They saw a sculpture of a monstrous black eagle mounted on a large stone. The stone base was engraved with the word *Saar*. A large chain that had tethered the eagle to a heavy iron ball was severed. This symbolized that the German state was no longer shackled and that the German region of Saar was reclaimed from the League of Nations in 1935.

My parents witnessed the evil combination of socialism, a warped nationalism, and ethnic persecution. Long since deprived of rights, Jews were slowly disappearing from Germany. Hundreds of Jews were being killed, and tens of thousands were being hauled in cattle cars to what the world later learned were extermination camps. *Kristallnacht*—or "The Night of Broken Glass"—soon followed my parents' departure. That was the night when Jewish stores, synagogues, homes, and hospitals were looted or destroyed, and thousands of Jews were put in concentration camps. Of course, after the war ended in 1945, the whole world learned the full, horrific story of Hitler's Holocaust.

While in Heidelberg during the summer, my parents visited a Jewish woman in her upstairs apartment in the back of a building. They were touched that she served tea from her meager supplies. My parents saw the words *Juden Verboten* ("Jews Forbidden") painted boldly on storefronts near her apartment. They saw "tears in the eyes of Jews who had nothing left in the world."[114] The outside world knew little then of all this.

My parents ached from the extent and immediacy of the situation, knowing that there was more perfidy to uncover about the Nazi oppression that was beginning to spread to other nations. They walked through a youth training camp where young men were brainwashed and marched like robots. In the dining hall, there was an altar with a swastika and a bust of Hitler. They viewed many of Hitler's favorite gaudy paintings that idealized the "master" Aryan race.

And after a late-night production of a Wagner opera, they watched one hundred soldiers march before and behind Herr Goebbels, the barbaric minister of Nazi propaganda and one of Germany's new demigods. The soldiers lifted torches while throngs of people raised their arms with the obligatory, "Heil Hitler!" Talk about crazy! In the play and follow-up movie, *Idiot's Delight*, by Robert E. Sherwood, a German scientist flees to Switzerland because he wasn't allowed to continue research in medicine. He laments that Nazi officials wanted him to put a swastika on every little germ and train them to say, "Heil Hitler!"[115]

Surrounded by this culture of madness, my parents trusted in God's protection and seemed unconcerned about personal danger. After visiting the Worms Cathedral in Wittenberg where Martin Luther is said to have nailed his ninety-five theses to the church door,[116] they headed back to Heidelberg, floating down the Rhein to Mannheim. They disembarked with their bikes, then peddled to a pub for a sausage sandwich. Upon entering the pub, my father lifted a stiff arm and loudly exclaimed, "Heil Roosevelt!" Not an uncommon thing for him to say in jest, but this was not the right time or place! Filled with admiration for Luther's boldness, his bravado was fueled by righteous anger at how Hitler had vandalized the German culture. My parents drew disapproving glares but were tolerated… until they ordered water. "*Frishe wasser*," my dad asked. Not very German!

They were brought bottled mineral water, a common substitute for non-beer drinkers, and more expensive than beer. My father ushered the waiter to a hose across the counter and requested the water that was used to wash beer mugs. Pointing emphatically, he repeated, "*Frische wasser, bitte*." His insistence offended the manager as much as "Heil Roosevelt!" Taking quick strides to the front door, the manager flayed his arms and shouted, "*Verschwinden ze hinaus!*" ("Disappear you! Out!")

With adrenaline flowing, my parents agreed they were no longer hungry but still plenty thirsty. Mom suggested they learn how to like beer! "It was a long bike ride back to Heidelberg in the moonlight," she said. Dad's only mention of this incident in his personal journal was that "back in Mannheim we had quite an experience that we'll remember." He was careful what he wrote while in Germany and downplayed this and other incidents that he could later speak of more openly. For example, he later had a great deal to say about the grotesque, torch-lit parade of Herr Goebbels (who met his demise with Hitler in the bunkers beneath the streets of Berlin.)

Assuming risks he considered more thoughtfully than the one he took in the pub, my father visited with church leaders at the Heidelberg Castle, just up the hill from my parents' apartment. Covered with ivy, the castle was crumbling (and like most castles, it still is). A section of the property had a restaurant and a large area where concerts and plays were held. There was also a room where my dad could freely converse with pastors and learn more about the specter of fear and uncertainty that hung over those who had not been brainwashed. My parents didn't know these visits were under scrutiny, and that they were likely in mortal danger. "Heil Roosevelt!" was definitely not a state-approved salutation! But they trusted God and accepted (and probably minimized) the perils of befriending those who opposed Germany's new chief god, Adolf Hitler.

There are many stories that can be told of faithful and fearless German pastors who refused to bend a knee to tyranny—leaders of the Confessing Church. Dietrich Bonhoeffer—whom we will hear more about in the chapter "Heroes by Choice II"—and other true Christians stood for righteousness and sanity in the face of crazed evil. Here are some glimpses of a few of Bonhoeffer's associates with whom my father was privileged to interact leading up to and after WWII. They helped defeat Germany through their influence and indomitable spirits, much as Christian influence was key in the lifting of the Iron Curtain across Europe forty-four years later in 1989.

Professor Martin Dibelius
God's Grace Is Enough

Before my parents' arrival in Germany, Martin Dibelius had been an interim preacher twice at Martin Niemöller's church in Berlin after Niemöller was imprisoned. Dibelius read Niemöller's sermon, written from prison, and then spoke from his heart to the packed Berlin-Dahlem Church while SS troopers jammed the aisles. Here is a brief excerpt:

> The beloved, courageous, and upright pas-
> tor of this church is in prison. We here in this
> house will pray for his welfare and the day of his
> return. You can do little for him now except pray
> that God will give him a firm heart. His arrest
> means the entire Christian church of Germany
> has been challenged before the courts.

On the following Sunday, Dibelius gave the same message: "I repeat, Pastor Niemöller's arrest means that the entire Christian church of Germany has been challenged before the courts... Are we to hear nothing but a German Christ from our pulpits?"

Needless to say, Dibelius was imprisoned—but not for long. My dad was anxious to meet him, and he soon did. During their meeting at his home, Dibelius wouldn't speak of his own imprisonment but spoke urgently of how the Nazis were harassing, expelling, and imprisoning pastors, and replacing elected bishops with Nazi sympathizers referred to as Reichbishops. Dibelius was among the German true followers of Christ who refused to drape the obligatory swastika over their pulpits, as did the collaborating pastors who led the Reich Church. Their congregants were called German Christians, and under the influence of the Reichbishops, they all worshipped Hitler above Christ.

A strange noise in the backyard cut short their visit. Dibelius' parting words to my dad were to the effect that Martin Luther's great "A Mighty Fortress Is Our God" was analogous to the US "Battle Hymn of the Republic." He quoted from the second verse of the former, followed by a stanza that isn't familiar to me:

> Let goods and kindred go
> This mortal life also
> The body they may kill

God's truth abideth still
His Kingdom is forever[117]

Let princes or human favor depart
If God's grace abides with me
Man's favor may come or not
But if not—let it to the Devil go!
God's grace is enough for me!

My mom said that Dad never forgot Professor Dibelius. "Odd, isn't it?" he would say. "Luther, Niemöller, and Dibelius—all Martins." Three Martins bravely stood for righteousness and against tyranny. Dibelius was not imprisoned again and taught at Heidelberg until his death in 1947.

He Could Not Be Silenced
Pastor Maas

Pastor Hermann Maas was the most well-known pastor in Heidelberg. Maas was one of the few pastors who would not pledge allegiance to Hitler and who also helped Jews escape from Germany. He was part of the Confessing Church that he, Bonhoeffer, and a few others helped to found.

My dad met Maas on the morning of July 17, 1938, at his church. It was then and there from this man that my father received most of the dark news that the rest of the world was not being told. When my father spoke of him in a sermon at a church near Oxford a few months later, he did not use Maas's name—for reasons which will become clear. Here's a passage from that sermon:

> "Why," we ask ourselves, "are we so far from peace and goodwill after almost two thousand years of Christian teaching?" The simple answer is that we have professed Christianity without being Christian… In Germany this summer, one of the splendid Christians with whom I visited

was the leading Protestant minister of Heidelberg. He was watched by the police. Still, he served his people. [In] the last visit I had with him he said he was going to Hamburg to try to get a passport so that he could attend a meeting in Oslo for international goodwill through the churches. His daughter naïvely said to me, "I hope they don't put him where we won't see him again," meaning a concentration camp.[118] [Unfortunately, this would be his fate.]

In the early 1940s, Maas helped many Jews escape death in Germany by enabling them to obtain exit visas. He was imprisoned in a forced-labor camp in France in 1944 that was liberated by Allied soldiers at the end of the war. It's hard to imagine his daughter's heartache when her worst fear for her father came to pass. But I think she did see him again!

Then They Came for Me
Professor Martin Niemöller

After the war, my dad hiked the Pocono Mountains of Pennsylvania with Martin Niemöller, the German theologian who was imprisoned at the time my parents arrived in Heidelberg. Niemöller had spoken to Hitler in the early thirties and was promised that Jews would be left alone. But he later wrote his now-famous piece of prose, acknowledging the ugly truth about Hitler. Different versions have been published, but here is what I believe to be the most common:

> First they came for the Communists and I did
>   not speak out
> because I was not a Communist
> Then they came for the Socialists and I did not
>   speak out
> because I was not a Socialist

Then they came for the trade unionists and I did
   not speak out
because I was not a trade unionist
Then they came for the Jews and I did not speak
   out
because I was not a Jew
Then they came for me and there was no one left
   to speak out for me.[119]

Niemöller and my father were both attending a conference where the founding of the World Council of Churches was being discussed. With evangelism as a primary unifying theme of the conference, hopes were high at the Inn at Buck Hill Falls. Niemöller and Dad shared frequent breaks, as neither was a voting member at the conference. Niemöller recalled his naïveté and gullibility when Hitler told him that no Jews would be harmed. After it became clear Hitler would not keep his word, Niemöller turned into one of his harshest critics.

Once while Niemöller was playing outdoors with his son in 1938, Gestapo agents drove up and took him away. He'd been temporarily detained before and expected to be home later that day. Instead, he was imprisoned in the Sachsenhausen and Dachau concentration camps, narrowly escaping execution by the war's end.

As Niemöller and my dad strolled by crashing waterfalls, it seemed he had left his naïveté and guilt behind. He reminisced about his young friend, Dietrich Bonhoeffer, who was hung at Dachau by Nazis shortly before American troops arrived. He wondered aloud whether God's justice would have been better served had the Nazis executed him instead: "Dietrich had more years ahead of him than I."

Niemöller and my dad agreed with the voting members of the conference: "Could we all be one," Niemöller said, "it would be as noteworthy as Martin Luther's nailing his ninety-five theses to the castle's church at Wittenberg."

These three men—Dibelius, Maas, and Niemöller—along with Bonhoeffer, Churchill, and thousands of notable and unsung heroes during Nazism's dark days knew what it was like to take great risks and live out principles that hold civilization together. They also experienced deepening faith through suffering. They had the same attitude as Teresa of Avila, a Catholic saint and theologian of the sixteenth century. Teresa had a vision of an angel thrusting a flame-tipped spear into her heart, creating both pain and a deep love for God. After this experience, she said, "Lord, either let me suffer or let me die."

As a footnote to Niemöller's life: perhaps his greatest foe was the most prominent *Reichbishop* in Germany, the self-aggrandizing Ludwig Müller. At one time a little-known pastor and theologian in East Prussia, Müller joined the Nazi party and rose to prominence. He wanted to "purge the Old Testament of the Jews" and establish a German national religion. This gave impetus to the *truly* virtuous Confessing Church. As the Allies entered Germany, Müller committed suicide. In his rise to "fame," he became the fly who conquered the flypaper.[120]

Others Who Stood against Evil

Most of us have friends or family who are every bit as courageous as these men, and they are making positive contributions to world order and peace. Uncle Bob and my other three uncles, as well as my father-in-law, were also war heroes and heroes in life.

My father-in-law, Bill, was a navigator on C-47s that flew missions to deliver supplies from India to China. C-47 crews could plot their course over the Himalayas by noting the scattered wreckage of downed planes. Imagine living for a few years knowing you could be blown out of the sky! About 590 aircraft were lost over this treacherous route, along with 1,314 crewmen and hundreds more declared missing.[121] Overall, approximately 80,000 American military crew members did not return from their missions during WWII.

My wife's brother, the younger Bill, watched a documentary with his dad that showed twelve C-47s flying over the Himalayas with only two returning. My father-in-law pointed at the screen and said, "That's my plane."

Young Bill said, "You mean you were in a plane *like* that?"

My father-in-law said, "No, *that's my plane.*" After that he was silent, secluding once again the memory he'd suppressed for years. The family had never known how much danger he'd been in.

My father had three younger brothers who were also in harm's way during the war. Uncle Wayne flew fifty bombing raids over southern France, Germany, and other countries. My dad wrote this about him:

> [He] lived through hell a number of times, walking on the heaviest anti-aircraft flack of the war at fifty thousand feet [sic] and seeing close buddies shot apart. He wrote me after one mission that when he put down, he noticed a hole the size of a grapefruit just a foot behind him!

Uncle Ethan was an infantryman, fighting from Northern Africa into Italy. Uncles Ethan and Wayne *just happened* to meet each other on the streets of Rome...*twice!* What were the odds? Uncle Kenneth served in the Pacific theater on a PT boat.

The Rest of the Story

Before I shift to stories of my brother Wayne, his former wife Nicki, and me, I'll add a bit more about my parents. They left Germany the day after they learned the German police had been watching them. I consider their timely exit from Germany a miracle, as much as I believe God's favor rested upon them throughout their time there. On their way to Oxford University in England, they breathed deeply of freedom as they crossed the Rhine into Switzerland to attend the Geneva Institute of International Relations. My dad wrote in his journal, "We were tired of soldiers, fear, and '*Heil Hitler!*'" He also wrote that as they "fled from the fury of our fears, we were loaded with guilt that we were speeding to safe borders while others were not."

Britain was preparing for war, and the American consulate advised my parents to leave England. But they decided to stay long enough for my dad to finish his studies. They boarded the *Aquitania* in January of 1939 and churned into harsh weather and sea swells of the Atlantic. They were passed by the SS *Athenia* that was later sunk by a Nazi U-boat in September, killing 117 people. It didn't take long for the Nazis to begin unrelenting predation of civilian and military ships plying the ocean between England and America.

My father served as a professor at Boston University and then at Baker University for four years. He then pastored three United Methodist churches for the rest of his career—two of them among the largest in the US. While he pastored North Methodist Church in Indianapolis and served on the DePauw University Board of Regents, he was able to engage British Prime Minister Harold MacMillan to speak at a commencement, where he received an honorary doctorate.

You can be sure my parents could tell many interesting stories typical of most pastors and their wives. One involved a mentally ill woman who thought my dad was Jesus Christ! (He always counseled her in an office with a back door!) I also heard about his life being threatened while he pastored the Methodist church at Harvard for a summer. Police officers attended services for his protection.

Then there was the corrupt bishop who made life and work difficult for my dad. I still have the newspaper article about how the church rallied to support my father against this bishop's desire to move him on to another church. A backstory is that my dad often beat this fellow in golf! Because of what I witnessed in the politics of the churches where my dad served, and because he never seemed to stop working, I swore I would never become a pastor. Of course, God had other plans for me *and* a sense of humor; so naturally, I've been an ordained pastor for years. More on this later…

Plagued his entire life by difficulty sleeping, Dad worked hard, helped people, and was a frequent radio minister, conference speaker, and community leader. He lived the life he'd always wanted. While a pastoral intern in Hull, Massachusetts, always one to "run to the battle," he stood at a town meeting and spoke against a proposed dog track that the Mafia wanted to bring in. The proposal was defeated, and Dad's stance became front-page news in Boston. Ever the visionary, he preached in 1949 that America would defeat Communism, which finally happened when the Soviet Union collapsed forty-two years later. I still have newspaper articles about these events.

Dad returned to Oxford in 1951 as a delegate to the Methodist World Council. While registering at a hotel, he found his and my mother's signatures from twelve years earlier! Tears filled his eyes, and I can imagine the flood of memories. On his way to the Council, he had been asked to speak in several churches in Scandinavia. Walking on the shores of Denmark with Pastor Sørensen, he learned the pastor had rescued sixty-two Jews during the war by hiding them in a hospital where people were not questioned by the Nazis. In the dark of night, an ambulance took the Jews far out of town to where Pastor Sørensen put them on a fishing boat to cross the Baltic Sea to Sweden. My father was stunned to hear of the bravery of yet another unsung hero!

In 1963, Dad served as a Methodist delegate to the World Council of Churches, which had been discussed at that earlier conference in the Poconos. But most important of his earthly achievements was his faith, encapsulated in his words from an Easter Sunday sermon: "Live now and always with complete devotion to Christ. Go toward the dawn of abundant life—now!"

My mother was a high school English teacher. I often awoke to find her surrounded on her bed by papers she was grading (the life of a teacher!). She also spoke at women's luncheons and directed plays in the church and community. I still enjoy reading newspaper articles about her speaking engagements, drama productions, and other achievements.

On a wall in our home hangs a photo of her wedding day. A scrapbook contains a picture taken when she was campus queen at Simpson College, where she met my dad. I loved to hear her sing and play the piano. She had considered an acting career but thought it better to marry Dad and join him in ministry. When I see old movies, I sometimes imagine how well she would have performed some leading roles.

God kept my parents safe in Germany and England and strong in the stress of ministry. Their trust in Him was constant, and in many ways, "bold righteousness" defined them. But in their mid-eighties, they both developed dementia such that Susan, my brother, and I decided to move them from Ohio to Tucson. With the help of skilled caregivers, we took care of them for four years in their own home before eventually moving them to assisted living.

Helping parents with dementia isn't typically easy, as many of you have experienced. But our times together were meaningful—sometimes fun—and I'm grateful their dementia was relatively mild. All in all, I have a rich inheritance—not as much monetarily as in what has been deposited into my spirit, which has much greater value. How I threw all that out the window for a period of my life is what I want to tell you about next.

Reflections on the Peaceful Life

Proverbs 11:3 says, "The integrity of the upright guides them." When guided by integrity, your life accurately reflects your character. There's a word we use in counseling that describes this: congruence. With people who are congruent, what you see is what you get. Throughout my life, people told me how much they loved my parents. What people saw in them is the same as what I saw in them at home. And their reward throughout their lives was peace. Hold to integrity and your reward will be the same!

Part 2
Pastures of Green, Tender Grass

Personal Miracles

Before I finally and fully committed myself to Christ, my life was far from showroom clean. Thankfully, I now have an inner joy that brightly contrasts with my dark laments of those troubled years. I'll first describe the shining aspects of my new life before I tell you about my drug and alcohol days and my battle with essential tremors.

First, a few snapshots of how Heaven has intersected with my life. We know that angels do the Lord's bidding. People have told me on three occasions that they've seen an angel with me. The first two were when church members reported seeing an angel by my side while I was preaching. I don't recall ever sensing the presence of an angel, but I did feel empowered as I delivered those messages.

The third angel was seen in my counseling room as I was talking with a client who had taken a lay counseling program I'd taught. During our conversation, the subject of angels came up. Quite casually, my client said there was an angel behind me in the upper corner of the office. She added that this wasn't the first time she'd seen an angel with me.

When I first read about angelic appearances, I was skeptical. Although I've been blessed throughout my life, I thought that with my luck—just when I needed a real angel to show up, he'd be on a coffee break! It turns out that a common thread in angelic appearances is that they often happen instantly after a person has prayed. Just as God knows the words we'll speak before they come out of our mouths, He knows what we're going to pray and sometimes has begun to answer already.[122]

I remember something else that occurred while I was singing and playing a song of mine after preaching. I had felt led to do this song because it dovetailed perfectly with my message. Because I hadn't sung to the congregation in a few years, I began rather tentatively. At the end of my message in the first service, something unusual happened. As I picked up my guitar and started to sing, I heard stringed instruments playing in the background. They nicely complemented my guitar, and my confidence quickly grew. I wanted to turn my head to see if the music director was playing the synthesizer, but I couldn't and still sing into the mike. So I decided to enjoy playing with the great backup and ask him about it later. But he told me that no musicians were on the platform and that he had not been playing along with me either! I heard no instrumental accompaniment in the second service, but I didn't need a confidence booster by then.

I submitted an account of that incident to a magazine that features stories of Heavenly interventions, and I was actually blessed by their letter of rejection! On the form letter was a checklist to explain rejections. The box that was checked for my rejection said, "We get a lot of stories like this." *Of course they do! What was I thinking?*

Another music-related incident occurred after "Chet and Dennis" (Dennis Lee was my musical partner for about six years) played to a small audience in Tubac on a Sunday night. A woman came up to me and said that while we performed, her mouth was completely healed of a serious abscess. Only God could have done that!

About that same time, more than twenty years ago, you'll recall that I frequently led worship at our church. Recently, my wife and I had lunch with Andy and Jennifer Cole, two close friends who were active in the church then. They helped finance my second contemporary Christian musical album, which was blessed with a lot of play on local radio. I'll never forget how happy I was when they forgave the debt!

During our visit, Andy shared a story he'd never told Susan and me. He said that when I was leading worship on a Sunday night, it was obvious that I'd come to the end of my musical segment. But I continued to lead spontaneous singing—which wasn't unusual in a charismatic church like this. Somehow, Andy said he was hearing incredible music even more beautiful than the rest of us were hearing as we sang and played. Andy whispered something about this to a mutual friend next to him, saying the music was *wonderful*. It was as if "a waterfall of refreshment poured through me," Andy said. "I realized that I was hearing an angel choir." Andy continued, "It was as if a door opened and allowed me to hear a choir of angels—and then it closed." Once he fully grasped what he was hearing, the Heavenly music didn't linger. But I've heard and read of many people hearing Heavenly music that wasn't heard by others. Whether one gets a quick glimpse of paradise or hears Heavenly music, such sights and sounds are enthralling and indescribable and leave a lingering sense of what's on the Other Side.

I've also experienced other Heavenly touches. I've had four dreams that I know were of God. One gave direction and three gave assurance. These dreams impacted me in a way that normal dreams do not. They were in vivid color, and on awakening, I immediately knew what they meant. Other times in the early eighties, I had visions of the feet and robe of Christ in the sky. The visions evoked in me a deeply comforting feeling of laying my head at His feet, which brought sweet relief to my mind and soul from years of alcohol abuse and repressed emotions.

I've had numerous other extraordinary experiences—some too personal to describe here. I know why folks sometimes won't let me write about certain miracles of theirs. Too personal to relate, they can be like fragrant flowers that may bruise with the slightest touch. Silence and holiness are often intertwined.

But now I turn to the years of alcohol abuse I subjected myself to, and the miracles God worked in my life to set me free. This happened in Tucson, where Susan and I still live.

Drug and Alcohol Abuse and a Life Redeemed

While driving once from Tucson to San Diego, Susan and I saw a solitary locomotive parked on a track next to I-8. I think the train was just plain stuck on that stretch of desert that was in the middle of nowhere. I told Susan it reminded me of how some people are marooned like a busted engine able to go nowhere. She said she thought of "power without purpose." Susan's metaphor resonated with me because it represented my life before I became a Christian. I was the little engine that *couldn't!* Any of my gifts and abilities certainly lacked purpose. My engine was busted; and because of the advantages of my upbringing, I should have been in fine working order.

My full name is Devereaux Chester Weld. I was named after an eighteenth-century Anglican minister named Devereux Jarratt. I never thought I could live up to his legacy. Nor did I think I could follow the example set by Theodore Weld, a distant cousin who is thought by many to be the greatest abolitionist of the 1800s. (You'll read more about him in the chapter "Heroes by Choice Part II.")

In my early years, I also didn't honor the influence and examples of my father and mother. My life drifted far off the course set by my ancestor, Cpt. Joseph Weld, who landed in New England in 1635. His brother, Thomas, helped write the first book published in the

United States—*The Bay Psalm Book.* Theodore Weld was descended from Thomas, and I was descended from Joseph.

I still haven't reached the high bar set by so many Welds, but I do sense God's pleasure in having done my best to be guided by the integrity He gave me since committing my life to Him. And I've experienced victories that sometimes only God hears me shout about!

Obviously, there are deeper roots to my vulnerability to anxiety than just my essential tremor. I'll soon tell you about that and more about my "corkscrew life."[123] But first, I think of these roots as self-inflicted damage that arose from unrealistic expectations of what personal success should look like. I measured success by recognition and financial rewards, and those expectations aren't worthy of anyone who lives with humility. I can relate to the lament of someone with such expectations: "We took what we wanted, and now we no longer want what we took."[124] My primary expectation now is that I will allow Jesus to live His life through me. Whatever money or recognition may accrue to me is in God's hands. I no longer want what I soon won't want.

My first memory is running across the grass from the parsonage to Elm Park Methodist, the church my father pastored in Scranton, PA. My brightest memory of Dad's next church in Indianapolis is a fish fry on another green front lawn. Memories like these awaken in me the sort of peace spoken of in Psalm 23. God makes us lie down in "pastures of [green] tender grass,"[125] and restores our souls.

My soul wasn't beset by self-inflicted wounds back then. Those came later. The more that life's harsh realities took their toll, the more I pursued peace—but in all the wrong places. And somewhere between the green grass and eventually being spiritually lifted by God on eagles' wings, my soul was shrink-wrapped inside pride and fear. I repeatedly tried to flap my trapped wings in more mud than I have space here to mention.

I've had persistent essential tremors for as long as I can remember. It was as if that condition alone could define my life and how much I could achieve. Twitches and spasms in my neck hit me like a freight train in my early twenties. That's when I discovered that alcohol could suppress them...and that marijuana could increase my enjoyment of music (which is no longer necessary). I couldn't get enough intoxicating classic rock as I often listened through all hours of the night—nor could I get enough of writing music. The constant hunger a songwriter feels to write the *next* song can be addictive. Melodies emerged from deep within me, usually in my sleep. I'd hear the melody and then arouse myself to record it with whatever lyrics that also bubbled up. But this feel-good escape from the tremors into alcohol and the thrill of musical expression detracted from my seminary studies in New York City that followed my graduation from Ohio Wesleyan University.

My tremors were bothersome during any eating or drinking situation, especially during the day with others when I couldn't drink alcohol because of classes or work. Eating a sandwich was no problem, but eating peas with a fork...*forget about it!* Also, there was a tightness in the side of my face that often made it difficult for me to look people in the eye for long.

Five years after seminary and the master's program in counseling that I finished in 1977, I saw no improvement in my tremor. My resulting angst was terrible. A girlfriend named Carol urged me to call out to God about it. "What should I ask Him?" I asked her.

"Ask Him anything you want!" she said.

Immediately, I silently prayed, "Lord, teach me how to love myself." I left Carol's house around 12:30 a.m., started my '72 Olds Cutlass, and reached for the radio dial. I said to myself, "Wouldn't it be something if there were a song about God's love on the radio right now?" I had never tuned in to a contemporary Christian music station, and I didn't even know they existed back then. I was about to be very surprised!

A song clicked on, telling how much God loves us. I cried for hours, knowing full well that it had been a "God-incident." The following Sunday, Carol took me to church. I started to attend regularly, pray, read the Bible, and search for the truth about God—and *for God Himself.* Carol told me that the same night I heard the song on the radio, she had asked a group of friends in Phoenix to pray for me. God had answered that prayer!

I never told Carol that three months before I met her—right after getting my master's from the University of Arizona—I had stopped using cigarettes, alcohol, marijuana, prescription drugs, and hallucinogens. I quit cold turkey in one day, and I was a detoxifying wreck when I met Carol. She couldn't help but notice, which prompted her to tell me to pray that life-changing prayer. I'd love to meet her again, this side of Heaven, and thank her for being the instrument God used to change my life. I wonder if she'd be surprised that my years of seminary and Bible college and my study of psychology culminated in my becoming a minister and Christian counselor and musician after I'd finally surrendered my life to God. Carol would no doubt give Him all the glory—just like I do!

After my genuine conversion—which far transcended singing at Methodist youth camps and saying occasional prayers in my undergraduate days—my healing began in every way: spiritual, emotional, and physical. And my healing continues today. Imagine that! As the saying goes, I'm still a work in progress. Aren't you? But it's good to remain under construction. Without drugs and alcohol to depend on, I worried less about my tremor and depended on God's power to help me do almost anything, including helping me find a way to make a living as a Christian counselor.

I learned what the psalmist meant when he said, "Deep calls to deep in the roar of your waterfalls."[126] I called out to God from my personal depths every day—often from moment to moment. The poet Percy Shelley put it this way in his poem "To":

> The desire of the moth for the star
> Of the night for the morrow,
> The devotion to something afar
> From the sphere of our sorrow

We know that Paul called out desperately to God when he had a severe affliction and that God gave him all the strength he needed to bear it. There's debate about what his weakness was, which he called his "thorn in the flesh."[127] In the last chapter, I called these thorns "grace-getters." They certainly keep us humble and dependent on God…which is a good thing! I once read about someone with a severe disability who called it his "difficult gift." You might even say that when surrounded by all manner of crazy, or even the crazy-hard, we can be at our best.

My tremors have never interfered with doing well as a pastor or therapist. I think my condition helped me be more compassionate. It invited more of God's grace into each ministry opportunity. No longer did I need to escape from reality or use a drug-induced cocoon as a buffer in my life. I've been learning to keep in step with eternal realities, such as living according to Christ's commands and seeing life more from God's point of view.

Viktor Frankl, a neurologist, psychiatrist, and Holocaust survivor, once said, "In the past, nothing is irretrievably lost, but rather, on the contrary, everything is irrevocably stored and treasured."[128] The motto of my family, *nil sine numine*, may have been temporarily lost to me—certainly not fully understood. But I believe God had it planned for me to embrace this truth all along.

New Life in Christ

After seventeen years in the church Carol took me to, and where I came to serve as the director of counseling and co-leader of the singles ministry (with my Susan), I began work at a Christian counseling agency. The main office was near Fourth Avenue in Tucson, where I'd previously frequented two bars: the Shanty (I loved the pool table) and the Buffet (I loved the country music that I never listened to anywhere else).

On my lunch breaks from the counseling center, I often ate at Time Market, a deli about a block away. I remember a truly kind fellow whom I ran into now and then there. He called himself "Tree." He had once worked on New York's Wall Street. Tree said he had quit his job and completely dropped off the radar. As an elderly man, he wore a colorful bandana around his forehead, a bright shirt, socks that didn't match, and patches that covered holes in his clothes. Tree was an imposing guy at about six feet, eight inches tall, so his name truly fit. He rode a bike with colored crepe paper woven into the wheel spokes. He was definitely "local color" in a neighborhood where bars like the Shanty, a feminist bookstore, and two coffee houses were located. You could say that the area was retro…and that Tree embodied the Fourth Avenue culture.

I tried twice to talk to Tree about faith in Christ, but he wasn't interested, so I talked to him about other things, like the weather. One time I asked him, "Tree, what time is it?" He showed me his watch. There were no big and little hands on the face of the watch, no digital display—just a round piece of paper with the word *NOW*. I think you can get why I liked talking to Tree! For a guy who didn't want to talk about God, I believe he understood one aspect of Christ's identity: that God lives in the here and now and wants us to do the same. Claiming equality with God, Christ called Himself the "I AM,"[129] God's archetypal name in the Old Testament.

Here's a recent "thin slice" of my own life: After thirteen years of practice at the counseling agency, I left to become the director of pastoral counseling at Casas Church. There, I was privileged to work with Drs. Roger and Julie Barrier whom I mentioned earlier in this book. To replace the retiring director who'd been there twenty-seven years, the ensuing search was spearheaded by Associate Pastor Jerry Wilkinson. At an early meeting over coffee at Starbucks, during the nine-month interviewing and hiring process, I said to Jerry, "I don't have a chance, do I [of getting the job]?" (Not a wise statement to make in a job interview!)

He replied, "Well, let's just say it's 'competitive.'"

To finally be chosen for the position was a thrill for me. Pastor Jerry became my supervisor. While discussing counseling situations, Jerry sometimes suggested that I ask myself, "What's the right thing to do?" Jerry had been the director of a large counseling agency in the past himself, so great advice from him was never a surprise! I made it a point to commit to memory Psalm 106:3: "Blessed are those who act justly, who always do what is right." This remains a principle in my life that undergirds everything I do.

My duties at Casas involved full-time counseling and supervision of three therapists, speaking at Bible studies, leading some of the traditional worship services, and overseeing other ministries. Jerry later added to my duties the oversight of the pastoral care department. As I met with Jerry less frequently, his role of supervisor became that of a coach who would be available for consultation.

My position at Casas was a comfortable fit for me. I loved the members and attendees, and I loved my daily contacts with the staff (I'm an extrovert that likes to talk to people!). But after nine years there, the direction of the church ministries changed, and the counseling and pastoral care departments were ended. This happened at a time when I felt I was in the center of God's call on my life...and I *was*, but God moved the center! I believe Lamentations 3:37 is true: "Who can speak and have it happen if the Lord has not decreed it?" Roger and Julie had moved on to their PreachItTeach.Org ministry a few years earlier, Jerry was moving on, and now God was moving me. I returned to the Christian counseling agency. Blessed to work with believing peers, I nevertheless experienced the shift as downward mobility because of the reduction of responsibilities and the scope of visible influence. Everyone goes through such times. Jeff Goins writes, "Every calling is marked by a season of insignificance."[130] And Alicia Britt Chole expands on this truth in her *Anonymous: Jesus' Hidden Years and Yours*. She states, "Rarely does hiddenness visit us only once in our lifetimes."[131]

My Seasons of Downward Mobility

An earlier season of seeming insignificance was when I worked as a janitor in the early eighties—*after* I had my master's degree and about three years of counseling experience, including in a church's outreach to down-and-outers (at the church where my old friend Carol took me). Those I helped had served as the church's janitors, as part of their rehab program. I was one of the supervisors. When the program ended, guess what job was available at the church? I could have done any number of things, but I felt led to take the janitor job.

Being a janitor is a noble calling for many, but because I'd already worked as a professional counselor with higher pay, I regarded this as a major demotion. On my first day, a fellow janitor, Brad, showed me how to scrub a toilet—then laughed at me while I did it! Though

Brad was a friend, I don't think I laughed with him! On my birthday, the janitorial staff gave me a present: a feather duster, to help me do better work. I think I cried! But God gave me the only hymn I've ever written while scrubbing a toilet in the men's room near the sanctuary. That was a blessing and more than a fair trade-off for my labor. Indeed, janitorial work was my noble calling at the time. Brad would say the same about his work. He later became a pastor too, and I'm hoping he's had to clean a few toilets in his own church!

Another example of my being fine-tuned to know God better while I was a janitor: After one Sunday morning service, I was vacuuming the elevated platform area. (I had no idea I would later speak and lead worship from there a couple of hundred times.) I noticed that a volunteer was restocking visitor cards on the backs of the pews, and I said, "God will bless you for that, Sue."

Sue said, "God will bless me anyway, Chet."

Sue was so right! Although good deeds add to our Heavenly rewards when we do them to please God and not man, God doesn't bless us because of our good works. I already knew that—but Sue's words still made that truth hit me between the eyes!

Humbling times can work for our good. It's worthwhile to heed the words of King Solomon, who said, "A clever man conceals his humiliation."[132] That is something I did until writing this book. But I now speak of some of my humbling experiences to encourage others whose lives *seem* to be shrinking in significance. Whenever you're downwardly mobile, you do more things in secret, and you detox from damage caused by needing to be known or rewarded. You also become freer to know God more intimately.

During this time, I attended Grace Bible College and received a three-year Bible diploma. Though the school is now closed, it was there I learned that biblical scholarship and a personal relationship with Christ are inseparable. Much good came of this season in a valley. Jesus was certainly downwardly mobile when He left Heaven and assumed the form of a man. Seasons of seeming insignificance are a necessary part of spiritual growth. Roger Barrier references a point by Hannah Hurnard in *Hind's Feet on High Places*: "Maturity means returning to the Valley of Humiliation and giving away our lives to bring in the Kingdom of God on Earth."[133]

As with most everything we do in confidence, each of my counseling sessions is a giving away of my life—and I'll never understand the full significance in this life of doing that. When I get to Heaven, I hope to find the diamonds I've scattered down here sparkling in my new home—not as rewards (though I will receive those) but as testimony that what we do on Earth has eternal consequences and can glorify God.

If you return to a Valley of Humiliation, don't sweat it! All work for God is of value, and when we're in God's will, He's pleased. Besides, we know that God works all things together for good, and what looks like disarray to us is often God's harmony. What may look like one demotion after another strengthens us for bigger challenges. And to meet those challenges, we need bigger miracles. Or as Bruce Wilkinson says in *The Dream Giver*, "You will need God's power to overcome a Giant, and sometimes you'll need one miracle after another."[134] If you've been humbled enough to know how much you need God's miracles, you're likely to receive one after another!

Learning the Music Belongs to God

Of course, I hope that God still has more miracles for me, including more songs to bless others. As valuable as counseling is, now and then I still wonder why God hasn't used the music He's given me in a greater way. If that were God's plan, I would love it. I mention this only because I've learned that most people also feel the same about unfinished tasks or gifts not fully used in their lives. Jeff Goins has a friend who told him, "We all die unfinished symphonies."[135] Nevertheless, living for God requires using our gifts and callings to give each day our best shot. When the music stops "down here," the symphony of our lives will be continued in Heaven.

I used to wonder why doors to record contracts didn't open to me. I've approached Christian musicians and a few studios, but to no avail. One time, a judge in a national songwriting contest called me from his New Jersey studio to tell me that every song on an album

I'd submitted was "great." However, when he found out that I was forty-four, he said the judges were looking for a younger musician. I later saw the contest winner perform on television but never heard from him again.

Perhaps Psalm 127:1 speaks to what is true for the winner and me: "Unless the Lord builds the house, the builders labor in vain." God wasn't building a career in music for either of us. I remember when a local radio station gave one of my songs regular airtime for two months. Listening to the station one evening, the song before it was about how God will give you your place in the sun. Most of the music on my two albums has been played on local radio, and that was my music's "place in the sun!" The music belongs to Him, and He's still doing with it what He wills.

One time, after I submitted a song to a publishing company, I received a rejection letter that was two pages long! The form letter offered detailed suggestions about how to write a song, ending with hollow wishes that my music would bless me in my quiet time. Susan and I still laugh about that. But I *still* wonder at times about closed doors, although worshipping and playing songs I've written *does* bless me *any* time!

But such is life for most of us. Charles Finney was a nineteenth-century American evangelist known for his exceptional singing voice—but he was called to preaching, not singing. King David was a skillful harpist and music composer, but his main assignment from God was not to be a musician. Even "Fiddling Bob" Taylor, mentioned in chapter 1, was called to be a governor rather than play the violin in an orchestra. I've known many skilled artists who pursued art as a hobby, not a livelihood, though their artistry seemed to be their greatest gift.

These examples remind me that God knows what is best for us and for His Kingdom, even when some of our hopes and dreams aren't fulfilled. What if my songs had reached a much larger audience but I had missed counseling one person whom He knew needed my influence? I would have missed His mark—and I do enough of that already. There are plenty of anointed and talented Christians who are being obedient to God's call to music ministry. I must answer God's specific call on *my* life, as must we all, if we're to continue growing closer to Him. *God's* call on our lives is always the *highest* one. In fact, no mission assigned to us by God is too small. And there's often a ripple effect that extends far beyond what we can know. When God one day reveals the results of our missions, we'll see clearly that any pain or disappointment we may have endured was more than worth it. In Shakespeare's "Sonnet 30," he summoned up the "remembrance of things past" and sighed "the lack of many a thing I sought." Yet when he thought about a single friendship, "All losses are restor'd, and sorrows end." In the same way, when we turn our thoughts to what there is to love about our lives, even just a single friendship, we can be assured that the sum of past regrets is overshadowed by hopeful shafts of God's intentions toward us. In many Bible teachings, I reference a favorite Scripture, Isaiah 49:4:

> But I said, "I have labored in vain; I have spent my strength for nothing at all. Yet what is due me is in the LORD's hand, and my reward is with my God."

The Healing Path through Heartache

I alluded to the "politics" that are part and parcel of almost all churches. There are many examples common to people in ministry over the years, although I haven't heard of this next one lately. My great-grandfather, William Morton Weld, was also a minister. At age thirty-six, William and his wife, Minerva, moved from Booneville, Maine, to Plainville, Minnesota. William had agreed to pastor a Baptist church for an annual salary of $100. The understanding was that the church would also raise an additional $200 each year for him.

But William didn't last long at that church. Here's why: He allowed non-Baptists to partake of Communion which caused quite an uproar. You can imagine the "pastor stew" consumed around the congregants' dinner tables after church! But William wouldn't budge from his belief that Communion was the Lord's table for *all* believers, not just Baptists. He left that church before his first year was up, and I don't think he ever got the additional $200! In those days, when so many ministers were itinerant, I'm sure he literally shook the dust of that place from his feet and moved on. Similarly, I try not to fill mental real estate with thoughts of unfair treatment. As with some of our exits from unpleasant circumstances, his exit was simply an exodus to a more fruitful promised land.

But before the turning point of my life at Carol's house, I knew little about perseverance or learning from the lessons of my ancestors. God allowed me to come to a place of pain and desperation before I could finally pray that He would teach me how to love myself. I believe that simple prayer was inspired by the Holy Spirit. If I hadn't been in deep emotional pain, I would not have sensed the Spirit's prompting. From God's perspective, my life was not bearing fruit for His kingdom. Since then, by His grace I've produced fruit that matters. I'm reminded of a newspaper clipping that was glued into an early sermon of my father's:

> Up in New York state [sic] they raise thousands of bushels of apples. Occasionally there is an apple tree which gives all of its energy to producing wood and leaves but bears no fruit. When that happens, the owner takes an ax and makes a deep gash in the trunk of the tree close to the ground. Almost always, that gash produces a change. The next year, that tree bears fine fruit. It is the fruit of suffering. Sometimes men are like that.[136]

As with millions of Christians, I'm like that "before and after" apple tree. It's only in looking backward that I've understood the purpose of the ax. But during the tough times, God's comfort abounds when we allow His love and forgiveness to rule our lives. That's the path through heartache—the "hard road of joy" I spoke of earlier. And even if we don't understand all of God's ways, how much of

God's light do we need to walk in, anyway? Here's the answer: just enough. He gives us all the light we need.

None of us asks for life's assaults on our psyche. But God is with us as we go *through* painful seasons. Jean Corbon in *The Wellspring of Worship*, referencing Psalm 88:12, speaks of God's glorious entrance into "the land of oblivion," which is Christ's entrance into our spiritually dark lives. Thereafter, God's intention to mold our character and change our lives becomes *unstoppable fulfillment*. Isaiah 43:13 says, "I will work, and who can hinder or reverse it?" (AMPC). God's promises throughout the Bible can become tangible, victorious realities. He pulls us out of spiritual oblivion, and He is with us!

Songs that Have Never Been Written

Sometimes I wonder about the many songs I *could* have written had I gone into music full-time. New music still awakens me from dreams. Earl Marlatt begins his poem "Overtones" with these two lines:

> Are they nowhere,
> The songs I did not sing?

Marlatt ends the poem with these words:

> Must all the music of infinity
> Be sung to be?[137]

I think the answer is simple. The music of infinity doesn't need to be sung to *be*. The songs I don't write here on Earth *are waiting for me to write in Heaven*. I look forward to lying down in endless pastures of green, tender grass…writing and playing that music… and listening.

Reflections on the Peaceful Life

Lloyd Douglas said, "If a man harbors any sort of fear, it per-colates through all his thinking, damages his personality, makes him landlord to a ghost."[138] Though I still have a vulnerability to anxiety, it's never interfered with meeting any challenge. I don't hesitate for long to follow God's leading. Many scriptures tell us to keep looking forward. God has plans to prosper us, not to harm us, plans to give us hope and a future.[139] While you let God conform you to His image, He will help you to fulfill your destiny in this life!

Part 3
My Trailblazing Brother

My older brother Wayne, like most of us, had his share of chal-lenges, heartaches, and victories. Though he was physically active for most of his life, he struggled with Parkinson's disease during his final seven years. His book *Wayne's Walk to the Grand Canyon (My Battle with Parkinson's Disease)* speaks of his *virtual* walk to one of his favor-ite national parks. For every mile he walked in Tucson, he kept his friends updated on his virtual progress to the canyon. He charted his progress with pins on a map. Many friends walked with him a few miles each day.

One piece of sage advice from Wayne's book is to "live as if you expect your prayers to be answered."[140] During his health struggles, I noticed that his faith grew deeper. Rather than focusing on symp-toms, he focused on his blessings, and he urged that all of us do likewise.

Wayne and his former wife, Nicki, lost their first daughter, Michelle Lee, to leukemia. She was diagnosed at age four and died at age five. Her parents felt deep heartache at their loss, and her absence has equally affected Michelle's younger sister, Dawn. I remember the joy that Michelle brought all our family.

I'm reminded of the Ian Maclaren quote, "Be kind, for everyone you meet is fighting a hard battle."[141] I recently spoke with a man in counseling who asked if I was Wayne Weld's brother. He didn't know

Wayne had died and said he remembered him as a robust, active, and influential man in Tucson. No matter how successful people may appear, we can't know what they might be going through. As I quoted my mother in chapter 1, sunshine exacts its penalty in shadow.

In this part of my family account, I turn to a few inspiring snapshots from Wayne's life story.[142] While these events don't speak of God's more spectacular interventions, keep in mind how God's favor can rest upon us in miraculous ways we don't always notice. It's noteworthy that Wayne ends his book with these words: "God treated me well! He gave me the talent and opportunities to serve others. For all my blessings, I am grateful."[143]

Seizing an Opportunity to Lead an International Corporation

After Wayne served in the Air Force near Seoul, he returned to the US in 1969 with his new Korean wife, Nicki. In less than a year, he was promoted to captain and then left the Air Force, moving back to Columbus, Ohio, where my parents still lived. He soon became the president and operations manager of Indian Hills Realty, a small real estate brokerage firm with three overworked sales associates.

Wayne didn't know much at first about real estate. When he showed a house, he got out his tape and measured the dimensions of a room while talking to people. I asked him why he did that. He said that it made him look busy as if he knew what he was doing. He also kept cinnamon rolls behind the front door to provide the aromatic experience of home. His methods seemed to work. Two years later, his firm had three offices and eighty salespeople...but there must have been more to his success than the tape-measure trick, or even more than the cinnamon rolls! But his time at Indian Hills was just the start of a remarkably successful real estate career that would be inspiring to many.

Wayne had never heard of Century 21 Real Estate LLC. Hardly anyone had back then. He happened upon an article about "two companies on the west coast that had a fresh approach to franchising that was transforming the way real estate was done... Century

21 and Red Carpet."[144] His instinctive response was to write both companies about establishing an Ohio branch. He didn't hear from Red Carpet, but a few weeks later, Bill McQuery from Century 21 showed up unannounced at Indian Hills to see Wayne.

Bill said he was in fact looking for someone to be an owner and regional director in Ohio. Wayne later said that Bill should've been completely unimpressed with his scant experience in real estate, sales, recruiting, and anything else that mattered and shouldn't have even considered him for such an ambitious venture. But Wayne was confident that he could surround himself with sharp people—and effectively *delegate*. He made it clear he would indeed like to take on Century 21, although he had no idea where he would get the start-up cash. Wayne says, "For something to change in your life, something has to change in your life." Then he made one of his most important decisions.

Wayne knew that every three months, Century 21 sent corporate executives to meet with regional directors all over the country. He found out the next meeting was to be in San Antonio. Wayne flew there and surprised co-founders Art Bartlet and Marsh Fisher, along with Bill McQuery and other bigwigs, and joined them at their table where they were having breakfast. Wayne made the most of his ten-minute pitch:

> I clicked off each point: that I was their man for the organization, that I could get the money, that I would recruit the needed staff, that I could carry their message to the marketplace and we would be their greatest success. After those ten minutes, I left for the airport and flew home, knowing that I had done my best to cover the important points.[145]

A week later, Wayne learned that Century 21 was going to bet on him. Keeping his cadre of four sales specialists, Wayne borrowed money and—with three others—financed the rollout of the Ohio office. Other regions typically used eight to twelve people to sell the franchise to independent real estate companies. Wayne decided his top four salesmen could do the job…and do it better, which they did. Right out of the gate, the team set a national record for opening a region. The previous record was thirty-two offices. Wayne opened with fifty-two offices "and dominated the marketplace everywhere we went."[146] For the next eighteen months, agents flocked to Columbus from other regions to learn how he did it. Wayne noted, "One of the lessons I learned from that experience was [to] hire the best, and with minimal guidance, let them do their thing."[147]

Wayne found out about the upcoming retirement of co-founder Marsh Fisher at a private meeting during a national convention in Las Vegas where twelve thousand sales associates and brokers were attending. The next thing Wayne knew, he was addressing the crowd! In short order, he became the new COO/executive vice president of Century 21 International! With Art Bartlet on the road a great deal, Wayne now essentially ran the company.

I wrote earlier of Wayne and Nicki losing their daughter, Michelle, to leukemia. It happened within six months of their move to Century 21 headquarters in California. I've noticed that great victories are often accompanied by great heartaches. I think of Proverbs 14:13: "Even in laughter the heart may ache, and rejoicing may end in grief." So, while Wayne and Nicki shifted to a more prosperous lifestyle, they were nonetheless suffering greatly. Amid this tension, both Wayne's and Nicki's lives went forward. Wayne quotes an unknown source in his Grand Canyon book: "Have faith to walk in the shoes God gives you."[148] Wayne kept walking. Prior to his struggle with Parkinson's, he had been able to complete several marathons, raising money then for the Leukemia Foundation.

As with all our stories, there's more to say about Wayne and Century 21…and so many more of his stories to tell. But we're thin-slicing. And I'm glad that Wayne gave glory to God for being treated well, not just in this situation but in others in the course of an overcoming life.

Wayne in Tucson

Years later, when Wayne moved to Tucson to help take care of our aging parents, Susan and I took a week off for a relaxing trip to Flagstaff while there was snow on the ground. For those of you who have taken care of parents with declining health, you know how much it means to get a break. During that week, I experienced normal energy for a total of only three hours, but it was better than nothing. By then, I was feeling continual pain in my lungs that one doctor attributed to flare-ups in scar tissue from the valley fever I'd contracted almost twenty years earlier. I'd gotten sick again as a result of the work and worry related to the care of my parents, as well as from the high stress of my counseling and pastoral ministries. But I viewed this as a small sacrifice to make for the time, energy, and love our parents had lavished on Wayne and me throughout our lives. Nevertheless, Wayne's arrival gave us a break at just the right time!

Wayne's business acumen enabled him to join a strong network of entrepreneurs and investors in Tucson. He was a sparkplug to the business and financial community. While acclimating himself to life in Tucson, Wayne golfed a good bit. He'd played in the number two position at Ohio University, won many tournaments, and took the low score in a casual round of eighteen holes with a Masters Tournament winner. With such a love for the sport, he was happy to enter a tournament at the Raven Country Club (now called the Arizona National Country Club).

Near the end of the summer-long tournament, Bomber—the club's reigning golf "czar"—paired Wayne with the three players who were the most competitive. Wayne said he started the round so poorly, including a double bogey, that the other three looked at each other as if to say, "What's wrong with Bomber?" Wayne was four over par after the first four holes. But he completed round five under par for an easy win. Bomber wasn't so stupid after all! And Wayne went on to win the tournament. At another course, Randolph Park, he won the longest-drive award for 325 yards (when golf clubs weren't as effective as the ones of today). He also won the prize for the straightest drive, landing his ball 2.5 feet off dead center.

Susan and I attended Wayne's seventy-fifth birthday party at Vivace Restaurant. We enjoyed listening to people tell how Wayne's life had impacted them. By then, everyone knew about his battle with Parkinson's. Wayne wrote five short books and published them through Amazon. He stopped writing when he could no longer read his computer screen without a magnifying glass. I loved Wayne because he was my brother and was an overcomer who acknowledged God's goodness to him through the thick and thin of life.

Onto His Next Adventure

Susan and I were in the Dallas-Fort Worth airport when we received a call saying Wayne was at Veterans' Hospital with aggressive cancer. Rather than receive treatment at the hospital, which probably would have been futile, he chose hospice care. After less than two weeks in the VA hospital, Wayne entered hospice on his birthday and was able to enjoy a party with about six of us. He had expressed hope that he would live for one final, earthly celebration. That hope was fulfilled, and he died two weeks later.

Since Wayne didn't say much about personal faith, I asked him on two occasions if he believed the essentials of the Gospel. He said that he did. Though I believed his eternal destination was secure, within days of his passing, I led him in a prayer to reaffirm Jesus Christ as his personal Lord and Savior.

I was pleased that Wayne had requested that I conduct his memorial service. A few days before the service, I had a vivid dream in which I saw a mural-like image of Wayne. He was young and dynamic as if he'd just finished another great round of golf. He wore a broad smile as he gazed at a beautiful angel. His hands were open and lifted as if he wanted me to also revel in the wondrous sight. Beneath this enthralling scene was a caption that read, "Now I have my vision in…" But I abruptly awoke before I could read the full sentence. As for the meaning of my vision, I believe it meant that Wayne no longer had double vision from Parkinson's and was enjoying complete and unimpaired Heavenly vision.

Nicki also was awakened by a vivid dream of Wayne smiling at her, the night before Wayne's memorial. He was wearing a red shirt and looked young. Oddly enough, in the more than forty years since their divorce, Nicki had never dreamed about Wayne. Susan also had a similar dream. Nicki, Susan, and I believe our three dreams were messages to us of hope and reassurance from God Himself.

Reflections on the Peaceful Life

Robert Browning wrote that a "man's reach should exceed his grasp."[149] Wayne's reach always exceeded his grasp. When he was struck with Parkinson's, I never heard him lament his decline. Despite double vision, he often drove to meet Susan and me for breakfast after church. His last words to me were, "I'll miss our breakfasts." For the last few years, he slept in a recliner, read emails with a magnifying glass, and wrote five short books. When he flew to Texas to make the surprise ten-minute presentation, which eventually landed him the COO position at Century 21 years before, his hope exceeded what he was likely to attain. In this way, he was always reaching and always finding. And when cancer struck, he quickly chose hospice care, making his final reach for Heaven. May all of us keep reaching and ever finding Jesus who said the kingdom of God is in our midst.

Part 4 From Traumatized Refugee

to Successful Entrepreneur

When my brother returned from Seoul, he brought with him a beautiful bride—the aforementioned Nicki. Their marriage in Seoul had been quiet, but then they had a second wedding at the Bexley, Ohio, church where my father served. That was a grand celebration.

Nicki is an on-fire follower of Christ and is arguably the best example in my family of an overcomer. Her joyful temperament often manifests in curiosity about people. Her joy belies the tragic events that had shrouded her growing up in Korea—the kind of trauma that mires most people in hopelessness. Nicki was born Lee Ok Chae.

Nicki's father was the chief of police in Seoul during the Korean War. He was executed before her eyes by Communists from the north. She also remembers the falling bombs and being frightened as she and her mother were shuttled among refugee camps. Her mother died along the way. Nicki remembers having friends who talked about their parents while she could not speak of hers. She was a deeply traumatized little girl; merely sharing this makes me grieve afresh for her.

At age eight, Nicki saw a movie about Christ at an Air Force base near Seoul and gave her life to Him. At age ten, she moved to a World Vision refugee camp. About twenty years later, she met my brother, who oversaw housing at one of those Air Force bases. They fell in love, married, and moved to America when my brother's deployment ended.

Nicki's new life in Ohio unfolded as my brother began his real estate career. Then came their move to Irvine, CA, with Century 21 followed by the loss of Michelle. Most folks realize there's no deeper pain than losing a child. To make matters worse, about 80 percent of couples who lose a child eventually divorce. Sadly, such was the case with Wayne and Nicki.

Soon after the divorce, Nicki was hired by Escada Boutique at an exclusive mall in Costa Mesa. She kept meticulous records of all her customers and stayed in close touch with them, which quickly made her a top sales representative. She went on to open her own fashion boutique in Newport Beach, which thrived and which she eventually sold.

On one of my trips to California for preparatory classroom time toward my doctorate, Nicki and I shared dinner overlooking the ocean from the deck of her home. I'll never forget watching the waves and walking on the beach. Nicki maintains a routine she's kept every morning for years—she walks the beach at sunrise.

But behind such peace, success, and victory has been yet more heartache and trauma, which Nicki and I agreed not to share here. It should be easy enough to grasp the long trip from the traumatic loss of her parents in South Korea, to the pain of losing her first child, to the divorce, and then to vibrant life in Christ on the shores of Newport Beach. Her dogged determination and her faith in God have been well rewarded.

Wayne and Nicki remained friends, despite their divorce, and she comforted him while he was dying with memories of how they first met in Korea so long ago. Though Wayne could not open his eyes, he managed a weak smile. Dawn, Nicki, and I sensed this signified their reconciliation.

Wayne's and Nicki's shared pride and joy has always been their second child, Dawn Elizabeth. She was a star gymnast who was so accomplished that she attracted the attention of world-renowned gymnastics coach, Bela Karolyi, when she traveled to Houston for a gymnastics meet. She studied at the Stella Adler Academy of Acting and Theater in Los Angeles, which produced notables like Marlon Brando and Al Pacino. She's had parts in television ads and motion pictures and now has screenplays in the works. In short, Dawn is a charming extrovert with a bright future. She loves the Lord, has helped in building houses for the poor in Mexico, and volunteers for a church ministry to feed the homeless.

And those are the thin-sliced cross-sections of how God has blessed my family!

As with many families, mine has lived through plenty of crazy, as well as the crazy-hard. Sometimes, we've soared above the crazy in the way all of us are created to. Don't most of us treasure victories and yearn for more? With the uplift and "thermals" from God through His Holy Spirit, there is no need to struggle to gain altitude and soar. Like the albatross or the eagle, we can circle effortlessly in the sky for hours, with barely the twitch of a wing. That's when we have more of God's perspective and can live with purpose, counting on Him to lift us up, even when we're being assaulted by all manner of crazy.

Reflections on the Peaceful Life

Roger Barrier likes to invite his listeners and viewers to imagine being the last Israelite in line when God parted the Red Sea so the Israelites could escape the Egyptian army.[150] Looking behind at the charging chariots, not knowing that tons of water would soon drown them, that last man would have been desperately crying out to God. You may feel like that man right now. That's how Nicki felt, as a child in South Korea, as have many others whose stories you've been reading. Ask God to help you, and He will!

Endnotes

112 Malcolm Gladwell, *Blink* (New York, Boston, London: Back Bay Book, Little, Brown and Company, 2005), 23.

113 Stories and quotes are taken from personal communication, author's father's journal, and from a book his mother wrote that author hopes to publish.

114 Hiram C. Weld, from an Advent sermon given at a church in Oxford, 1939.

115 Robert E. Sherwood, "Idiot's Delight." 1936 and 1939, cited by Hiram C. Weld in a sermon, "The World-Minded Man," The Hull Village Church, 5/5/1939.

116 See Eric Metaxas's *Martin Luther: The Man Who Rediscovered God and Changed the World* to learn of possible myths that surround this world-changing event that marked the beginning of the Reformation.

117 Martin Luther, "A Mighty Fortress Is Our God," accessed 12/13/2020, https://en.wikipedia.org/wiki/A_Mighty_Fortress_Is_Our_God.

118 The sermon is titled "Advent—1938." The author has six typewritten pages of his father's notes.

119 "Holocaust Memorial Day Trust," accessed 12/27/2017, http://hmd.org.uk/resources/poetry/first-they-came-pastor-martin-niemoller. Numerous websites contain the same quote or slight variations of it.

120 Peter Marshall, "From Peter Marshall's Pulpit," in *The Best of Peter Marshall*, ed. Catherine Marshall (Old Tappan, New Jersey: Chosen Books, 1983), 335. Marshall probably had in mind the parable of the fly who thought he saw safety in the number of flies gathered on a piece of paper.

121 Lyon Air Museum, "Flying the Hump during World War II," accessed 11/08/2019, http://www.lyonairmuseum.org/blog/flying-hump-during-world-war-ii.

122 Psalm 139:4 and Isaiah 65:24.

123 The phrase "corkscrew life" is from poet Rob Matte Jr.'s *Rasdale at 70*, "Time" (Unpublished). Used by permission.

124 Anonymous, quoted by Peter Marshall, "From Peter Marshall's Pulpit," in *The Best of Peter Marshall*, 212.

125 Psalm 23:2, *Young's Literal Translation*, accessed 3/23/2019, https://biblehub.com/ylt/psalms/23.htm. "Green" is inserted, as this is the most common translation of the Hebrew adjective that describes "grass."

126 Psalm 42:7.

127 2 Corinthians 12:7.

128 Viktor Frankl, *Man's Search for Meaning*, "Viktor E. Frankl Quotes," Goodreads, accessed 4/25/21, https://www.goodreads.com/quotes/7950095-in-the-past-nothing-is-irretrievably-lost-but-rather-on.

129 John 8:58.

130 Jeff Goins, *The Art of Work* (Nashville, Tennessee: Nelson Books, 2015), 122.

131 Alicia Britt Chole, 114.

132 Proverbs 12:16, *The Tanakh*.

133 Roger Barrier, *Got Guts? Get Godly: Pray the Prayer God Guarantees to Answer* (United States: Xulon Press, 2011), xvii.

134 Bruce Wilkinson, *The Dream Giver* (Sisters, Oregon: Multnomah Publishers, 2003), 139.

135 Goins, *The Art of Work*, 186.

136 Quoted in a sermon delivered by Hiram C. Weld at the Hull Village Church, circa 136–1940. The source is not identified.

137 Earl Marlatt, *Cathedral: A Volume of Poems*, "Overtones," 2nd. ed. (New York and London: Harper & Brothers Publishers, 1937), 123. Marlatt was one of the author's father's professors at Boston University. They were lifelong friends. Marlatt gave Weld a copy of *Cathedral* in 1935.

138 Lloyd Douglas, accessed 8/17/2020, https://www.quoteswave.com/authors/lloyd-c-douglas.

139 Jeremiah 29:11, spoken to the Israelites before they were taken into the seventy-year captivity.

140 Wayne R. Weld, *Wayne's Walk to the Grand Canyon: My Battle with Parkinson's Disease* (Amazon, 2017), beginning of chapter 3.

141 Ian Maclaren, Wikipedia, accessed 12/13/2020, https://en.wikipedia.org/wiki/Ian_Maclaren.

142 Wayne R. Weld, *Wayne's Autobiography: It Doesn't Suck to Be Me!* (Amazon, 2018), 34.

143 Ibid., 80.

144 Ibid., 34.

145 Ibid., 37.

146 Ibid., 40.

147 Ibid.

148 Wayne R. Weld, *Wayne's Walk to the Grand Canyon: My Battle with Parkinson's Disease*, Chapter 2 introductory quote.

149 Robert Browning, Dictionary.com, accessed 3/27/2021, https://www.dictionary.com/browse/a-man-s-reach-should-exceed-his-grasp.

150 Roger Barrier with Briana Barrier Engeler, *Got Guts? Get Godly* (United States: Xulon Press, 2011), 267.

Chet's father, Hiram Chester Weld, professor and United
Methodist minister. Photo by Olaf Carlson.

Chet's mother, Mary Elizabeth Weld, teacher and
public speaker. Photo by Olaf Carlson.

DR. WELD GIVES FINAL ELM PARK INSTITUTE LEC-
TURE—The Rev. Dr. Hiram C. Weld, pastor of Elm Park
Methodist Church, gave the main lecture last night at the
close of the six-week, 20th annual Mid-Winter Institute,
discussing "Christianity Challenges Communism." Said he:
"Christian America, as the leading nation of the world, will
defeat Communism when it takes the offensive."

'Christian America' to Defeat Communism, Dr. Weld Says

This photo (without the newspaper article) is from Feb. 17, 1949. Without television newscasters in those days, and with the American culture being influenced more by Christianity than in our time, ministers had more of a platform.

Chet's mom was the campus queen at Simpson College in 1934. She was the captain of the debate team and competed in national competition.

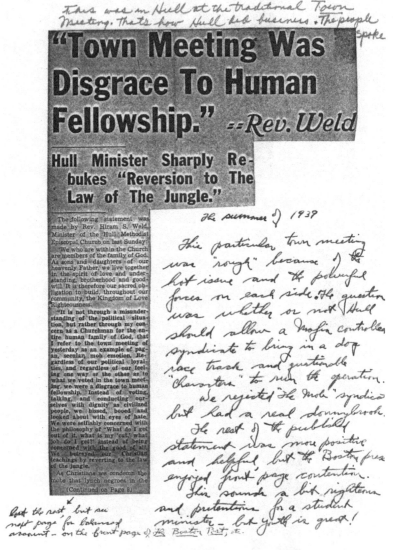

This was in Hull at the traditional Town Meeting. That's how Hull did business. The people spoke.

"Town Meeting Was Disgrace To Human Fellowship." ==Rev. Weld

Hull Minister Sharply Rebukes "Reversion to The Law of The Jungle."

The following statement was made by Rev. Hiram S. Weld, Minister of the Hull Methodist Episcopal Church on last Sunday:

"We who are within the Church are members of the family of God. As sons and daughters of our heavenly Father, we live together in the spirit of love and understanding, brotherhood and goodwill. It is therefore our sacred obligation to build, throughout our community, the Kingdom of Love Righteousness.

"It is not through a misunderstanding of the political situation, but rather through my concern as a Churchman for the entire human family of God, that I refer to the town meeting of yesterday as an example of pagan, secular mob emotion. Regardless of our political loyalties, and regardless of our feeling one way or the other as to what we voted in the town meeting, we were a disgrace to human fellowship. Instead of voting, talking, and conducting ourselves with dignity as civilized people, we hissed, booed and looked about with eyes of hate. We were selfishly concerned with the philosophy of "What do I get out of it, what is my 'cut', what job do I get?' Instead of being concerned with the good of all, we betrayed our Christian teachings by reverting to the law of the jungle.

"As Christians we condemn the mobs that 'lynch negroes in the

(Continued on Page 8)

The summer of 1939

This particular town meeting was "rough" because of the hot issue and the powerful forces on each side. The question was whether or not Hull should allow a Mafia controlled syndicate to bring in a dog race track and questionable "characters" to run the operation.

We rejected the Mob "syndicate" but had a real donnybrook. The rest of the public statement was more positive and helpful, but the Boston press enjoyed front page contention. This sounds a bit righteous and pretentious for a student minister — but youth is great!

Read the rest, but see next page for balance of account — on the front page of the Boston Post, etc.

(Continued on Page 8)

While attending graduate school in Boston, Chet's dad pastored a small church in Hull, Massachusetts. At a town meeting, he stood against the Mafia's attempt to build a dog racetrack in Hull. He was surprised to see his words make headlines in a Boston newspaper the next day.

Dr. H. C. Weld Named New Elm Park Pastor

The Rev. Dr. Hiram C. Weld has been named pastor of the Elm Park Methodist Church, the official board of the church announced last night. He succeeds the Rev. Dr. Harold C. Case who left in November to assume a pastorate in Pasadena, Calif.

Dr. Russell T. Wall, who made the announcement in the absence of Chairman H. R. Van Deusen, stated that the pastoral relations committee was unanimous in its call of Dr. Weld, who has been serving as interim minister since Nov. 1. His appointment was made by Bishop Fred P. Corson of the Philadelphia area.

Dr. Weld, 33 years of age, follows such distinguished churchmen in the leadership of Elm Park as Drs. Joseph M. M. Gray, Henry H. Crane and Harold C. Case. He comes to the post with a wide background of training, travel, educational service and pastoral experience, and follows in the spiritual footsteps of his own grandfather, a clergyman of distinction before the turn of the century, and his father, a lay leader in the Chicago area.

BORN IN CHICAGO

Born in Chicago, Dr. Weld graduated from Simpson College in Indianola, Iowa, and did seminary work at Boston University School of Theology. There he received a master of arts degree.

Dr. Hiram C. Weld ... call is unanimous

Chet's dad left academe to co-pastor Elm Park Methodist Church in Scranton, PA with Harold Case who later became the president of Boston University. When Case left Elm Park to pastor another church, Chet's dad assumed the role of senior pastor.

EUROPEAN DPs JOIN CLERGYMAN'S FAMILY CIRCLE—Mr. and Mrs. Gregor Chandochin (center) who have been married just a year, are pictured at the parsonage of Elm Park Methodist Church with the Rev. Dr. and Mrs. Hiram C. Weld. The DPs arrived here late Monday and yesterday got their first good look at an American City—Scranton. They plan to live here and will start night school tonight. They came under auspices of the Methodist Committee of Overseas Relief. They are Greek Orthodox. By his father's knees is Devereaux Weld, frisky son of the clergyman and his wife.—Tribune Photo by Olds.

DPs Get Temporary Haven at Parsonage

the young couple and the clergyman and his wife opened new vistas to one another. While Mrs. Weld showed Dorothea America's modern home appliances, Dr. Weld took George to the Church office to meet his staff. ... until they have a home of

Chet's family welcomes two "displaced pilgrims" from Eastern Europe after WWII. Chet, or "Devereaux," is at the bottom right. Wayne must have had more important business to tend to at the time!

DARTMOUTH SUMMER NEWS　　　　　　　　　　AUGUST 9, 1965

SUMMER TERM FAMILY RETURNS — CHET, WAYNE, DR. AND MRS. WELD

Four Welds Here For 'Recharge'

The Dartmouth summer term is a family "battery charger" for the Rev. and Mrs. Hiram C. Weld and their two sons, now in Hanover for their third summer.

According to Dr. Weld, of the Bexley Methodist Church in Columbus, Ohio, the family has been taking courses and participating in other summer term activities for three years now, because "we have some roots here. . . this is where we get re-created."

This summer Dr. Weld is taking a course in drawing at the Hopkins Center. His wife, Mary, a summer term student two years ago, has must finished her first year teaching high school English in Columbus.

Both their sons, Chet, 17, a high school senior, and Wayne, 22, a senior at Ohio University, are studying here.

Dr. Weld has been familiar with the Hanover area since he was a student at Boston University some 30 years ago. At that time he spent his summers as a counselor at a nearby boys' camp, and has been returning to the area, off and on, ever since — "for the physical and spiritual refreshment that sustains me in the rigors of public life through the rest of the year."

"Now that Dartmouth has a summer term," he added, "each member of the family has enjoyed tremendously increased enrichment and stimulation."

"We hope to be back next summer."

Chet's family was welcomed in Hanover, NH for the summer where they studied at Dartmouth. Chet audited a psychology course, produced a radio program for the college, won a tennis tournament, and sang in the Dartmouth summer choir. Pictured here: Chet, Wayne, Mom and Dad.

Photo of Chet on the back of an album he made in the 1990s.

Chet's brother, Wayne, snapped this picture of Chet
when he and Susan visited him in California.

Chet and Susan in their early forties.

Typical tourist picture of Chet and Susan.

Chet and Dennis Lee sang and led worship at their church, city events, and Arizona venues for about nine years. Photo is from their album back in the day.

Wayne and Dad were the golfers in the family. They drove together in 1959 to watch Dad's friend, Art Wall, win the Masters. Wall had attended Elm Park Methodist Church when Chet's dad was the pastor.

Christopher Kotecha's story, *Danger on the Road to Maine*, is featured on page 249. Christopher is shown here in New York with his wife, Sarah, and his two children, Abigail and Noah, in the fall of 2021.

Nicki in America after marrying Wayne. They met at an Air Force base in South Korea where Wayne served as an officer.

Wayne, Nicki, Dawn, and Michelle.

Nicki, Dawn, and Wayne soon after Wayne moved to Tucson.

Theodore D. Weld

Largely unknown but measured by his influence, Theodore Weld
is thought to be the greatest of the abolitionists. Weld is a distant
cousin of Chet's, each descended from different brothers who came to
America in the early 1600s. You'll read his story, "The Most Mobbed
Man in the United States" in Chapter 8: Heroes by Choice 2.

SECTION 4

DESTINED TO CONQUER CRAZY WITH HEROIC LIVES

7

HEROES BY CHOICE

Man is in reality what he is before God; no more and no less.
—Curé d'Ars

Some heroes we know well. Others, we've never heard of. Common denominators to them all are that they don't care who's ever heard of them, they face impossible odds, and they are willing to accept death but not defeat. They have the kind of character that comes from *acting* on the conviction that principles are more important than personal safety. One could say that many of them live by the premise that God is in the crazy and in the crazy-hard, and He will provide the courage to face all of that. Such are the heroes and the overcomers mentioned throughout this book.

While writing this chapter, I came across the online article "Heroes by Choice" by Lisa D. Healy that tells the story of five "coasties" or servicemen and servicewomen of the Coast Guard Station at Cape Charles.[151] "Despite howling winds and unruly seas, the crew of Coast Guard Station Cape Charles 41502 went in search of a tugboat in distress." Led by their officer-in-charge, Joe Habel, the crew of five volunteered for the mission to save three seamen from their boat that was floundering off Virginia's eastern shore near the station. The five coasties flung ropes and life rings to the tug's crew who had jumped into the thirty-eight-degree water. Within two minutes, all three seamen were hauled to safety.

At the ceremony honoring the five brave volunteers, "no one asked for autographs, and there weren't any balloons, banners, or T-shirts. But the coastguardsmen didn't mind, because these heroes prefer not to be honored that way." Healy does not give a date in her article of this episode, so I called the Coast Guard Station in Cape Charles. I was told Chief Habel served there from 1997 to 2002, so the rescue must have happened in that five-year span.[152]

John Wesley, an Anglican founder of Methodism, was grateful to seamen of the same caliber when he sailed to America. He was unaccustomed to seas of any kind and admired the men who bravely fought the rough and temperamental waves. In his journal, Wesley mentions that he was awakened on that voyage by a great noise. As it turned out, there was no reason for concern, but he comments "the bare apprehension of it gave me a lively conviction what manner of men those ought to be who are every moment on the brink of eternity."[153]

Let's now turn our attention to the lives of historical figures, known and less known, who did much good for civilization by living near the brink of eternity. They accomplished their missions and survived by God's grace.

The Flag Never Touched the Ground
Sergeant William Carney

William Carney had lofty plans for his life. The son of a slave who had escaped slavery through the Underground Railroad, Carney settled in New Bedford, Massachusetts.[154] But when the Civil War came along, he believed the best way to serve God was to join the military in order to free the oppressed.[155] He gave up his pursuit of Christian ministry to join the Army. In an 1863 edition of the abolitionist newspaper *The Liberator*, Carney stated, "Previous to the formation of colored troops, I had a strong inclination to prepare myself for the ministry; but when the country called for all persons, I could best serve my God by serving my country and my oppressed brothers. The sequel in short—I enlisted for the war."[156]

In May 1900, *Sergeant* Carney became the first African American to receive the Congressional Medal of Honor. A record of his brave deed is sculpted on the Saint-Gaudens Monument on the Boston Common. But what was his brave deed, one of the most heroic of the Civil War? As an infantryman in the first African American regiment in Massachusetts, Company C of the Fifty-Fourth Massachusetts stormed Fort Wagner from a beach near Charleston, South Carolina. As seagulls flew above and waves gently lapped the sand, the Fifty-Fourth led the charge against the formidable Fort Wagner, which up to that time had never been taken. Half of the brave Fifty-Fourth were mowed down in short order by bullets and grapeshot (clusters of small, round balls fired from cannons).

I recently watched the movie *Glory*, which tells the story of the Fifty-Fourth Regiment. They had trouble even getting fitted out with shoes, socks, and uniforms. Despite the ignorant prejudice of white officers who did not want to fight with the Fifty-Fourth, Carney and his comrades had one goal: to fight to preserve this great nation and the fundamental freedoms put forth in the Declaration of Independence.

When the flag bearer was injured, Sgt. Carney passed off his gun and took up the colors. He was soon alone with the dead and wounded surrounding him, lying on top of each other. He knelt on the beach. With bullets and grapeshot whizzing around him, he raised the flag high and looked for survivors of his regiment who'd somehow found shelter behind the carnage. Someone offered to carry the flag for him, but Sgt. Carney refused, although he had suffered some head wounds. He did not relent until he finally rejoined the men in his regiment who were still standing. As soldiers cheered for him and the flag, Sgt. Carney exclaimed, "Boys, I only did my duty; the old flag never touched the ground!" He then fainted and collapsed on the sand. He had risked his life to protect America's flag and what it symbolized.[157]

But there's more to his story, and it happened between his heroism and his death. In 1866, civilian Carney was put in charge of streetlights for the city of New Bedford. After briefly going to California, hoping to improve his finances, he returned to New

Bedford in 1869 and took a job as a postman. He served the postal service for thirty-two years before retiring. He next was hired as a messenger in the Massachusetts commonwealth capitol where, after serving seven years, he tragically died after his leg became trapped in an elevator.[158]

The story of Sgt. Carney reminds us that greatness can emerge from humble circumstances yet still end in death and lingering questions. Why didn't Sgt. Carney find success in California? Death itself can raise questions for many, as does Carney's by a freak accident. I still wonder why Elisha the prophet died from an illness while Elijah, his predecessor, was taken to Heaven in a whirlwind by chariots of fire.

We seldom judge a life by external measures—certainly not by how someone dies. And was Sgt. Carney less of a hero as a mail carrier? Of course not! Whether we're janitors, artists, mail carriers, politicians, professors, or hold any other perceived "rank" in society, we are known by our deeds—both good and bad. People most remembered are usually known for acts that contribute to the good of humanity, especially when such acts occur in difficult circumstances. But many good deeds are not known or are totally forgotten. Either way, God sees worthy deeds and motives and enables us to hold our heads high,[159] carrying dignity with us wherever we go. Even Abraham Lincoln referred to himself as "a man without a name, perhaps without a reason why I should have a name."[160] Yet he carried dignity with him, as well as God-given humility.

Being fondly remembered is often encouraging and a blessing to those who follow. But *not* being remembered is of no consequence. As Curé d'Ars said at the top of this chapter, "Man is in reality what he is before God; no more and no less."[161] Although Sgt. Carney was relatively unknown in his time, his reputation is now common knowledge, and "who he was before God" remains an inspiration to us all.

Foreordained to Found a New Nation
George Washington

George Washington is regarded as the father of our nation. Preceded by indigenous peoples, the English, and then colonists from other nations, Washington led the charge against British colonial domination and unfair taxes. Most of us know his armies endured great hardships and lost many battles before ultimate victory. But history books are mostly silent on the miracles that God performed in Washington's trajectory to greatness. Peter Marshal and David Manuel wrote in *The Light and the Glory* about a succession of miracles that enabled America to be born. What follows are three examples from Washington's life.

The Miracle of Survival and of Prophecy

Before the American Revolution, Washington became well-known during the French and Indian Wars. In the Battle of the Monongahela that took place July 9, 1755, Washington's regiment was decimated, and the commanding officer, General Edward Braddock, was killed. Fifteen years after that battle and five years before the American Revolution, Washington and a close friend, Dr. Craik, were exploring the Ohio River Valley. They were approached by a band of Indians and an interpreter. The tribe's elderly and venerable chief wished to have words with Washington. A ceremonial fire was kindled, and then the chief said,

> I am a chief and ruler over my tribes. My influence extends to the waters of the great lakes, and to the far blue mountains. I have traveled a long and weary path, that I might see the young warrior of the great battle. It was on the day when the white man's blood mixed with the streams of our forest, that I first beheld this chief. I called to my young men and said, "Mark yon tall and daring warrior? He is not of the red-coat tribe—he hath an Indian's wisdom, and his warriors fight as we do—himself alone is exposed. Quick, let your aim be certain, and he dies." Our rifles were leveled, rifles which, but for him, knew not how to miss...'Twas all in vain: a power mightier far

than we shielded him from harm. He cannot die in battle. I am old, and soon shall be gathered to the great council fire of my fathers in the land of shades, but ere I go, there is something that bids me speak in the voice of prophecy: Listen! The Great Spirit protects that man and guides his destinies—he will become the chief of nations, and a people yet unborn will hail him as the founder of a mighty empire.[162]

Washington's journal and other sources confirm that the twenty-three-year-old colonel "had two horses shot out from under him and four musket balls pass through his coat."[163] "There was nothing wrong with the Indians' marksmanship!"[164] Washington wrote his brother, Jack. "Death was leveling my companions on every side of me, but by the all-powerful dispensations of Providence, I have been protected."[165] Reverend Samuel Davis also wrote of Washington's action in this battle, and it was even heard of in Great Britain. A man named Lord Halifax said that Washington behaved "as bravely as if he really loved the whistling of bullets."[166]

The Miracle Escape from Certain Death or Imprisonment

After the Revolutionary War began, only one thing stood in the way of the British capturing the key territory of New York: the town of Brooklyn on the western end of Long Island. British troops needed to capture Brooklyn in order to control the Hudson River, the gateway to the north. Twenty thousand troops (higher estimates have been given) under General Howe faced eight thousand Americans under Washington. Half of the latter were not even trained!

After five days of fighting, many Americans died, and the rest were pushed to the northern tip of Brooklyn. Rather than press his advantage and overtake Washington's forces, General Howe inexplicably held back and did not fully surround them as he could have by sailing his ships into the East River. Further, Howe allowed a day and night to pass without attacking. Then another day went by quietly, except for the cold and pelting rain. A northeast wind then prevented Howe's fleet from entering the East River. Washington decided to evacuate his men in a flotilla of small boats. Fortunately, the last men to join Washington were expert oarsmen who had grown up on the shores of Massachusetts Bay. His soldiers from Salem had similar abilities. Every ounce of their strength, skill, and ingenuity was needed to maneuver the makeshift evacuating armada back and forth across the mile-long stretch of the East River.

When the sun rose, the Americans still needed three more hours to escape. But a dense fog rose off the ground and river, blanketing that whole area. It was so dense that visibility was barely six feet. When the fog lifted, the British were shocked to see the last few boats disappearing to the far shore. Firing upon the Americans did little good, for they were out of range. So "thanks to a storm, a wind, a fog, and too many human 'coincidences' to number, there still was a Continental Army!"[167]

No Bullets Could Touch Him

A victory over Hessian mercenaries in the middle of winter was a turning point in the war. "Washington's rag-tag army [had] shrunk from 25,000 at the beginning of the year to 3,335 now."[168] With other generals wanting to replace Washington and the enlistments lapsing for many of his men, he made a bold move. In the predawn hours of December 26, 1776, Washington defeated a force of one thousand Hessians in less than an hour at Trenton, New Jersey.

General Cornwallis was about to return to England to visit his ailing wife when he received orders to proceed to Trenton and engage Washington. On January 2, 1777, Washington temporarily repulsed the British. Cornwallis could have pressed on to victory, but—as with Howe—he inexplicably hesitated and delayed a full attack until the following day. By then, Washington and his men had slipped away, as their campfires burned through the night.

Marching on to Princeton to take a British garrison, Washington encountered a support column on its way to join Cornwallis. While driving the redcoats back, Washington "deliberately rode in front of his troops to within thirty yards of the British line, in order to steady his force of wavering recruits."[169] At six feet, three inches, Washington was an easy target. But miraculously, he survived volleys of fire. As the Indian chief had said, "He cannot die in battle."

Washington won other battles, but actually, he lost more than he won. And we all know the improbable outcome of the war between a "rag-tag" army of patriots and huge divisions of the then greatest army in the world. An interesting postscript is that when King George heard that Washington planned to resign his commission, he said, "If he does that, he will be the greatest man in the world."[170] When Washington's own officers asked him to proclaim himself king, Washington donned his spectacles, appearing to be frail. Tears welled up in the eyes of his officers. All talk of "kingship" ceased.[171] No wonder Robert Frost said of him "that he was one of the few in the whole history of the world who was not carried away by power."[172]

Many others have done great things by eschewing power or acclaim. After David's victory over Goliath, King Saul's son, Jonathan, was pleased to honor David above himself. "And Jonathan stripped himself of the robe that was on him and gave it to David, and his armor, and even his sword and his bow and his belt."[173] Jonathan esteemed David more highly than himself in order to please God. Philippians 2:3 exhorts us to "Consider others better than yourselves." 1 Peter 5:6 says, "Humble yourselves, therefore, under God's mighty hand, that he may lift you up in due time." God lifted up George Washington because faith in God compelled him to pursue a noble cause.

We know from Washington's own notes in the margins of *Daily Sacrifice*,[174] a small book of prayer found in the Yale Library, that he had the kind of faith that would inspire him to stake his life and the destiny of America on God's perfect providence.

Finally, here are two quotes from *Daily Sacrifice* that attest to Washington's deep faith in Christ:

Monday Morning

Direct my thoughts, words and work, wash away my sins in the immaculate blood of the lamb, and purge my heart by thy holy spirit… daily frame me more and more into the likeness of thy son Jesus Christ.

Monday Evening

Thou gav'st thy Son to die for me; and hast given me assurance of salvation, upon my repentance and sincerely endeavoring to conform my life to his holy precepts and example.[175]

One Man Saved the World from Darkness
Winston Churchill

Man of Vision

Murland Evans was a close friend of young Winston Churchill. Evans was so struck by one of sixteen-year-old Winston's statements that he immediately wrote it down. Years later, Evans shared it with Randolph Churchill, Winston's son and official biographer:

> I see further ahead than you do. I see into the future… This country will be subjected somehow to a tremendous invasion, by what means I do not know. But I tell you I shall be in command of the defenses of London, and I shall save London and England from disaster.[176]

Evans asked Winston, "Will you be a general, then, in command of the troops?"

Winston responded, "I don't know… Dreams of the future are blurred, but the main objective is clear… I repeat—London will be in danger and in the high position that I shall occupy, it will fall to me to save the Capital and save the Empire."[177]

Churchill was clearly a visionary from his childhood to his service as the prime minister that began May 10, 1940. Charles Krauthammer considered Churchill the greatest leader of the twentieth century and thought he should have been named *Time* magazine's "Person of the Century" rather than Einstein[178] because Churchill saved the world from "darkness the likes of which it had never known."[179] One Churchill biographer states, "The burdens of America's cause, as well as Britain's, fell on Churchill's shoulders."[180]

Of course, other great world leaders and millions of ordinary people (if there are such folks) sacrificed and gave their lives for victory in WWII, but "above all, victory required one man without whom the fight would have been lost at the beginning. It required Winston Churchill."[181] With his eyes wide open to the evil he'd seen in the world, Churchill knew that Hitler was a particular threat to civilization. Churchill spoke of the dangers of Hitler in the early 1930s, long before Hitler's intentions became obvious. Prior to Churchill's leadership, everyone in Great Britain had accepted that the invasion of England was inevitable.

Like Washington who rode between opposing armies firing bullets at each other, Churchill seemed heedless of danger. One of several examples of courage occurred during the Nazi blitz of England, which lasted from September 1940 to May 1941. While bombs rained from the sky, killing more than twenty thousand civilians in London alone, Churchill often walked the streets, encouraging citizens to stand strong. He knew that his destiny had already been established and nothing could derail it.

Faith and Grit Trump Others' Expectations

Although Churchill brimmed with admiration for his parents, they had little relationship with him. His father, Lord Randolph, a former Chancellor of the Exchequer (think "Secretary of the Treasury") and one of the upper crust of the British aristocracy, was especially distant and rarely spoke to Winston. His mother was an American debutante, known for her beauty as well as rumored extramarital affairs. Nonetheless, Churchill adored them both and wrote them almost daily, begging them to visit him at Harrow, the boarding school where he spent most of his younger years. All his letters went unanswered. Though privileged, Winston had what would be considered a deprived childhood.

For those who've been Downtown Abbey fans, you see that such treatment by upper-middle-class English parents was commonplace in the Edwardian culture that followed the end of the Victorian period in which Churchill was raised. In Churchill's case, the lack of normal parental nurturing that characterized these times may have actually helped create the grit and perseverance that defined his indomitable character. As Eric Miller, a businessman and friend of mine, has said of successful entrepreneurs, "The people who have the most grit and resilience usually have drivers [inner strength] that stem from the most severely negative or traumatic childhood circumstances."[182] Also, what therapists refer to as attachment theory posits that caretakers who are more avoidant of a child, in spite of resultant negative effects, can make for a more self-reliant and decisive adult.[183] Such was the case with Churchill.

Despite his emotionally deprived childhood, Churchill never saw himself as a victim. This self-possessed man was well-known for his rapier wit. He was once told that a political opponent of his—a man disliked by many for his self-righteousness—had just stopped smoking cigars. Churchill commented, "Too bad. Those cigars were his last contact with humanity."[184] On another occasion, Churchill saw this same man pass by and remarked, "There, but for the grace of God, goes God."[185]

But his wisdom excelled his wit. Long before Hitler made clear his ambition of world domination, Churchill had gotten a foreshadowing of this intention by seeing the German war machine in action during WWI. He was in several battles during his younger days but escaped death and was never seriously wounded. "Churchill knew where the ultimate outcome of the struggle rested—in the hands of God. This, as much as anything, distinguished Churchill's confidence from Hitler's arrogance."[186]

The Least Likely to Succeed

Even after being elected to the House of Commons and following his father's footsteps into the halls of power, Churchill was ridiculed as the least likely member of Parliament to become prime minister. He didn't seem "dignified" and was regarded as just a "common man." Churchill was laughed at by many fellow politicians for not admiring Hitler's "energy." He was hated by his own party, the opposition party, *and* the press, which made him an unlikely candidate to build the bulwark against what could have become centuries of darkness around the world!

Such ridicule must have reminded him of his father's recurring words of disdain. For example, when Churchill's father encouraged him to join the military, Churchill was filled with pride that almost compensated for his father's aloofness. Churchill later discovered that his father advocated for the military because he thought his son was "not clever enough to go to the bar."[187] Then, after Winston graduated from the military institute at Sandhurst, his father lambasted him for not passing a test to enter the infantry, saying this "demonstrated beyond refutation your slovenly, happy-go-lucky, harum-scarum style of work."[188] Winston entered the cavalry. That meant he would fight from horses and not be carried around in vehicles.

As the Twig Is Bent

Alexander Pope said that "as the twig is bent the tree's inclined."[189] Winston was "bent" from childhood toward faith in God. His nanny, Elizabeth Everest, helped him to overcome the negative effects of parental neglect, capitalize on how the neglect could work for good, and discover his deep faith, which became the bedrock of his character. Everest accompanied him to Harrow. She helped transform him into more than just the "bulldog" and man of wisdom that history records. They began each morning with prayer and the reading of Scripture. Churchill memorized Scripture and adopted the moral principles of the Bible.[190] He was forever thankful for the woman he considered his closest companion. Her picture is displayed to this day in the study of Chartwell, his landmark home in the southeast county of Kent.

> Her role in the formation of Churchill's worldview was still evident later in his life when he often paraphrased or quoted Bible passages in his speeches. Even in seasons of doubt, he instinctively saw through eyes formed with a biblical outlook. This is why he could inspire hope, call for strength and faith, and most importantly, grasp the true meaning of Nazism and its threat to civilization.[191]

With the "tree" so inclined to God and England, Churchill held forth against his naïve English contemporaries and their political leaders. He especially defied Neville Chamberlain, who tried to make peace with Hitler. But as a man of grace, Churchill later gave Chamberlain a cabinet position, and when Chamberlain died only one year after Churchill became the prime minister, Churchill wept openly and honored him at the memorial service for his peace-loving nature.

Of course, Churchill was finally vindicated over political rivals who wanted to appease Hitler and would have surrendered to him. His well-known determination and bravery rallied all his countrymen. And let's not forget how God mightily used Elizabeth Everest to help develop Churchill's character and fulfill his destiny. Everest's Heavenly reward is surely as great as Churchill's!

The Delayed Pilgrims
Heroes from the Ashes of Eastern Europe

By the end of WWII, many refugees were desperate to escape the Russian army that was advancing on Eastern Europe. My parents ended up housing a couple who were the first of four thousand people to be evacuated by the Methodist Church from Eastern Europe to the United States. They began their new American life in the parsonage of Elm Park Methodist, where our family lived.

Gregor Chandochin, twenty-seven, was from Ukraine, and his wife, nineteen-year-old Dorothea, was from Bavaria. After a ten-day voyage in 1951 from Bremerhaven, Germany, they were given $2 apiece in New York. They arrived at Scranton on the midnight train. As Greek Orthodox believers, they were among the "Delayed Pilgrims" or "DPs" who were saved from the Russian threat. The Chandochins were tired yet relieved to be safe in America. *The Scranton Tribune* reported, "They can't go back unless they want to be liquidated."[192] I still have the newspaper article with a picture of my parents, the Chandochins, and baby Devereaux. At first, the Chandochins and my parents communicated by gestures but soon discovered they could converse in German.

Gregor's parents had been "swallowed up behind the Iron Curtain,"[193] and he never saw them again. Dorothea's father was killed in the war, and she heard that her mother had died in a hospital. Whether she saw her forty-year-old brother again, I never heard. Such is the story of but one couple out of tens of millions of people who suffered Hitler's brutality, followed by the Russian occupation of most Eastern European countries and all three Baltic States.

The good news is that many people like the Chandochins overcame great odds and contributed to America's greatness as well as to their own success. Gregor was a skilled mechanic, using this skill to save himself from execution by working in a slave labor camp when he was too young to fight. Gregor and Dorothea eventually made their home in Detroit. In more recent years, I was able to locate a daughter of theirs and sent her a copy of *The Scranton Tribune* article, which she was grateful to receive.

Reflections on the Peaceful Life

God's destiny for your life is far bigger than any harm that might befall you. As with Abraham of the Old Testament who was told by God that he would be the father of God's chosen nation of Israel, Carney, Washington, Churchill, and the Chandochins gained an eternal perspective on this life as well as eternity itself. They all had many setbacks and suffered greatly. But all these heroes had assurance they would receive an inheritance here on Earth and then enter "the city with foundations, whose architect and builder is God."[194] You can have the same assurance! With righteous zeal for a noble cause, neither your mission on Earth, nor your eternal inheritance can ever be blocked!

Endnotes

[151] Lisa D. Healy, "Heroes by Choice," "Coast Guard Stories," "Jack's Joint," accessed 12/23/2017, http://www.jacksjoint.com/heroics.htm.

[152] Unknown employee at the Coast Guard Station, Cape Charles, interview by author, December 19, 2017. Author could not find a way to get in touch with Healy.

[153] John Wesley, *John Wesley's Journal, Abridged Edition* (London: The Epworth Press: London, 1735, 1903) October, Fri. 31, 8. Note: Author's father accompanied coasties who attended his student church in Hull, Massachusetts, out to sea. This quote is underlined in his copy of Wesley's journal.

[154] "History Net," "William H. Carney: 54th Massachusetts Soldier and First Black U.S. Medal of Honor Recipient," accessed 12/13/2020, http://www.historynet.com/william-h-carney-54th-massachusetts-soldier-and-first-black-us-medal-of-honor-recipient.htm.

[155] Katie Lange, US Army, "Meet Sgt. William Carney: The First African-American Medal of Honor Recipient," accessed 12/13/2020, https://www.army.mil/article/181896.

[156] Ibid.

[157] Tyler Durden, "First Black Medal of Honor Recipient's Act of Defiance': He Never Let The Flag Touch The Ground," *Zero Hedge*, September 24, 2017, accessed 12/12/2020, http://www.zerohedge.com/news/2017-09-24/first-black-medal-honor-recipients-act-defiance-he-never-let-flag-touch-ground.

[158] Ibid.

[159] Psalm 3:3, Leviticus 26:13.

[160] David Donald, *Lincoln* (New York, London, Toronto, Sydney: Simon & Schuster Paperbacks, 1995), 275.

[161] John Marie Vianney (Curé d'Ars was a designation of Vianney's position as the pastor of Ars, France, nineteenth century), cited in William Kelly, *Youth before God,* adapted from French and German texts by Lelotte & Pereira (Westminster & Maryland: The Newman Press, 1958), 52. Author's father gave him this book on his father's fifty-third birthday.

[162] Peter Marshall and David Manuel, *The Light and the Glory* (Old Tappan, NJ: Power Books, 1977), 285–286. Marshall and Manuel state that this incident is confirmed by George Bancroft, *History of the United States of America, from the Discovery of the American Continent* (Boston: Little, Brown, and Company, 1854–1878). See numerous websites that report this same story.

[163] Kistler, *This Nation*, 54, cited by Marshall and Manuel, 286.

[164] Marshall and Manuel, 286.

[165] George Washington, George Bancroft (*History, IV*, 190), cited in Marshall and Manuel, 286.

[166] Marshall and Manuel, quoting Samuel Davies, a Virginia clergyman (no reference cited), 286.

[167] Ibid., 313–315.
[168] Robert E. Buxbaum, "You are Cornwallis, Dec 29, 1776. What should you do?", REB Research Blog, accessed 11/28/2019, http://www.rebresearch.com/blog/you-are-cornwallis-1776/.
[169] Marshall and Manuel, 318.
[170] Accessed 11/23/2017, http://althouse.blogspot.com/2007/08/if-he-does-thathe-will-be-greatest-man.html and many other internet sites.
[171] Ibid.
[172] Robert Frost, "Brainy Quote," "Robert Frost Quotes," accessed 11/23/2019, https://www.brainyquote.com/quotes/robert_frost_151822.
[173] 1 Samuel 18:4.
[174] George Washington, *Small Book of Prayers*, cited in Marshal and Manuel, 284.
[175] *George Washington's Prayer Book*, "Classic Prayer Texts," 23–28, accessed 3/18/2019, http://prayer1.org/home/409/classic-prayer-text/george-washingtons-prayer-book/. Some pages from this prayer book may have been lost.
[176] Jonathan Sandys and Wallace Henley, *God and Churchill* (Carol Stream, Illinois: Tyndale Momentum, 2015), 4.
[177] Ibid.
[178] Charles Krauthammer, "Winston Churchill: The Indispensable Man," from *Things That Matter* (New York: Crown Publishing Group, 2013), 27.
[179] Ibid., 28.
[180] Martin Gilbert, *Churchill: A Life* (New York: An Owl Book: Henry Holt and Company, 1991), 816.
[181] Krauthammer, "Winston Churchill: The Indispensable Man," 29.
[182] Eric Miller, *The Owner's Compass* (2017), 38–39.
[183] Peter Lovenheim, *The Attachment Effect* (New York, New York: TarcherPerigee, 2018), 21.
[184] Winston Churchill, cited by Os Guinness, *The Call: Finding and Fulfilling God's Purpose for Your Life* (Nashville, Tennessee: W Publishing, 1998, 2003, 2018), 165.
[185] Winston Churchill, cited by Os Guinness, *The Call: Finding and Fulfilling God's Purpose for Your Life.*
[186] Sandys and Henley, *God and Churchill*, 95.
[187] Ibid., 11.
[188] Ibid., 12.
[189] Alexander Pope, "Oxford Reference," accessed 1/14/2017, http://www.oxfordreference.com/view/10.1093/oi/authority.20110803110350386.
[190] Sandys and Henley, Ibid., 8.
[191] Ibid.
[192] Gordon Williams, "DPs Get Temporary Haven at Parsonage," *Scranton Tribune*, 1951, day unknown.
[193] Gordon Williams.
[194] Hebrews 11:10.

8

HEROES BY CHOICE II

When Jesus calls a person, He bids him come and die.
—Dietrich Bonhoeffer

Paying the Ultimate Price
Dietrich Bonhoeffer

Dietrich Bonhoeffer was a German pastor and theologian who was hung—at the personal order of Hitler—just days before his concentration camp was liberated by American soldiers. In the early 1930s, Bonhoeffer attended Union Theological Seminary on the upper west side of New York City where he studied under Reinhold Niebuhr. I was blessed to walk the same gothic halls for two years. I regret not giving more time to my studies and less time to marijuana and alcohol. But I later made up for this profligacy at Grace Bible College (mentioned in chapter 6).

Bonhoeffer, of course, became one of Union's most celebrated students. His most well-known work, *The Cost of Discipleship*, stresses that, although eternal life is a gift of grace through faith, grace is not cheap. Bonhoeffer coined the concept of "cheap grace," which is grace that some believers take for granted, believing in Christ while not truly living for Him. This is the grace that people grant themselves without believing basic tenets of Christian faith, such as the atonement for sin by Christ's death on the cross—grace without letting Christ live in and through them. Bonhoeffer is also well known for his books *Ethics* and *Letters and Papers from Prison.*

While attending Union, Bonhoeffer was especially impressed by the Abyssinian Baptist Church, a black church in nearby Harlem where he worshipped on Sundays. There he experienced passionate worship unlike any he had known before, with "clapping, shouting, and dancing"![195] Bonhoeffer wished that believers in Germany could learn to worship God with anything close to that deep fervency and reverence.

Though Bonhoeffer was disappointed in Union's lack of emphasis on the inerrancy of Scripture and the importance of a personal relationship with the risen Christ, he was impressed by the professors' academic rigor and Union's emphasis on ethics and practical Christianity. But the attraction to Union or the United States was not enough to keep him in New York, so he returned to Germany to join in solidarity with other believing pastors against Hitler.

As a lecturer at Berlin University, he became the most prominent leader of the Confessing Church (composed of virtuous Christians, spoken of in chapter 6). Two days after Hitler fully seized power, Bonhoeffer denounced him in a radio broadcast. He clearly saw what Churchill saw: that Hitler was a ruthless dictator. As Churchill did, Bonhoeffer said it out loud; but before he could finish the broadcast, he was mysteriously disconnected from the airways.

After working with pastors who were true disciples of Christ and were not yet imprisoned, Bonhoeffer had a brief hiatus in England. Theodor Heckel, a bishop of the Reich Church, visited him and other German pastors there in 1934. Heckel's mission was to set the "rebellious" German pastors straight. Speaking at London's St. George Church, Heckel essentially advocated purging anything related to Judaism and morality from the Old Testament. His bald heresy was most disturbing to these members of the Confessing Church. Bonhoeffer denounced Heckel and the false pastors of the Reich Church who willingly hung swastikas from their pulpits. He spoke boldly against all that the heretical church stood for. "We German pastors in England," he said, "are not willing to be party to heresy… We would rather split away than risk our salvation."[196]

Heckel made sure that an official record was made of Bonhoeffer's emphatic resistance.

Bonhoeffer's conscience would not allow him to remain in England, so he returned to Germany. Working undercover within the German government in order to bring it down, he helped his own sister escape Germany. And as part of the German resistance, he participated in a still-controversial plot to assassinate Hitler. The actual attempt took place soon after Bonhoeffer was engaged to be married. When his part in the plot was discovered, he was arrested by the Gestapo and imprisoned. As a conspirator condemned to death, Bonhoeffer demonstrated inner contentment and grace that baffled even his guards, and he was a constant encouragement to his fellow prisoners.

Bonhoeffer wasn't certain his participation in the assassination attempt was the right thing to do. He "never implied that the assassin and his accomplices were not guilty, that they weren't under the judgment of God. Indeed, they were to be considered 'bloody men,' like King David in the Bible."[197] Paying the ultimate price, he exemplified that grace, indeed, is not cheap. God gave him grace to live a righteous life, and whether the attempt to assassinate Hitler was right or wrong, the cost to Bonhoeffer was to lose his life by the hand of evil. Bonhoeffer walked to the gallows with evident peace. As he faced execution, he said, "This is the end—for me, the beginning of life."[198]

A Builder for Eternity
Dr. Ben Carson[199]

When eight-year-old Ben Carson's mother told him and his brother, Curtis, that their father was never coming home again, it was a profoundly sad day for the boys. Though Ben had seen little of him, his father was a source of encouragement, sometimes taking him and Curtis on Sunday afternoon visits to another family and their children. Seemingly a responsible member of the community, Ben's father worked at the local Cadillac plant and preached in a small Baptist church on Sundays. But appearances were deceiving. As it turned out, the family that Curtis and Ben visited was their father's *literal* other family. As if living in a poor section of Detroit with rats that were bigger than cats in the backyard wasn't bad enough, Ben's father abandoned his mother, Curtis, and him. Ben's future wasn't looking good.

Another hindrance to Ben's personal growth was his extreme anger problem. He once even drew a knife on a fellow student and thrust it at his stomach. Fortunately, the knife hit a belt buckle and no harm was done. Realizing the potential seriousness of his violent act, Ben went home and cried and prayed. Not long after this, Ben was in church and listened carefully to the sermon. The hymn that he remembers was "He Hideth My Soul." Ben took the song's message to heart and concluded, "That's exactly what I should do—get sheltered in the cleft of the rock." He began to read the book of Proverbs, a book in the Bible that emphasizes honorable behavior and character and speaks bluntly of the consequences of living without a moral compass.

Ben and Curtis later concluded life was actually easier without their father around. While their father had talked much of material things and "looking good," their mother, Sonya, often asked them, "What did you learn in school today?" Sonya worked more than one job, including as a maid to wealthy families. By carefully observing the lives of her employers, Sonya grasped the importance of education even though she was uneducated.

Acting on what she'd witnessed, Sonya returned from work one day and announced that each week, Ben and Curtis could only watch three television shows and had to submit two book reports to her. Her new demands rocked Ben's world since he regarded himself as the dumbest guy in his fifth-grade class. But Sonya was committed to seeing her boys rise above the kind of lives their environment would lead them into. The boys didn't know that their mother could barely read (although she later learned to read quite well)!

The good news is that Ben and Curtis quickly developed a hunger for learning and began going to the public library every Saturday. Ben especially liked to learn about minerals. One day in class, the teacher held up a large, black stone and asked the class what it was.

Ben's was the only hand that was raised. "Obsidian," Ben answered and then explained lava, and how obsidian was formed when lava hit water. The class was stunned. So was Ben! Suddenly, the dumbest guy in the class sounded like the smartest! The only reason Ben later graduated third in his high school class, instead of first, was that in his sophomore year, he'd been more occupied with wearing name-brand clothes than his studies. One can't help wondering if that temporary preoccupation wasn't the last vestige of his father's influence.

Ben's diligence opened the door to Yale University on a full scholarship. As he looked around the campus and met fellow students, Ben was surprised by how many people appeared smarter than him (!), even though his IQ was undoubtedly on the high end.

Ben had decided when he was still a youngster that he wanted to become a doctor. However, one thing at Yale seemed to stand in his way: a chemistry test. The night before the test, he simply wasn't "getting it." He studied until he could stay awake no longer. He had to pass this test to get into medical school, and he fell asleep with only the barest grasp of concepts he'd need to understand the next day. Then he had a dream.

In his dream, he saw chemistry problems written on a black-board. Along with the problems were the real answers. When he went to take the test the next day, the test questions were precisely the ones he'd dreamt about! Of course, he passed the course and went on to medical school at the University of Michigan. Oh, and Dr. Carson would probably say the very *best* thing that came from his time at Yale was meeting a beautiful violinist who shared his love for classical music. Her name was Candy, and she became his wife.

After graduating from medical school, Ben was accepted into an internship, then residency, at Johns Hopkins Hospital. Fortunately, his vulnerability to anger had subsided as he continued to grow in his relationship with the Lord. During his surgical residency at the hospital, a fellow resident who was prejudiced against Blacks pushed Ben to the limit. But with some difficulty, Carson maintained an attitude of grace and forgiveness. He was finally able to conquer the anger that had been a major weakness of his in the past. Of course, if he had injured that boy from way back with his knife, we likely

GOD IS IN THE CRAZY

never would have heard of Dr. Ben Carson, who later thanked God for that belt buckle!

During his internship at Johns Hopkins, Dr. Carson appeared on one of the hospital floors in his scrubs. Thinking that he was an orderly because of his skin color, the prejudiced unit nurses told him they didn't need patient transport right then. Another time, while wearing his white coat, he was told that there was no need then for respiratory therapy on that unit. In both instances, the nurses apologized when they saw his name tag with "M.D." on it.

But prejudice continued. One family, after meeting Carson, refused to allow him to perform surgery on their son. The department chief invited the family to go to a different hospital, but they relented and let Dr. Carson operate. The surgery went well. Clearly, Dr. Carson didn't view himself as a "victim" of the slums of his youth or of his skin color. He continued to patiently overcome obstacles and challenges to God's plans for his life.

Some years after his training, Dr. Carson was the first pediatric neurosurgeon in the world to separate Siamese twins conjoined at the head. He also made the news as the first to successfully perform a hemispherectomy (removal of half of the cerebrum) for a child whose severe and incessant seizures would not respond to any other treatment. Dr. Carson also performed the first successful neurosurgical procedure on a fetus inside its mother's womb.[200]

After becoming, perhaps, the world's pre-eminent pediatric neurosurgeon, his autobiography, *Gifted Hands*,[201] was made into a movie starring Cuba Gooding Jr. I saw it soon after its release in 2010 and later eagerly read the book twice. Some of my favorite books are by physicians, including neurosurgeons, and they agree with Dr. Carson that it's a gift to be able to understand the brain in three dimensions.

Dr. Carson spoke at a Presidential Prayer Breakfast in 2013 (he never speaks from notes), and by 2015 he was persuaded by many of his admirers—who saw the replays of his speech on the news—to run for president in 2016. For months, the polls had him among the leading candidates. We know who finally won, but Dr. Carson was appointed Secretary of Housing and Urban Development. One can hardly imagine a better choice to improve urban development than a man who grew up in a ghetto and was committed to making inner cities better places to live and grow up.

Most of us have listened to Dr. Carson or read his writings. We've seen excerpts from speeches, watched presidential debates, or seen interviews on the news. Obviously, he's a soft-spoken and humble man, which is reflected in a favorite poem of his. He begins chapter 7 of his book *Think Big* with a poem by R.L. Sharpe titled "A Bag of Tools." It speaks of those who build their lives for eternity:

> Isn't it strange
> That princes and kings
> And clowns that caper
> In sawdust rings,
> And common people
> Like you and me
> Are builders for eternity?
>
> Each is given a bag of tools,
> A shapeless mass,
> A book of rules;
> And each must make—
> Ere life is flown—
> A stumbling block
> Or a steppingstone. (R.L. Sharpe[202])

Giving thanks to his mother and to God, Ben Carson—who once thought himself the dumbest kid in the fifth grade—made stepping-stones out of his bag of tools, life's book of rules, and the rubble of his growing-up years. Scripture says that God looks upon the lowly. That was a great day when God lifted up the lowly Ben Carson from the streets of Detroit. I'm sure Dr. Carson would want us to know that the lowliest among us can be builders for eternity, realizing destinies of impacting the world for the good of all and for His kingdom.

The Most-Mobbed Man in the United States
Theodore Weld, Abolitionist[203]

Few have heard of Theodore Weld, but his influence in abolishing slavery is historic. "Measured by his influence, Weld was not only the greatest of the abolitionists; he was also one of the greatest figures of his time."[204] Poet Carl Sandburg called Weld "a storm bird in the making of American history."[205]

Other contemporaries agreed with these opinions. Frederick Douglass stated that "one of Weld's books, *American Slavery As It Is*, was as influential in the earlier period of the antislavery movement as Harriet Beecher Stowe's *Uncle Tom's Cabin* was in a later day."[206] In fact, Weld was used by God to convert Stowe to the Christian faith, and her classic is partly based on his text.[207] *American Slavery As It Is: Testimony of a Thousand Witnesses* records unspeakable cruelty to slaves. No one can read these accounts and not feel outraged by the acts of murderous bigots. I have the book, but I can't bear to read more than a few stories.

Theodore Weld has gone largely unnoticed in the accounts of the antislavery movement. This anonymity was by his choice.

> Weld would never accept an office of authority or honor in any antislavery organization. He refused to speak at antislavery conventions or anniversaries, or even attend them if he could avoid it. He shunned the cities, and chose to labor in the country districts, where newspapers were few, and his activities were seldom reported except by abolition journals. His writings were published anonymously, and he would seldom allow the content of his speeches or his letters from the field to appear in print at all.[208]

The primary reason we've heard of Weld is that Gilbert H. Barnes, a student of the antislavery movement, discovered multiple references to him in other documents, establishing him as an unsung hero in the elimination of slavery in America. After tracing clues further, Barnes discovered a trunkful of letters in a farmhouse attic near Allston, Massachusetts. These letters proved that the primary impetus for the antislavery movement was by a group in New York City whose prime mover and inspiration was Weld.

Talk about downward mobility! Weld tried to keep his legacy hidden in a trunk rather than seek recognition for it! And now his humility has become a crown. His passion for the righteous cause that God inspired him to champion was its own reward.

Our snapshot of Weld's life and influence begins with his near-drowning in Alum Creek, barely a mile from where I grew up in Bexley, Ohio. As the carriage he was riding in began to cross the creek, which was at flood stage during a thunderstorm, the vehicle tipped over and was swept downstream. Weld rose from the muddy water, only to be kicked back under by a frantic horse's hoof. He came up for air and was kicked yet again by a flailing hoof. He was finally able to grab hold of a tree branch and pull himself ashore. He called for help amid the din of pounding rain, expecting no response. But three men in a solitary log cabin nearby heard his cries of distress.

Weld already thought of himself as an instrument of God, and this divine deliverance left him with an added sense of special protection and an "indebtedness to God that was beyond his power to ever fully repay."[209]

Weld was accident-prone during childhood, breaking many bones, and was slovenly and unkempt in manner as an adult. His memory was bad, especially for people's names. He even had trouble remembering the month or season. Weld was known for his "severe" face that he referred to as a "streak of lightning."[210] One person said he looked like a pirate. Weld recalled how a four-year-old girl took one look at him and ran screaming to her mother!

Weld had other quirks that might have been thought to disqualify him from a productive life. He liked to go deep into the woods and childishly jump, hop, and scream. In the mornings, he would plunge his head into a bucket of cold water half a dozen times then allow his hair to "straggle in all directions like the quills of a porcupine."[211]

Obviously, Weld had severe "grace-getting" limitations for which he needed God's power to overcome. Weld is yet another example of how God chooses the weak and humble people of the world to confound the wise and shame the strong. He seemed to be an especially unlikely candidate to do God's work! Weld was therefore just the kind of man God might choose for a historic task—one that would glorify God. After all, what could this very unusual and eccentric man possibly do in his own strength?

With such handicaps, one might not expect that "to know him was to feel the warmth of his benignity, to sense his charm, to yield to his persuasiveness. His voice was rich, full, mellow; his presence breathed an almost godlike power." After meeting him, the sister of a prominent poet said, "His smile has been haunting me…ever since he left us."[212]

His father and grandfather were pastors who infused in him a strong reliance on biblical principles and a hatred of sin. "Moral courage was Weld's by cultural inheritance."[213] But given his many quirks, as one trained in psychology, I wonder how we might "diagnose" him today!

As an adolescent, he earned enough money from managing his father's one-hundred-acre farm to attend what is now Phillips Andover Academy. But after two years, he had to drop out because of failing eyesight. Chalk up *another* limitation!

Despite his memory problems, he lectured for three years on mnemonics, a tool to improve memory (without notes, of course!). Along with compelling subject matter, he had power with words and a presence that drew large audiences. His riveting messages were surely inversely commensurate with his great weakness in the memory department!

After becoming an admirer of evangelist Charles Finney, Weld helped found Lane Theological Seminary in Cincinnati, Ohio, in 1833 where he also became a student. After shifting his attention from there to the cause of abolishing slavery, "angry reactions reached a point that Weld eventually was nicknamed 'the most-mobbed man in the United States.'"[214] His contemporaries, many known as "Weld's crusaders,"[215] were also terrorized and insulted. As I consider how

John Wesley and his early Methodist followers were also mobbed, many barely escaping death, this thought occurs to me: Show me a righteous man in a groundswell of ignorance and I'll show you an angry mob.

Weld suspended his studies in 1834 to represent the American Anti-Slavery Society, which he also helped found. Weld ceased lecturing after he lost his voice in 1836 and began editing books and pamphlets for the Society. He married Angelina Grimke in 1838. She became an almost equally prominent spokesperson for the cause of abolition and an advocate for women's rights. From 1836 to 1840, Weld served as editor of *The Emancipator*. And it was in 1839 from a farm with Angelina and her sister that he published *American Slavery As It Is: Testimony of a Thousand Witnesses*.

In 1854, Weld helped establish a school, the Raritan Bay Union at Eagleswood in Perth Amboy, New Jersey. The school accepted students of all races and both sexes.[216] In 1864, he moved to Hyde Park, New York, where he helped open another school in Lexington dedicated to the same progressive principles.

Most noteworthy is that despite his near drowning, poor memory, odd behavior in the woods, poor eyesight, abuse by angry mobs with "nails, eggs and stones,"[217] and finally the loss of his voice and his legacy hidden in a trunk—Weld's influence only increased.

Other men and women who have demonstrated abundant righteousness and accomplished great things have tended to suffer extreme limitations and unfavorable circumstances. As alluded to in Dr. Carson's story, God does lift the lowly to positions of influence so that His light might shine through them. Certainly, the world is a better place for this man's difficult life that elevated the dignity of all men and women.

Living for a Higher Cause
James Garfield

Consider one more historical figure who regarded a noble cause to be of greater importance than his own life: On April 15, 1865, the day of Abraham Lincoln's death, a relatively unknown congressman named James Garfield stilled a mob of fifty thousand people gathered in the area we now know as Wall Street. The rabble was intent upon destroying the offices of the World, a newspaper said to sympathize with the South. Two people already lay dead in the street.

This is what Garfield was recalled to shout:

> Fellow citizens! Clouds and darkness are round about Him [God]! His pavilion is dark waters and thick clouds of the skies! Justice and judgment are the establishment of His throne! Mercy and truth shall go before His face! Fellow citizens! God reigns, and the government at Washington still lives![218]

These were stirring and anointed words. Lincoln had lived for a high cause: It was for God's kingdom and for the rightful government of free people to unite for the good of all people. As the volatile mob caught that vision, rationality and hope stilled the tumult.

Sixteen years later—on July 17, 1881—President James Garfield was also slain by an assassin's bullet. Before dying, he asked for a piece of paper and wrote his name followed by *strangulatus pro republica*, which meant "tortured for the republic." No wonder Garfield had spoken so eloquently years earlier. He too esteemed a noble cause higher than personal ambition.

When I enter the counseling center, I often prepare my heart by telling myself, "My life is not my own." Should any of us do less in any of our endeavors? Most of us will never be known heroes like those I've spoken of. My highest goal is to let Christ live in me, and through His power to imitate Him. Whether I'm perceived by others as a hero is not important. What matters is God's opinion of me and my actions—and we are all equally valuable to Him.

Heroes Epilogue

When I consider well-known war heroes as well as unsung soldiers and civilians who have perished, I wonder, "How many of them had other incredible gifts that could have benefitted humanity?" Those who die young, long before they have a chance to fulfill all their dreams, do not escape God's notice. God knows the measureless peace and fulfillment that awaits believers beyond our brief earthly lives. He also knows that eternity is forever! Who knows what gifts any of us will further develop or newly acquire in eternity? Bonhoeffer was a skillful musician. Perhaps we'll find him making music when we join him someday!

I think especially about anyone whose life was cut short. Someone once said that the cure for cancer was probably extinguished in the Holocaust. Who can comprehend such senseless loss? But God sees the measureless impact of all inhabitants of Heaven. Who can comprehend the eternal gain? Even the gain of the prayers of the dying?

In this fallen world, God allows death to cast its dark shadow until Christ returns to judge the living and the dead and to establish a new Heaven and a new Earth.[219] Till then, God can keep us from living unproductive lives and help us make our lives count. He is even able to give us joy in endless empty days. The author of the book of Hebrews says that God has placed the world under Christ's authority, but we don't presently see that happening…BUT WE SEE JESUS. In seeing Him, we know God is with us.

In Sgt. Carney's case, he survived to keep contributing to society as a humble letter-carrier. He inspires us all to perform any service that's valuable to humanity and to do it with excellence and all our might. Sgt. Carney did not seek his own glory. He imitated Jesus, who came to serve and served with all his might, even in washing the feet of his disciples.

Washington survived miraculously, more than once, to become the first president of the greatest country in history. The Declaration of Independence and our Constitution have become a beacon for all who want to live in freedom and determine what their government will look like. Though Washington did not sign the Declaration because he was in New York preparing to defend against the English, he was the only man who could have presided over the 1787 Constitutional Convention of fifty-five state delegates. It was recorded that:

> In those four months [of the convention], Washington watched over the debates from a chair that had a sun painted on the back of it. Benjamin Franklin was unsure during the convention if the sun was rising or setting. As the constitution was being signed, Franklin was famously quoted as saying, "I have the happiness to know that it is a rising and not a setting sun."[220]

As with Washington, Churchill helped steer the world on a course of righteousness. While the United States seemingly didn't understand that Russia could quickly morph from our ally during the war to become our enemy, Churchill warned in his famous "Iron Curtain" speech in 1946 that this is exactly what would happen: We needed to prepare for the Cold War. He saw that Russia was preparing to draw an iron curtain down around Eastern Europe. Just as he'd spoken prophetically of Nazi ambitions to dominate the world, he was equally emphatic about similar intentions of Communist Russia. With such a legacy, it's little wonder that a half-smoked Churchill cigar recently sold for $12,000![221]

Bonhoeffer didn't live as long as others in this chapter. But as with us all, "The measure of life is not its duration, but its donation."[222] Bonhoeffer's donation has an ever-broadening impact in that his faith, character, and life still inspire us. His vision of an ecumenical church burned in the hearts of many; it was also a passion of my father, who gave his best efforts to unite churches of different denominations, as I referred to earlier in "Nil Sine Numine." This vision was never to come to fruition, and in our time, it seems less likely than ever to succeed. But Bonhoeffer never gave up his desire to see God's kingdom established on Earth. To that end, he never stopped exhorting all true Christians of Germany to fight evil in all forms. Nor did he stop doing all the good he could in Christ's name.

Heroes like those I've described are usually pursued by plagues of folly, be they words that "lie in wait for blood,"[223] overt smear campaigns, or attempts on their lives that sometimes succeed, as with Lincoln and Garfield. They live for a cause higher than their own interests, usually knowing the cost will be high. As a call to true believers, Bonhoeffer said, "When Jesus calls a person, He bids him come and die."[224] The grace God extends to all people came at the cost of the death of His Son, Jesus Christ. Therefore, God desires our all—ourselves as a worthy offering.

Many people of integrity illustrate what we can call the principle of exponential opposition: the more good you plan to do, the more you'll be attacked. The more good you actually do, the more you'll be attacked more. Through perseverance, you will either finally breakthrough or God will make it clear that you've fulfilled your mission, and He will be pleased. Jesus began his ministry by reading from Isaiah and announcing the good news of His coming. For speaking of God's good plans, a crowd attempted to throw him off a cliff. When He began performing miracles, the opposition increased exponentially, ending in His crucifixion and breakthrough resurrection. He completed His mission, and God was pleased!

Wherever God Has You, Endure There for One More Moment

Once, while taking a break from writing, my wife and I shared some great Chinese takeout. I resumed writing, and within minutes, my wife returned to my study and read me her fortune cookie message. I searched for the quote on the internet, and it came up immediately. It was a quote by George F. Kennan: "Heroism is endurance for one moment more."[225] As I ponder what we've learned in these two heroes' chapters, besides what's been mentioned, I see another common thread: These heroes lived what they believed when times were the toughest. They kept enduring for one moment more—over and over. We can do the same. When we feel we just don't matter, it's good to respect God's refining process to prepare us for something that will best suit His purposes. As Alicia Britt Chole said, most of us will endure more than one season of insignificance, but they will pass—because "God changes times and seasons."[226]

George Washington became our country's first president, was hailed as a truly great man, and was urged to make himself king. David in the Old Testament was promoted from shepherd to king. Jonathan, the son of King Saul, had been in line as the next king of Israel. He and David became dear friends, and what mattered most to Jonathan was who he was before God. That's why he didn't hold onto his right to inherit the throne from his father. Jonathan certainly received rewards in Heaven greater than any throne.

Chapters 7 and 8 presented a few intentional heroes. Surely, in the course of world history, there have been multitudes like them who would encourage us not to demand our rights but to yield to God's will to become all that He intends us to be, fighting for causes He equips us to fight, and finding joy in lives lived with reckless abandon.

Reflections on the Peaceful Life

All our heroes by choice were passionate about their mission. We know Washington was passionate about establishing a new nation founded on principles of justice and God-given individual rights. But many of his short-term goals weren't achieved, and he lost important battles. Despite battles you have lost, keep your "eyes on the prize" and on your mission! Goals are important, but it's good to ask yourself, "What is my mission that's bigger than my next goal?" Keep looking to that. Then, when you reach your next goal, you'll never stop fulfilling your mission. There will always be a next goal. My mission is to encourage people to faith in Christ. Every goal fulfills that mission. What's yours? And don't worry about your legacy. Tell people about Jesus's legacy and God will take care of yours as you follow His example…even if you leave it hidden in a trunk like Theodore Weld did!

Endnotes

195 Michael Van Dyke, *The Story of Dietrich Bonhoeffer* (Uhrichsville: Ohio: Barbour Publishing, Inc.), 53.

196 Michael Van Dyke, 90.

197 Ibid., 181.

198 Ibid., 205.

199 Ben Carson, *Gifted Hands: The Ben Carson Story* (Grand Rapids, Michigan: Zondervan, 1990). This portion of *God Is in the Crazy (with Extraordinary Miracles and Wisdom for a Peaceful Life)* is derived from this book by Carson; from the movie, *Gifted Hands*; from television interviews of Carson; and from numerous internet sites such as Biography.com, "Ben Carson," accessed 3/26/2019, https://www.biography.com/people/ben-carson-475422.

200 Wikipedia: The Free Encyclopedia, "Ben Carson," accessed 12/13/2020, https://en.wikipedia.org/wiki/Ben_Carson.

201 Ben Carson, *Gifted Hands: The Ben Carson Story.*

202 R.L. Sharpe, cited in Ben Carson, *Think Big* (Grand Rapids, Michigan: Zondervan, 1992), 99. Also, see PoetryNook.com, "Poetry for Every Occasion," "A Bag of Tools," accessed 3/26/19, https://www.poetrynook.com/poem/bag-tools. Little is known about R.L. Sharpe or the publication date, and no sources are referenced in *Think Big*, PoetryNook.com, other internet sites, or YouTube readings of the poem. Edward Burra states the publication date is likely 1890, "Redtree Times," accessed 12/12/2020, https://redtreetimes.com/2015/10/20/bag-of-tools/.

203 Benjamin Thomas, *Theodore Weld: Crusader for Freedom* (New Brunswick, New Jersey: Rutgers University Press, 1950). Most information from this portion of *God Is in the Crazy (with Extraordinary Miracles and Wisdom for a Peaceful Life)* is obtained from Thomas's book.

204 *Dictionary of American Biography*, cited in Benjamin Thomas, *Theodore Weld: Crusader for Freedom* (New Brunswick, New Jersey: Rutgers University Press, 1950), v.

205 Thomas, *Theodore Weld: Crusader for Freedom.* The quote is a portion of Sandburg's quote on the book cover.

206 Ibid., v.

207 "Theodore Dwight Weld," Wikipedia, accessed 3/27/21, https://en.wikipedia.org/wiki/Theodore_Dwight_Weld.

208 Thomas, *Theodore Weld: Crusader for Freedom*, vi.

209 Ibid., 5.

210 Ibid., 7.

211 Ibid., 6–7, cited from Weld's letters to his future wife, Angelina Grimke and her sister, Sarah.

212 Elizabeth Greenleaf, quoted by Henry B. Carrington, *Theodore D. Weld and a Famous Quartet*, 6. No other publishing information is given. Cited by Benjamin Thomas, 8.

213 Thomas, *Theodore Weld: Crusader for Freedom*, 10.

214 Susan Down, *Voices for Freedom/Abolitionist Heroes: Theodore Weld, Architect of Abolitionism* (St. Catharines, Ontario; New York; Hove, United Kingdom; & Coburg North, VIC, 2013), 5.

215 Owen Muelder, *Theodore Dwight Weld and the American Anti-Slavery Society* (Jefferson, North Carolina and London: McFarland and Company, Inc.), 52.

216 "Theodore Dwight Weld," Wikipedia, accessed 12/13/2020, https://en.wikipedia.org/wiki/Theodore_Dwight_Weld.

217 Susan Down, 4.

218 "Soundings," "The Blog of Douglas B. Skinner," "God Reigns, and the Government at Washington Still Lives!" accessed 1/14/2018, https://dougskinner.wordpress.com/2016/11/07/god-reigns-and-the-government-at-washington-still-lives/.

219 Isaiah 65:17, 66:22; 2 Peter 3:13; and Revelation 21:1.

220 "George Washington/Mount Vernon," "Presiding Over the Convention: The Indispensable Man," accessed 12/8/2017, http://www.mountvernon.org/george-washington/constitutional-convention/convention-president/.

221 BBC News, "US and Canada," "Half-smoked Churchill cigar sold for $12,000," accessed 12/8/2017, http://www.bbc.com/news/world-us-canada-41604511 and other internet sites.

222 Peter Marshall, "Brainy Quote," "Peter Marshall Quotes," accessed 10/28/2019, https://www.brainyquote.com/quotes/peter_marshall_382640.

223 Proverbs 12:6.

224 Michael Van Dyke, 112.

225 George F. Kennan, "George F. Kennan Quotes," "Brainy Quote," accessed 12/31/2020, https://www.brainyquote.com/quotes/george_f_kennan_142133.

226 Daniel 2:21.

SECTION 5

GOD INSIDE AND OUTSIDE EVERY CRAZY

9

REMAIN AMAZED!

The pursuit of truth and beauty is a sphere of activity in which we are permitted to remain children all our lives.
—Albert Einstein

Jim Rohn offers a reason why many people are not leading satisfying lives. Rohn states that it's because "they keep trying to get *through* the day. A worthier challenge is to get *from* the day." He suggests that "we must become sensitive enough to observe and ponder what is happening around us. Be alert. Be awake. Let life and all of its subtle messages touch us."[227]

I think we can train ourselves to be continually alert to God's presence and to what may seem to be the smallest of miracles. The man in the following story learned to be attentive to what most of us ignore.

Listen for the Cricket![228]

During the turn of the nineteenth century, a pioneer husband and wife were driving their wagon over the prairie. In the back of the wagon lay their baby boy. As the wagon lurched over the trackless prairie, the baby came loose from his cocoon and rolled out onto thick tall grass. An hour later the mother and father discovered their loss and turned back, but they couldn't find him. Some Indians had rescued their baby, and the tribe came to adopt him.

As the boy grew, he learned the secrets of the wilderness from his Indian family, including how to distinguish the songs of birds, the chirping of insects, and other sounds of nature. Years passed, and eventually, the tribe allowed the boy to leave. He somehow got to New York City where he became educated. But the young man never lost his keenness of eye and ear in this strange new place. He was standing once with a friend at a busy intersection where the elevated railway clattered overhead and taxis honked their horns. Grabbing the arm of his friend, the young man said, "Listen, I hear a cricket."

His friend said, "Ridiculous! No cricket could live here, and if it did, you couldn't possibly hear it."

"Wait," said the youth again...listen."

He took his companion by the hand and crossed the street to the opposite corner. There on a windowsill were some flower-pots. Searching through the plants, the young man found a cricket. "Amazing," cried his friend, "Incredible!"

"Not at all," said the other, taking a silver coin from his pocket and flipping it into the air. As it hit the pavement, a score of New Yorkers immediately started searching for where the coin had fallen.

"You see," said the young man. "Everyone hears what he is listening for."

While I attended seminary in New York City, I lived about two blocks from where subways emerge to street level from underground, crisscrossing trains coming from the opposite direction. I know how easily the clamor of trains and traffic could drown the chirp of a tiny cricket. But the only way to hear the cricket—or the still small voice of the Spirit of Christ[229]—is by carefully listening for it. Jesus said, "If anyone has ears to hear, let them hear."[230] Jesus also said that God's invisible kingdom is in our midst, but not everyone will perceive it. William Winter puts it this way: "As much of Heaven is visible as we have eyes to see."[231]

Let's shift to accounts of people who notably had ears to hear and eyes to see. God doesn't need to prove His existence to anyone. Even when He acts in powerful ways, we don't *see* Him. Psalm 77:19

says of God, "Your path led through the sea, your way through the mighty waters, though your footprints were not seen." God Himself may not be visible, but His miracles and their effects are perfectly real.

Rather than arrange the following stories in neat categories, I present them in the varied order I usually encounter them—with biblically-based messages or life lessons embedded in each of them. All the miracles related in this book remind me that I'm inherently limited in ability and understanding. Some quite clearly highlight the reality that I'm mortal and subject to the possibility of death at any moment. If we weren't mere mortals, we wouldn't need such reassurances that *it is God* who ultimately is in control and can aid us— or intervene—anytime! Put more simply, these narratives remind all of us that *God is God and we are not!* My final story crystallizes that theme and helps nail down the fact that we need not fear death *or dying*—when the Lord is with us. Remember Psalm 23:4: "Yea, though I walk through the valley of the shadow of death, I will fear no evil: for thou art with me; thy rod and thy staff they comfort me."

Angel on the Hood

I was getting a haircut from Lois on Tucson's east side in 2006. She'd cut my hair a few times, and we'd had some deep conversations. After many years of counseling, I've gotten good at detecting a "big fish" story, so when Lois told me of a possible brush with death, I believed she was speaking from a pure heart.

In 1997 Lois was en route to evening church in a small town in Arizona when she stopped for a bite to eat at Taco Bell. After getting her bag of food from the drive-through, Lois prepared to pull out into traffic. She looked both ways, and then prepared to go, but with the car in gear and her foot pressing on the accelerator, the car would not move. Equally bewildering, she saw the front of her car pushed down as if an invisible force was keeping it from moving into the street. Lois said, "It was like something big and powerful was sitting on my hood." Suddenly, a car sped in front of her. She realized instantly that she'd been spared a broadside collision that could have killed her. After shedding tears of gratitude about God's evident protection, she went on to church with a powerful testimony to share. That next year, she delivered a beautiful baby boy who is her pride and joy and now loves Jesus too!

Patricia at the Yellow Light
Intuition or God?

Another friend of mine had a similar experience. It didn't seem to defy laws of nature, but it was as equally lifesaving as Lois's was. While taking one of her frequent trips to the airport to pick up friends who've been especially drawn to Tucson during the winter, Patricia was with her husband who happened to have Hodgkin's disease. Pat told me that as she was driving down Kolb Road toward Valencia, she approached a blinking yellow light. There was a red light for crossing traffic. Patricia was driving about fifty miles per hour, and she began to slow down for the yellow. For no reason, she braked to a dead stop. At that very moment, as her husband began to yell at her for being a stupid driver, *woosh!* A red truck zoomed in front of them and ran the red light. If Patricia had not stopped, their car would have been broadsided and her husband likely killed. Who knows if either of them would have survived? Patricia could not explain why she stopped at the blinking light. She never had before. Her only thought was that they had both been saved by an angel for whatever purpose God had in mind.

Most of us have had an experience like what Patricia described. Coincidence? Intuition? An angel? When *you* are the one whose life is saved, you're more likely to look heavenward for an explanation—and give deepest thanks.

The Divine Appointment

Michael Hastings's life was deeply impacted by a woman who heard the still, small voice of God. It was a clear prompting with specific instructions. I attended Grace Bible College with Mike in the early 1980s, so we've been friends for over forty years. In the

244

early 1980s, Mike earned his BA in Theology from Oral Roberts University while also attending Rhema Bible Training Center for one year. He later earned an MEd from Point Loma Nazarene University (1989) and an MS in Educational Technology from the University of Arizona (2012). In addition, he spent a year studying library science (2013) and almost a year of an MBA program (2014) at the University of Arizona. (Mike and I have spent *far* too much time in school!) In addition, Mike was a church counselor for three years and taught school for ten years in various locations throughout the US.

Mike also played a military character on the popular TV show *The West Wing* and received lots of media attention, even though he never spoke a word of the script. He still looked great in his captain's uniform on the set of Warner Brothers. Here's Michael's story in his own words:

> I will never forget an experience that took place in 1984. While juggling financial tuition at two schools—Oral Roberts University and Rhema Bible Training Center in Tulsa, Oklahoma—I received letters from both schools stating that if I did not come up with $250 for each one by March 12, I would be dropped. I barely had money to live on, and this amount seemed impossible to obtain. I had only two days to come up with it, so I immediately went to prayer. I prayed according to the admonition of Hebrews 4:16: "Let us then approach God's throne of grace with confidence, so that we may receive mercy and find grace to help us in our time of need." I began walking around my room, boldly reading scriptures out loud (and I mean loud!), and addressing the angels in Heaven (Hebrews 1:14).
>
> The next day something incredible happened...something I will never forget. It was a Sunday morning, and I went to one of the morn-

ing services at Victory Christian Center which was held at the Mabee Center Stadium on the Oral Roberts campus. I expected to be all "fired" up by some dynamic message, but instead, I felt nothing. I returned home, and as the hours progressed, I began to realize that I was going to be kicked out of both schools.

Suddenly, a profound heaviness came over me. I wasn't bitter, but I realized that this *really was* the end of a dream. It meant I wouldn't graduate from either of the schools. It also meant I would have to resign from my position as the missions director to Kenya, East Africa, which I had been chosen to lead. I became very quiet and somber.

But Jan Hears the Voice of God

As the hours ticked by, I decided I may as well go to the evening service at the church. I walked over (I didn't have a car) and attended the service. It was a nice sermon, but nothing seemed to move the heaviness that was upon me. As I was leaving the stadium, a woman named Jan came up to me. I met her at a Bible study several months before, but she was just an acquaintance. She turned to me and said, "It's beginning to rain. Can I give you a ride home?" I could barely hear the question since I was so absorbed in my inner world of trying to figure out how I was going to solve my crisis. I thought I had cast my cares on the Lord and was choosing to trust God. But the reality was that I really believed God had abandoned me, and I was now reaping the harvest of poor planning. I felt so much defeat at that moment and really didn't want to be bothered by anyone—or be with anyone. I turned to her and said, "No, I'm fine, I don't live that far."

I kept walking but then realized that getting a ride was probably a good idea. I turned back to Jan and said, "Yes, the ride to graduate housing would definitely help!" I got in her car, and she began to drive me to the graduate housing where I lived. We talked about the Lord and the sermon, but I made no mention of my crisis. When we arrived, she turned to me and said, "Michael, is everything okay?" I told her everything was "just fine." (I genuinely felt my situation was too burdensome and complex for anyone to help.) As I began to get out of the car, she turned to me and said, "Wait!" I stopped in my tracks and leaned back into the car to hear what she had to say:

"Michael, while we were in the service tonight, the Holy Spirit spoke to me and said, 'Give Michael Hastings $500.'"

My eyeballs just about popped out of my head! I couldn't believe it! "You've got to be kidding!" I said. I slowly sat back in the car seat and told her the whole story about the $500 that was needed for the two schools. She opened her purse, wrote out a check for $500, and handed it to me. I was stunned…flabbergasted! How could this have possibly happened?

In that shocking moment, I realized how real God was, and that this woman heard from God—and obeyed what He said! Not only was my prayer answered, but it set into motion a series of outstanding events. Jan's obedience helped me to continue my education at both schools and graduate from them in May of 1984. Her obedience also allowed me to continue my role as missions director to Kenya that summer. But there was more to the story…

And That Was Dining with the President

During that summer in Africa, our mission team produced much fruit: hundreds of people were saved, and dozens of people shared testimonies of healing when we prayed over them. In addition, we were invited to dine with the president of Kenya (President Moi) at his home which was like our White House in the USA. We were his honored guests at a three-hour tribal celebration in his backyard. When I returned from Africa, my story was featured in the December 1984 issue of Oral Roberts' magazine, *Abundant Life*. Without Jan's $500 gift, not only would I have not graduated, but I would not have dined with the president!

None of these things would have happened without Jan's obedience.

What was so striking about this miracle:

1. The timing. I needed the money in a matter of hours;
2. The exact amount that was needed—$500;
3. The chances of running into Jan after leaving a stadium filled with *thousands* of people streaming through multiple exits; and
4. The precision of God's words. Jan didn't get a "sense" that she needed to help some person in need. God specifically called my name—"Michael Hastings"—and told her exactly how much to give. There was also a sense of urgency on Jan's part to "act on

the word NOW," not a week or month later when it would have been too late.

I still marvel that Jan was practically a stranger to me. She knew very little about me, my life, or my finances. And an interesting back-story is that Jan's mother accepted the Lord a few weeks after Jan gave me the check. The blessings never stop!

An important lesson of this story is that God wants to be INVOLVED in the events of our lives, especially in our hours of crisis. We need to TRUST God in difficult times and not be surprised when He shows up to part our Red Sea.

In retrospect, I look back and reflect: I learned God can move mountains when we cooperate with Him. I had chosen a lifestyle of diligently seeking God, and God rewarded me... just like He will reward you, if you diligently seek Him (Hebrews 11:6). Our daily decisions will either qualify us for favor, breakthroughs, and miracles...or they will disqualify us from them. So, we must choose wisely! Remember, "God is able to do exceedingly abundantly above all that we ask or think" (Ephesians 3:20)!

(Note: I'm still good friends with Jan who is a Christian author and holds a Doctorate in Ministry from ORU. Our friendship spans forty years, and I'm so thankful God sent her across my path those many years ago!)

Danger on the Road to Maine

We know it's no accident that the Big Dipper points toward the North Star. God's invisible hand often produces visible highlights that indicate His precise and intentional design. This next story contains a series of events that show yet again how God works in specific and wondrous ways for our benefit.

In 2009, my wife Susan's nephew, Christopher Kotecha, was serving as the director of the All Rockland Kids for Christ in Rockland County, New York. Chris was taking sixteen children, aged nine to fourteen, to Camp Good News in Maine on August 1 and driving an old borrowed fifteen-passenger 1984 Dodge van. Still, the van looked quite new with fresh paint and had only forty thousand miles on its odometer.

Before receiving his master's in counseling and entering children's ministry, Chris had worked at a car repair shop. Although the business was well-equipped, he always brought along his own kit of favorite tools, like any picky mechanic does. But it turned out he'd need more than a few tools to deal with the van's pending mechanical meltdown!

As the caravan of three vehicles left Nyack and crossed the Hudson River on the Tappan Zee Bridge, Chris's windows were down, and the children on board expected a relaxed and fun trip. After several hours, he noticed an odd sound that seemed to be coming from one of his van's wheels. Fear gripped him as he considered how they would manage a major breakdown so far from home—and in a caravan to boot.

The vans stopped for lunch in Connecticut, then continued a bit further on I-95 before switching to Route 1 to avoid heavy traffic on the interstate. As they crossed Massachusetts and entered New Hampshire, Chris noticed difficulty slowing the van down at traffic lights and sensed that something still wasn't right. Then one of the kids blurted, "Hey, is that smoke?" It looked like smoke was rising from under the hood, near the windshield. Chris pulled over. But when he popped the hood, he saw no smoke, nor where it might've come from.

Driving on the road again at about forty to forty-five miles per hour, Chris was now approaching a traffic light at Provident Way in Seabrook, NH. The very name of that cross-street was a providential sign! When he put his foot on the brake pedal, the Dodge Ram would not slow down. Chris quickly downshifted into low gear, but that didn't help either. He stomped on the emergency brake, but he still could not stop the van. Chris was moving ever closer to the bumper of his dad's minivan that was stopped in front of him at the red light…and there were more kids in that van.

Hoping to avoid a rear-end collision, Chris jerked the van off the road and turned sharply to the right, honking all the way as he headed onto a wide sidewalk running parallel to the roadway. Fortunately, there were no telephone poles, parking meters, pedestrians, or anything else in his way—and the van with its precious cargo finally stopped.

Of course, the kids immediately went nuts, exclaiming things like, "We could've been killed!" and "That was like a roller coaster ride!" and "I'm gonna call my mom!" Chris breathed a sigh of relief that he and his passengers all seemed unharmed. A few began throwing a Frisbee outside the van while Chris gathered the other kids in a circle for prayer. Chris told me, "It was the shortest, worst prayer I ever prayed: 'God, thank you for keeping us safe. Now we're stuck and we don't know what to do. Please help. Amen.'"

It was Saturday evening, almost dark, and their destination was still about 130 miles away. Even if there was a motel close by, Chris didn't know if he and the other adults had enough money to pay for all the rooms they'd need for the entire gang. Plus, he had no idea where to find a replacement van. So he began to jack up the front driver's side where the smoke seemed to be coming from. Maybe he could figure this thing out.

Then a stranger appeared. He said his name was Bob, and he'd been eating in a restaurant nearby. He saw much of the drama unfold and asked what was going on. He touched the van's wheel and said, "Oh my god! That wheel must be a thousand degrees!"

After Bob's other choicer words, Chris asked him to curb the expletives around the kids. "Maybe you're our answer to prayer," Chris said.

"I doubt that," Bob responded.

However, it turned out that Bob was a truck mechanic at the truck and auto repair shop just across the street. But it was closed on Saturdays, and Bob didn't have a key.

At that moment, the shop's manager just *happened* to pull up. Bob said, "I don't believe it!" The manager just *happened* to be selling a boat to someone that night. And of course, he had the shop key! Chris gingerly pulled the van up to the shop while Bob donned his overalls. He quickly discovered the problem and saw what was needed to fix it: the brake had seized up and needed replacement brake pads and a piston caliper. Bob explained that this was common in older vans that weren't used a lot. But where could they get these parts? Easy! From the Auto Zone—just around the corner!

Chris returned with both needed parts, despite it being unusual for an auto supply to have what such an old van required. But Bob discovered that *another* part was needed: the wheel seal had melted. Chris had done many brake jobs on his own, but he was not familiar with a wheel seal. So back to Auto Zone he went, where they had the exact wheel seal that was needed! Bob promptly installed the new parts and lubricated the chassis. *Problem solved!* Chris dug into his wallet and found only $136 in cash and no credit cards. Bob refused the money and told him to "just get these kids safely to camp...and write my boss a letter to say I did a good deed, so I won't get fired for this."

Chris and the weary entourage finally arrived at the camp near midnight. The weeklong retreat was a wonderful success, with four children committing their lives to Christ and several others receiving assurance of their salvation.

Chris is still in awe of the number of unusual circumstances that made for a safe arrival:

1. No dangerous incident while driving the roads
2. The wide sidewalk just off the roadway
3. Bob the truck mechanic who saw the whole thing and left the restaurant to offer help
4. The repair shop where Bob worked being right across the street
5. The manager who showed up and had the keys to open the closed shop

6. The Auto Zone around the corner that had exact parts needed for the old van

Chris gives glory to God for having His hand on every aspect of a potentially disastrous situation. Every need was perfectly and timely met, and no one was hurt. God was surely in charge of this trip to Maine that unfolded in such a crazy way!

An Ordained Pastor, Songwriter, and Farmer

Many of you know the song "You Are My Hiding Place," written in the 1980s by Michael Ledner. It's one of the world's most popular contemporary Christian songs, having been transposed and sung in many languages and countries. Its compelling beauty speaks for itself.

Written in the 1980s, I was happy to hear it again on radio *and* television recently. Very few songs get airtime almost forty years after they're released! And I notice that more than three million people have viewed different versions of "You Are My Hiding Place" on YouTube. I got to thinking that the story behind this song illustrates how God moves powerfully yet invisibly.

I knew Michael back in the eighties. We attended the same church for a few years, and I met him through his mother, Dottie, who also attended there. Dottie was the receptionist at the Student Counseling Center at the University of Arizona, where I did an internship. I got to know Michael as we hung out together with other church musicians. All of us loved "You Are My Hiding Place."

I'd heard from Michael back in the day about that song's rise to popularity. But I'd forgotten the details and was curious about what he might have to say about the song now. So I gave him a ring. Michael was excited that the night before, he and his wife, Lylah, had just hand-delivered a breech goat on their three-acre farm. He "gloved up" and successfully delivered the baby by its hind legs. This ordained pastor-musician-farmer was just as excited about mom and baby goats doing well as he could've been with a new song!

Along with songwriting and farming, Michael pastors a home church that meets in a remodeled, three-car garage on his farm. But Michael and Lylah's livelihood depends on their caramel candies and the goat's milk soaps they sell online and at a local market. I believe that Michael is ordained to be a farmer and entrepreneur as much as he is to be a songwriter and pastor!

His inspiration for "You Are My Hiding Place" came when he was sitting on his bed and idly strumming his guitar with his Bible open to the Psalms. It was January 1980 while he was enduring a painful divorce. God helped him compose the song from deep within his soul's distress. Michael shared the song with a few friends right after he wrote it but then shelved it for about a year. I know from my own experience how mystical, wondrous, and drawn out that process can be!

That September, Michael went to Israel to live and work on a kibbutz[232]—no great surprise, given the Jewish roots of his family name. I suspect that's where he learned to love farming. Two months into his stay, he led Messianic worship one evening for his group and sang "You Are My Hiding Place." It was soon sung by others not far north in the Golan Heights, where fighting was raging at that time. The song comforted many Israelis amid the sounds of war against their country.

A woman from his worship group returned home to California and shared his song at church, which happened to be attended by agents from Maranatha! Music. They traced the song back to Michael and contacted him at his kibbutz—via one telephone that was shared by four hundred people. Michael's song landed on the label's Praise 6 album. Michael wrote and published five other songs through "Jews for Jesus" and continues to write Christian music.

Michael radiated joy throughout our hourlong conversation. Before we hung up, he said his primary aim in life is the instruction of 2 Corinthians 5:9: "So we make it our goal to please him, whether we are at home in the body or away from it." Happily married to Lylah, he has two children and seven grandchildren. Michael is thrilled to be about God's business, whether pastoring, writing music, or delivering a goat![233]

Not His Time to Die

Our last four miracle accounts are of answers to prayer. The first account is one that Dr. Roger Barrier has graciously allowed me to share. Again, it illustrates God's power as well as the importance of individually heeding God's special word to us. The following is excerpted from *Got Guts? Get Godly*[234]:

> One of our Wycliffe Bible Translators went into anaphylactic shock immediately following an insect bite. By the time he was airlifted to the hospital, the oxygen loss to his brain meant likely brain damage and probable death. When I arrived to pray with the family, I sensed in my spirit that this sickness was the misfortune of a broken world. So, I prayed accordingly: "Lord, there is no reason for this sickness to end in death. He needs to finish his Bible translation. He has children to raise. This is not the time to die. Heal him and make him well."
>
> Several days later, the family asked our church elders to anoint him with oil and pray for his healing according to James 5:14–16. With his doctor's permission, our elders entered the intensive care unit. We all felt strongly from God that this sickness was not unto death. We anointed him with oil and prayed in faith for his healing. Three hours later, he was sitting up in bed, eating. Today, his children are raised, and his translation is finished.

The Audible "Crack" and the Healing that Was Witnessed and Confirmed

Ivan Rudolph is a retired teacher and author of twelve books who now lives in Australia. He's a disciplined student of God's Word

255

who has presented scrupulous research on the extraordinary—notably near-death experiences (NDEs). He has researched thousands of NDEs for the last forty years. His *Living Beyond: Making Sense of Near Death Experiences* is the most comprehensive book I've read on this subject. It presents a solidly biblical overview and interpretations of NDEs aimed at addressing confusion in both returnees and those interested in life after death.[235]

Since the book was released some time ago, Ivan and I have corresponded. When I wrote him to discuss the book you're now reading, he told me about another book he was writing (now published) called *Your Origin and Destiny.* It is an intriguing work that builds on scriptural descriptions of the difference between God's time and man's understanding of time. Ivan has allowed me to share from this new book the next two miracle accounts. The first is a modestly edited report of miraculous healing.[236]

Ivan first met a young boy named Graeme Stokes at a Pentecostal church in Rhodesia (now Zimbabwe) in the mid-1970s. Graeme had a dental condition called a "bulldog bite." The Stokes family brought Graeme to the capital city of Salisbury (now Harare) so that the child could be examined and treated by a skilled dentist named Dr. Bowker. But the family had also read in the local newspaper of miraculous healings at a Pentecostal church. After an evaluation by Dr. Bowker, they took Graeme to a service there to request prayer for his rare condition.

Ivan attended a service a week later at that church, where he saw Graeme and heard his parents and Pastor Bill Anstruther describe Graeme's complete and instantaneous healing the previous Sunday. They told the large congregation how Pastor Bill had invited those who would like prayer for healing to come forward. Graeme went forward with his mother. When the pastor put his hand on the youngster's head and prayed for him, people close by could hear a distinct cracking that seemed to come from Graeme's head. The boy's jaw contour had changed, and his bulldog bite had completely disappeared! Everyone rejoiced, amazed over this immediate reconstruction performed by God!

At the close of the service, Ivan sought out Graeme and his parents. He had a special request: Would the family be willing to return to the dentist so he could re-examine Graeme and verify the miracle? Ivan had been investigating other miracles reported at that church, and because of this commitment to scientific credibility, he wanted to document Graeme's and other accounts as thoroughly as possible. So Graeme's parents agreed to take him to visit Dr. Bowker the following week.

Ivan took documentary pictures of Graeme's now-perfect jaw contour and waited in the reception area for him and his family to emerge from their meeting with Dr. Bowker. Mrs. Stokes came out with a broad smile, saying, "Dr. Bowker didn't believe it was Graeme, at first. He told his nurse that she must have brought him the wrong card [patient record]. The nurse told him it was definitely the correct one—and he looked very confused." Mrs. Stokes continued, "Graeme told him that he had been prayed for and healed, and I added that I'd very much like a letter from him to confirm this. Dr. Bowker's face went all funny, and he plopped down into his chair. We all looked at him and waited for him to say something, but he was speechless. It's the first time I've seen someone actually speechless."

Ivan finally asked, "Did he verify the miracle?"

"Yes, he did. He re-examined Graeme and told us the healing was perfect. He was amazed. He questioned Graeme further. Finally, he said he would prepare a letter for me to collect later."

Dr. Bowker's letter appears in its entirety in *Your Origin and Destiny*, along with a more comprehensive account of his experience. The dentist explained how his original treatment plan for Graeme was going to include doing several fillings and giving him "an appliance to wear to correct this malocclusion and I estimated it would take between six months to one year to correct his bite." He confirmed that Graeme's dental alignment was now normal and added that Graeme said, "I asked a man to pray for me and he fixed my teeth." God healed Graeme through the believing prayer of that pastor!

This reminds me of the blind man whom Jesus healed. When the man was questioned by the Jewish teachers as to who had healed him, the blind man said that he didn't know who Jesus was. All he knew was that *he once was blind but now could see!*

Dr. Bowker's letter conclusively ends like this: "To repeat, I am delighted to have been able to see this divine cure for myself." Ivan adds, "Many of the dentist's colleagues would not have been prepared to record on paper their scientific observations of a miracle for fear of ridicule. Of course, true investigative scientists are not afraid of facts and do not ignore or hide them, but are prepared to record them."

Come Away and Rest

The next account involves the humble prayer of one man, followed by an audible answer to that prayer, and God's use of another man who longed to be of service to God.[237] Many years ago, missionary Rev. Frank Mussell wanted to build a retreat center in Rhodesia (now Zimbabwe—again!). He had no idea how to obtain the land. So he put his head in his hands, closed his eyes, and prayed out loud, "Lord, who can I ask for land?" He immediately heard a clear, audible voice: "Try Mr. Webb." Sitting back in his chair, repeating the words "Try Mr. Webb," Frank asked himself and the Lord, "Who is Mr. Webb?"

As Frank pondered this strange experience, he remembered two years earlier, when he'd met a Mr. Webb at a social event. Frank had a vague recollection that Mr. Webb attended a Baptist church, and with some reluctance, Frank mailed a letter to him, in care of the church. Meanwhile, unbeknownst to anyone, Mr. Milton Webb had committed to God in prayer a beautiful valley on his farm—"for whatever you decide to use it for." This secret promise to God was in gratitude for the desperately needed financial help he'd recently received.

Milton Webb responded enthusiastically to Rev. Mussell's letter, and a Christian center with cottages for a youth camp began to take shape in the valley. The retreat was given the same of Resthaven, based on Christ's invitation to His weary disciples in Mark 6:31 to come away for a while and rest. Ivan Rudolph learned this backstory as he came to organize youth camps at Resthaven. Ivan says, "Over the years, many lives have been transformed, enriched, and even rescued at Resthaven…the center seemed to have a special, peaceful atmosphere, and good things always happened." Ivan regards Resthaven as a monument to God's "continuing voice intervening in our world."

Gwen's Story
Prayers Terrorize the Darkness

When I met Gwen in my counseling office, I noticed each hand was joined into two fingers and a thumb—rather than five normal digits. Gwen was born with Apert Syndrome[238] which presented challenges and necessitated many surgeries during her younger years. Considering what she was up against, I was curious where she got her great smile and dynamic personality. She definitely seemed comfortable in her own skin.

I later learned she had been healed of four separate identities called "alters" or dissociated "parts" and delivered from five demons. Each new alter emerged within a day of another childhood trauma, often associated with being bullied. Personality fragmentation began at age three…the demons came later. Thirty years of confusion and drama locked her in a prison of depression.

As a child, Gwen began to see a clinical psychologist who was no help at all. He didn't even report the abuses to her parents. Nor did he tell them about the multiple identities, which would have explained Gwen's frequent bouts of rebellious behavior and poor memory about various life events. Gwen's life was, as she says, "a walking conflict"[239] with blank periods lasting sometimes for weeks that were due to the influence of the alters and/or demons.

Gwen had a severe case of dissociative identity disorder (DID), which used to be called multiple personality disorder and affects approximately 1.5% of the world's population (although underdiagnosing and misdiagnosing may be skewing the percentage). Gwen was among an extremely rare group that may also be demon possessed. Most mental health professionals discount demon possession, and I was among the skeptics of most such reports. Also, as with therapists of many years ago, I thought multiple personality disorder was beyond rare. But after reading about Gwen's grueling journey toward healing in *Shattered Secrets*,[240] I became convinced Gwen had suffered from both DID and demonic possession.

Gwen's torment ended and her healing began during intercessory prayer with a small group of Christian believers (prior to the start of counseling with me). As she was being prayed over, Gwen felt like she was being dragged through the floor into an abyss of darkness. This is not an uncommon experience for someone who is being delivered from demons. In the early twentieth century, for example, God moved mightily on a group of Chinese orphans in the southeast corner of Yunnan. Missionary H.A. Baker tells of a schoolteacher's deliverance at an orphanage in Adullam:

> I questioned him when he was able to rise, as to why he wept and why he fell. He said, "I wept from sheer terror. Something awful happened. Everything became black; I was myself about to go in a black pit at the base of a terrible mountain." When on the floor, he saw himself being bound by demon chains and about to be carried off into terrifying darkness, but he was set free again."[241]

As with the schoolteacher and many people Jesus healed and others from whom He also cast out demons, Gwen returned to the land of the living and to true freedom. She's been telling everyone about her new freedom in Christ ever since. Gwen's message is that the power of prayer in Jesus' name is stronger than mental illness and spiritual darkness. Since her release from bondage, Gwen has been rejoicing as she's been productive in several jobs, including one that involved skilled typing (she's very fast!).

In the face of life's cruelties and even spiritual oppression, any of us can pray—sometimes in intercessory prayer for others—and expect deliverance into the healing light of God's presence and His perfect plan for our lives.

Nothing to Fear in the White Release

Except for Beth's near-death experience, mentioned in chapter 4, I've not written about them. But I mention them here to remind us that the miracles I've reported point us to a heavenly realm that others have visited in instances of NDEs. There are innumerable, truly encouraging accounts of people who've been transported to paradise.[242] Two of my favorite books by those who've written of their NDE are *To Heaven and Back* by Dr. Mary C. Neal and *Flight to Heaven* by Captain Dale Black. I've also talked with other people who shared their own profound NDEs. The apostle Paul was himself taken to paradise during his earthly life. He summarized his impressions in 1 Corinthians 2:9:

> No eye has seen, no ear has heard, and no mind has imagined what God has prepared for those who love him. But it was to us that God revealed these things by his Spirit. For his Spirit searches out everything and shows us God's deep secrets. (NLT)

We can't fathom the ways our infinite God can intervene for us in our finite dimensions of space and time. It's even harder to grasp matchless, eternal provisions that await those who are His children. I urge you to allow the reality of the stories you've read to saturate your soul with confidence that eternal realms are the ultimate destiny of believers.

A friend of my father's, whose poetry I quoted in chapter 6, was a professor and well-known hymn writer of the mid-twentieth century. Dr. Earl Marlatt's poem "Mountain Communion"[243] gives an enticing glimpse into wondrous realms from which God's miracles flow:

> If you have once seen ripples
> Upon a mountain lake,
> You will not marvel that love can fill

Hearts until they break.

If you have once seen granite
Above the highest grass,
You will not grieve that fragile things
Blossom and seed and pass.

If you have once seen birches
Rise, star-lit, from the snow
You will not fear the white release
Beyond the afterglow.

At over ninety years old, Myra was one who didn't fear the white release. She was wheeled into Dr. Robert Lesslie's emergency room in Rock Hill, South Carolina, with a broken hip. Dr. Lesslie's son, Jack, was observing in the ER for the summer; and both he and his father quickly recognized her kind face. She'd been Jack's Sunday school teacher years earlier. Although she looked healthy, because of her age and the loss of her husband of over seventy years, Dr. Lesslie sensed—and Myra *knew*—she didn't have long for this world.

When Jack visited with her, she said, "Jack, it's important to live well, and it's important to leave well." She repeated herself so that Jack would understand. Then she told him to go home and look up a passage of Scripture. Jack opened his Bible that night:

> It was just before the Passover festival. Jesus knew that the hour had come for him to leave this world and go to the Father. Having loved his own who were in the world, he loved them to the end. (John 13:1)

As a woman of strong faith who, indeed, lived well, Myra soon left well.[244]

Follow That Chariot!

The following is a story that's precious to me and should comfort anyone who lost a loved one to the coronavirus during the pandemic that began in 2020. [245]

Esther Reynolds grew up in Mexico. She lived in California for a while, then moved with her family to Tucson where she lived for thirty years. Her greatest joys were her husband of forty years, her six children, twenty grandchildren, and twenty-four great-grandchildren. She loved God's great outdoors and all manner of travel. She often flew to Minnesota where she'd visit her daughter, Charity, a physician then back to Tucson to be with her other children and family. As the beloved matriarch of such a large family—and a friend to many—her influence was profound.

Amid the raging pandemic, Esther and her clan suffered a shocking blow on June 24, 2020, when she tested positive for COVID-19. Esther was tested because of a cough she'd developed a week earlier. With an upcoming trip to Minnesota at the end of the month, she didn't want to risk infecting Charity and her family. The long-awaited trip was originally scheduled in February, but due to the pandemic, it was postponed again. Esther and her family exchanged daily phone calls to assure everyone she was "okay." But it wasn't long before her breathing became painful and labored.

Esther was admitted to the hospital but did not improve despite aggressive medical care. Her physician-daughter Charity, as expected, kept close touch with the treating medical team. As her mother's blood oxygen level remained dangerously low and her breathing labored despite all measures to that point, it became clear that Esther needed to be intubated and placed on a ventilator. She naturally didn't want that but agreed it was necessary to save her life.

In the 1990s, Esther experienced a vision of a white chariot. She wasn't feeling well when Frances, a friend from church, felt prompted to call her. When Frances couldn't reach her by phone, she went to Esther's home, found her very ill, and called 911. As she lay awaiting the ambulance, Esther had a vision of a white chariot in her room.

She told Charity she was grateful that God guided Frances to check on her. It wasn't her time to go.

Esther was a diligent student of God's Word and knew well the account of Elijah being taken to Heaven in a chariot. So she knew where the chariot in her vision was bound. Before she was put on the ventilator, she told Charity, "I saw the white chariot. It left me once again." Unlike her feeling of relief when the first chariot left without her, the second vision left Esther sad. She wanted to be *on* that chariot and knew it would carry her to live with her Lord and Savior Jesus forever!

Esther then contracted a stubborn bacterial pneumonia on top of the coronavirus infection. She improved for a while—which heartened everyone—but then the pneumonia worsened. Esther's other daughter Rebecca was the last person to speak with her mother before she was intubated. Esther was far too weak to hold the phone, so her nurse made the call. Esther breathlessly asked Rebecca to take care of her brother and requested that she "tell them all that I love them." "Her last words are forever engraved on my heart!" said Rebecca, and now they're engraved on the hearts of all Esther's children and loved ones.

After three trying weeks, Esther peacefully passed into eternity to join her husband, Joseph, a baby daughter, her parents, sister, and others who had preceded her. Although the chariot left her twice, the family believes that, indeed, it returned once more to take her home. The two visions previewed her ultimate ride to her heavenly home! Her family is certainly comforted to know that their mother's desire to ride the white chariot all the way was fulfilled!

On the night her mother died, Charity had a dream. In it, she saw her mother at the foot of her bed—looking young, vital, and radiant. Charity felt a deep peace and assurance that her mother "was happy and watching over each one of us." As Esther's family from time to time may still wonder about *what might have been* for her, another daughter, Sara, told me they're always reminded Esther's greatest desire was to enter life eternal and receive her ultimate healing—white chariot or not!

What My Mother Saw

I mentioned at the beginning of the book that I wanted to say more about my mother and a gift God gave at the end of her life that helped her reconcile with hard things in a dark world. When I visited her in assisted living the night she died, we had a memorable time of prayer. She couldn't talk, but we had deep eye contact. She weakly waved to me as I left her room, and I will never forget that final wave.

As I walked down the hall, leaving her for the last time, I realized I'd forgotten my glasses. So I returned to my mother's room and found her pointing at a corner of the ceiling. She wasn't aware of my presence, and her eyes and mouth were open wide in wonder. She was obviously awed by something she saw. I believe she was seeing an angel, or my father, or some glorious vision of paradise. Whatever she was seeing, the diaphanous veil between Heaven and Earth was beginning to part for her. Like Esther Reynolds, she did not fear "the white release beyond the afterglow!" A few hours later, I received the call that my dear mother had slipped through that veil to the Other Side.

Living Joyfully in the Meantime

As the years go by, I try to stay alert and fully open to anything in my life that is amazing: like different seeds that contain information to produce millions of varieties of trees and vegetation; like colorful hummingbirds flitting through the rainbow-producing spray of our garden hose; or like the luminous vermilion flycatcher that visits our birdbath. My wife Susan has been teaching me about birds and other wonders that we can readily enjoy right in our small yard.

We once spent an anniversary weekend near Wilcox, Arizona, where we were treated to the spectacle of huge flocks of sand-hill cranes settling for the night in orderly groups on ponds and marshes. Our vantage point was a small hill by a pond. To one side of the pond was a desert with mesquite, ocotillo, and cacti stretching to the horizon. On the other were marshes and a golf course. Bird watchers there told us that hundreds of cranes usually landed on the pond every evening. But not that evening.

The flock of ducks already on the water was a pleasant enough sight. But the cranes had apparently headed south instead of toward the Chiricahua Mountains where the famous Apache chief Cochise once had a stronghold. I wonder if he was ever awed by the cranes and the sunset like those of us gathered at the pond. The migration of birds is a remarkable phenomenon. In many cases, migratory birds sense and follow magnetic fields that surround the earth to their seasonal destinations. Isn't God's creation on this side of Heaven amazing?

Look Beyond the Horse Thieves

We all can find the sorts of stories I've shared in magazines, books, or newspapers. We can also hear them from family, friends, and acquaintances. And though our own family tree might reveal a horse thief or two, we can invariably find examples of family members who overcame adversity through a supernatural event or experienced a dramatic answer to prayer.

Most of us have had good things happen for which there is no rational explanation. But life's heartaches and stressors can blind us to a kaleidoscope of miracles, big and small—some we might have just ignored. It behooves us, therefore, to be *expectant* of God's beautiful gifts that invite reverence—much as the man I told you about earlier in the book who attuned himself to the chirping of the cricket across the street in the middle of a big city.

Purity of Worship

At the first church I served, I was the director of counseling and then director of the adult singles group in tandem with Susan. I trained over two hundred forty people to serve as lay counselors at the altar of our sanctuary. I attended that Tucson church for seventeen years, serving on the pastoral staff for twelve. I loved every one of the ministries I was involved in. My counseling schedule was routinely full, and the singles ministry thrived with dear folks who constantly were learning how to better serve God and one another. I taught many Bible studies, often on Sunday mornings. If I ever had to miss a Sunday when I'd been scheduled to teach, I'd ask a pastor or church member to stand in for me. Geoff Lucas, a highly skilled woodworker, was one such friend. Geoff was also a diligent student of God's Word and a gifted teacher.

Geoff once concluded a class with this story: While camping in the vast Sonoran Desert west of Tucson, he had an interesting experience. Because of the need to minimize light pollution so that the nearby Kitt Peak telescopes can function optimally, the streetlights in Tucson are sparse and specially designed. On a clear moonless night, it's so dark that you can see millions of stars, planets, and other heavenly bodies.

Geoff had built a small campfire for warmth and to keep critters away. By dawn, only a few smoldering embers remained that sent wisps of smoke skyward. But they weren't ordinary wisps of smoke. In that still and peaceful place just before dawn, the smoke ascended high into the morning sky—a thin, arrow-straight column. Geoff drew the parallel that our worship and praise to God can have such purity that it ascends to Heaven as straight and direct as that line of smoke. "Straight as a pencil lead," he said.

Geoff linked the illustration to his message concerning one of Elisha's miracles. Elisha is an Old Testament prophet among others who performed many miracles and gave all the glory to God. In just this way, when we believe God for miracles and the gift of eternal life, we can more fully love, worship, and serve Him.

Miracles with Purpose

Pastor Lee Strobel hired a highly respected polling service in 2018 to determine how many American adults have experienced a miracle. The survey concluded that about 38 percent have experienced at least one miracle—events they could explain in no way other than as a miracle. That's more than ninety-four million people in America alone![246] Hopefully, you've concluded that the Creator of billions of galaxies is in the miracle-working business!

How does this relate to you? Despite the turbulence and uncertainty swirling about your life, whether or not God performs the miracles you pray for, you can experience inner peace. This peace is a result of your faith in His power and love. God sent His Son, Jesus Christ, to die for your sins and then to rise again to extend both His love and power to you.

As you express faith by thanking, praising, and worshipping Him, and in serving others, you will sense an exchange of your weakness for His strength. Your sacrifices of worship and praise ascend directly to the throne of God and are a sweet smell to him. Even if we're confined in jail or in a failing body, we can experience peace that only God can give and that surpasses all understanding. We can *feel*—and we *are* truly—FREE INDEED!

Jesus said that if we follow Him, we'll know the truth, and the truth will set us free.[247] His miracles confirmed the truth of these words and validated all He said, did, and promised to do! Clearly, the purpose of God's miracles is to show His power and inspire intimacy with Him. God can shine His *essence* through *you!* You can channel your time, talent, and worldly goods from what He has lavished on you. You can also give generously the blessings of friendship, love, encouragement, and so much more. Many gifts we've been given aren't tangible or quantifiable, yet they are glimpses of the attributes of our holy, loving, sovereign, and gracious Heavenly Father. We can know and love and serve Him in response. Just as the stars and all creation declare the glory of God, *you can too!*

Once a year the president of the United States gives a State of the Union speech. But right here, I'll give you a State of the Universe address in a couple of sentences. Here is the text in its entirety: "God is in the crazy—even in the crazy *hard*—and He's in charge. Remain amazed!"

Reflections on the Peaceful Life

Take *daily steps of faith* and acknowledge God's creative power as revealed in the Heavens and the many ways you've already been blessed. Your life's journey can be helped by an amazing spectrum of miracles and *even more* blessings that can only emanate from God's heart. They invite us to respond with gratitude, surrender, and worship. Let blessings and miracles give you hope. May you grow in an intimate relationship with Him, and may everyone you touch in this life catch the overflow.

What small step of faith can you take today to let His light shine through you? As trauma therapist Rachel Lohrman sometimes asks clients, "What's the smallest change that will make the biggest difference?"[248] Right now—in faith—commit to making that change. Keep doing that every day, and you will see the glory of God!

Endnotes

227 Jim Rohn, *The Five Major Pieces to the Life Puzzle* (Southlake, Texas: Dickinson Press Inc., 1991), 27.

228 From a sermon by the author's father's at the Methodist church in Hull, Massachusetts, circa 1936–1940.

229 1 Kings 19:11–12 KJV. God did not speak to Elijah in extraordinary ways that we might expect but in a "still small voice."

230 Mark 4:23.

231 William Winter, "Great Books Online," Bartleby, accessed 11/29/2018, https://www.bartleby.com/348/authors/594.html.

232 *Kibbutz*: a communal settlement in Israel, typically a farm.

233 Ledner, Michael. Interview with author, 3/3/2018.

234 Barrier with Engeler, *Got Guts? Get Godly,* 214–215.

235 Ivan Rudolph, *Living Beyond: Making Sense of Near Death Experiences* (Bloomington, Indiana: WestBow Press, 2015), x.

236 Ivan Rudolph, *Your Origin and Destiny* (Mount Pleasant, South Carolina: Bublish; co-published by Ivan Rudolph, 2020), 40–43.

237 Frank Mussell, *The Resthaven Story of Answered Prayer,* first ed, (Arthur James Limited, The Drift: Evesham, Worcs, England, 1968), cited in Ivan Rudolph, 148–149.

238 For a thorough explanation of Apert syndrome, see WebMD, "Apert Syndrome," accessed 6/6/2020, https://www.webmd.com/children/apert-syndrome-symptoms-treatments-prognosis#1.

239 Laura Steffens, Gwendolyn and Dorothy Egan, *Shattered Secrets* (Bloomington, Indiana: CrossBooks, 2011), 96.

240 Laura Steffens, Gwendolyn and Dorothy Egan.

241 H.A. Baker, *Visions Beyond the Veil* (New Kensington, Pennsylvania: Whitaker House, previously published under the title *Visions of Heaven*, 2006), 59.

242 Near-Death Experience Research Foundation (NDERF) has recorded over four thousand seven hundred NDEs from around the world, accessed 5/27/2020, https://www.nderf.org/index.htm.

243 Marlatt, *Cathedral,* 5.

244 Robert D. Lesslie, *Angels on Call: Inspiring True Stories from the ER* (Eugene, Oregon: Harvest House Publishers), 23–28. Though tragically taken from this Earth on 4/10/21, Dr. Lesslie was also one who left well. It's well known that he was looking forward to praising his Savior in Heaven. The author has read many of his books and greatly admires Dr. Lesslie for living a life of integrity and faith.

245 Reynolds, Sara, Interview with author, August 17, 2020, and subsequent email exchanges with daughters Sara; Reynolds-Richardson, Charity; and Reynolds, Dulce Rebecca.

246 "Lee Strobel: The Case for Miracles," YouTube video, 58:05, message uploaded March 6, 2018, accessed 5/6/2019, https://www.youtube.com/watch?v=y3VSIWHZtOI.
247 John 8:32.
248 Rachel Lohrman, LPC, NCC; in a conversation with the author circa January, 2021. Lohrman is the founder and director of Joshua Tree Counseling, Tucson, Arizona.

Chet and Dad along the shores of Lake Webb
in Weld, Maine. Chet was age 14.

EPILOGUE

*I am the Alpha and the Omega, the First and
the Last, the Beginning and the End.*
                              —Jesus Christ, Revelation 22:13

You've just read a selection of miracles. If you reflect on any one of them, I think you'll conclude, "If God can do that, he can do anything! *Anything!*" That's my natural response to standing on the ocean shore and looking toward the horizon. Whether it's the ocean, a flower, the view from a high mountain, a caterpillar becoming a butterfly, melodies that echo in our spirits, or the biochemistry of living things, a natural reaction to beauty and mystery is a speechless wonder. That's often how I feel just waking up in the morning and appreciating the miracle of my eyes! When a man named Brother Lawrence gazed at a single tree in winter and considered that leaves and fruit would soon be renewed, he came to complete faith in Christ through that simple realization. He had a constant awareness of God's presence that he cultivated while working in a monastery kitchen. Some of Brother Lawrence's writings comprise the three-hundred-year-old Christian classic *The Practice of the Presence of God.*

As you reflect on the truths unveiled in miracles, I hope you've already joined me in believing that regardless of the depths of our hardships or uncertainties, they're only temporary. There's an Unseen Hand that can alter circumstances in surprising ways. God really does draw straight with our crooked lines. He really does know and understand that the broad sweep of all we do can only make sense when looking back. He truly does evoke heroism from the weakest among us—even the most "downwardly mobile!"

We're all on life's journey together—each day striving and resting, knowing and not knowing, risking and finding safety, and loving and guarding our hearts against harm. Fortunately, as the world gets even crazier, there is a God who lives both inside and outside time and space. He is sovereign and artfully molds each of us as He wills. This same God *loves* His most unique creation—mankind—and He daily draws all people to Him. Jesus, who predicted His death on the cross and His resurrection, said in John 12:32, "And I, when I am lifted up from the earth, will draw all people to myself." Sadly, not all respond, but if you're not among the millions of Christ's followers in the world today, I hope you will soon commit your life to Him and to an adventure greater than you can imagine!

ACKNOWLEDGMENTS

My mother spent almost fifteen years writing a book about my father. Quite naturally it's from that book that I garnered some of the information included in this one—especially from my parents' time in Germany. My mom never named her book, so I christened it *A Beautiful Stride*. More than one journalist researched my dad's history in athletic competition and discovered that he had been named as captain of both the golf and track teams at Simpson College. In track and field, he ran the anchor in a 440-yard sprint relay that set a national record. He also won events in the famous Drake Relays and other major track meets throughout his college career. One journalist said that my dad had "a beautiful stride"—and I believe it even though I never saw him run in competition. When I "thin-sliced" his life, I didn't speak of his golf achievements. One of the founders of the Professional Golf Association encouraged him to turn pro. But as the pages about my parents explain, my dad's sights were not set on professional golf; nor were my mother's set on acting. I'm a beneficiary of how both Mom and Dad chose to invest their lives in God's specific call to help build His kingdom on Earth.

I'm deeply indebted to the subjects of the book who benefitted from God's miracles, along with many others who submitted stories that weren't included. I hope to publish some of them in a follow-up work. If you have a story that you would like considered, send it to me at docdevereaux@gmail.com. Please include your email address. I'm extremely grateful to my friend Cheyenne Self, who told me a few years ago, "God is in crazy." The moment she said that I knew I had the title for the book I'd been thinking of writing for almost fifteen years.

Someone said there are three secrets to writing a good book: edit, edit, edit! I've worked with excellent editors who have inspired me to look for ways to say it simpler and better. Pamela Cangioli and Kim Jace of Proofed to Perfection made many good edits and suggestions. Also, my friend from high school days, Dr. Sam Williams, added untold hours of fine-tuning and "literary surgery" to my efforts. We were in the awesome Bexley High School class of '66 and got confirmed at—and joined—Bexley Methodist Church where my dad was pastor. He is a retired surgeon based in Virginia who's been serving the Lord all over the world with his wife Liz through Samaritan's Purse. Also, I've been in frequent dialogue with my wife, Susan, who combed through the chapters as I wrote them (and rewrote them!). She was an undergraduate English major, as I was, and she has an intuitive sense of what is put well—or not! Susan supported me in many ways while I was holed up in my study most evenings for four years. And in the early stages of writing, Ivan Rudolph's wife, Brenda, and Mary Kennedy made helpful edits. Tragically, for us who remain on Earth, Mary recently died from a heart attack. She was eagerly looking forward to new life in Heaven! And my friend from Australia—author, teacher, and Bible scholar—Ivan Rudolph endorsed my book and offered tips on publishing.

I wrote this book for Jesus Christ, my Lord and Savior. I am grateful for the work that many of you are doing to spread the news of God's goodness and the message of salvation through Christ. You all have rewards on this Earth and in Heaven that won't be measured until we get there. For those of you who are diligently searching for the real God, I hope this book has helped you on that journey. I pray that your diligence will be rewarded by the gift of faith in Christ.

APPENDIX

This poem was written by a WWII Spitfire pilot for the Royal Canadian Air Force who fought the Luftwaffe alongside the British over the North Sea. The author was overcome with battle fatigue and at one point had contemplated aiming his plane straight toward the waters to put himself out of his misery. But growing up with Christian missionary parents, he must have had a reservoir of faith to help him stay in the fight and, soon after, write this enduring poem.

High Flight[249]

Oh! I have slipped the surly bonds of Earth
And danced the skies on laughter-silvered wings;
Sunward I've climbed, and joined the tumbling
    mirth
Of sun-split clouds,—and done a hundred things
You have not dreamed of—wheeled and soared
    and swung
High in the sunlit silence. Hov'ring there,
I've chased the shouting wind along, and flung
My eager craft through footless halls of air…
Up, up the long, delirious, burning blue
I've topped the wind-swept heights with easy grace.
Where never lark, or even eagle flew—

And, while with silent, lifting mind I've trod
The high untrespassed sanctity of space,
Put out my hand, and touched the face of God.

—John Gillespie Magee Jr.

Magee died in a midair collision in 1941 at the age of nineteen. He had a full scholarship to Yale but chose to fight instead.

Endnotes

249 John Gillespie Magee Jr., "Poems to Share," National Poetry Day, accessed 12/12/2020, https://nationalpoetryday.co.uk/poem/high-flight/. Public Domain.

ABOUT THE AUTHOR

Chet Weld has been intrigued by God's secret and astounding ways since experiencing his first miracle. As a marriage counselor, therapist, and pastor, he's learned about how the natural and supernatural realms ebb and flow in people's lives. He comes alongside hurting people to encourage and attribute dignity to them.

As a songwriter and worship leader, music is his first love. He loves all music that's inspired but listens to—and writes—mostly contemporary Christian songs. He credits God for lifting him out of the pit of drug and alcohol abuse into a life of purpose.

He's been a night watchman, emergency room orderly, hotel clerk, janitor, warehouse worker, delivery driver, camp counselor, and tennis instructor. He's attended seminary and Bible college, studied counseling and psychology, and earned his EdD in Counseling Psychology.

He's authored articles for journals, PreachItTeachIt.org, and Crosswalk.com. He's a member of the American Association of

Christian Counselors, certified by the International Board of Christian Counselors as a board-certified professional Christian counselor and a member of the Society for Christian Psychologists. He's a licensed professional counselor and an approved supervisor in Arizona. He maintains a blog on his website at drchetweld.com. You can listen to some of his music by searching on YouTube for "Chet Weld."

He lives with his wife and soul mate, Susan, in the foothills of the Tortolita Mountains in Tucson, Arizona. He loves the sunsets and surrounding mountains, but he misses the green grass of the Midwest where he grew up. He relates to owls on a first-name basis but has yet to interpret what lonely coyotes howl at the stars.